RUSSIA'S TRANSITION TO DEMOCRACY

IN

This
rec
l

Russia's Transition to Democracy

An Internal Political History, 1989–1996

G. D. G. Murrell

Foreword by
Sir Brian Fall

sussex
ACADEMIC
PRESS

First published 1997 in Great Britain by
SUSSEX ACADEMIC PRESS
18 Chichester Place
Brighton BN2 1FF

and in the United States of America by
SUSSEX ACADEMIC PRESS
c/o International Specialized Book Services, Inc.
5804 N.E. Hassalo St.
Portland, Oregon 97213-3644

British Library Cataloguing in Publication Data
A CIP catalogue record for this book is available from the British Library.

ISBN 1–898723 57 5 (hardcover)
ISBN 1–898723 58 3 (paperback)

1973, 4263

Printed and bound by Biddles Ltd, King's Lynn and Guildford

Contents

———

Foreword by Sir Brian Fall

The period covered by Geoff Murrell's book – from 1989 to the Presidential elections in June/July 1996 – was a tumultuous one for Russia. There always seemed to be something new to pack the front pages and television screens of the Western media; and, inevitably, much of the analysis which accompanied the reports was of the instant variety.

Beyond the action, there was the plot; and, underlying that, a need to understand the motivation of the principal characters. They, with the numerically insignificant exception of the former dissidents who remained active in public life in Russia, were people who had cut their political or bureaucratic teeth while working within the system controlled by the communist party of the Soviet Union. They were not all prisoners of the past, but they remained influenced by it. The extent of that influence, and its power to attract or repel, varied from case to case; but it was more often than not the starting point for any political analysis likely to prove accurate and robust.

Russians, when they talked politics among themselves, knew that instinctively; and they rarely found it necessary to spell out what it was about the past that was serving to shape a judgement about the future. Russians talking to Westerners could rarely rely on this shorthand, and the quality of the message suffered in consequence.

Geoff Murrell was an exception. The years that he spent in Moscow following this dramatic story, often literally from hour to hour, marked his fourth posting as a political specialist at the British Embassy in Moscow; he had spent much of the rest of his career working on Soviet affairs in what, under different names, was the Research Department of the Foreign Office; and his knowledge of the country and language enabled him to move easily among the Russian politicians, political scientists and journalists who were shaping as well as analysing events. He was the right man in the right place at the right time.

In this short history, he has squeezed a lot into a small space: sometimes by selection; mainly by condensation. It is not a book that one can very usefully skim; the effect of careful reading is cumulative; and, while neither the intention nor the style are inflammatory, the result is a bonfire of the falsities. Up there in the flames, if I am not mistaken, is the idea that Gorbachev-the-reforming-statesman was pushed prematurely off the stage by an ambitious autocrat from Sverdlovsk; the idea that there was anything very democratic about the 1993 version of the defence of the White House; and the idea that all the things that hindsight suggests that Gorbachev and Yeltsin *should* have done, were also things that they *could* have done, and done successfully, in the circumstances prevailing at the time.

My own view is that Russia has been in the throes of a benign, and still incomplete revolution; and that history will rate Gorbachev and Yeltsin – at different times, and in different spheres of activity – as its crucial leaders. They inevitably made enemies; and, because they rejected the Leninist inheritance of firing squads and labour camps, those enemies were able to regroup after setbacks, and to use the machinery of democracy against the reforms required to make democracy safe. If Gorbachev and Yeltsin had been able to work constructively together in harness, and if democratic and reformist politicians more generally had been willing to do likewise, it would all have been much simpler. But Geoff Murrell records things as they were.

It has not been easy, and difficulties remain; but we should not assume with the pessimists that they will prove greater than those that have been successfully overcome over the last few years. Russia's new constitution is at the presidential end of the democratic spectrum, but it is nevertheless recognisably democratic; the new institutions, including the parliament and the constitutional court, are beginning to find their feet; there are now good prospects for economic growth; and, above all, we have seen political battles fought out as they should be: two parliamentary elections and two rounds of presidential elections, in less than three years, have taken place on schedule and in satisfactory conditions. Yeltsin deserves more credit for that than his critics have been prepared to acknowledge.

Sir Brian Fall GCVO KCMG
HM Ambassador, Moscow, 1992–1995
Principal, Lady Margaret Hall, Oxford

Preface and Acknowledgements

This book was originally written as an internal FCO memorandum to provide background briefing and a work of reference for diplomats dealing with Russian affairs in London and Moscow. My aim was to produce a reasonably concise history of the astonishing sequence of events which led to the break-up of the USSR and the troubled birth of the new Russia, accompanied by an analytical commentary discussing the reasons why Russia's transition to democracy had proved so traumatically difficult.

For the historical part, I decided to focus primarily on the dynamics of the internal political process and therefore adopted a largely narrative, chronological approach. I believe this provides a relatively clear perspective which, in view of the complexity of recent Russian history, tends to be lost in a more comprehensive thematic study. The disadvantage is that I have had to neglect or touch only tangentially on important issues such as economic policy, relations in the CIS, federalism and regional politics as well as the constant succession of often ephemeral new political structures and institutions which have appeared during this tumultuous period.

I chose to begin the story in 1989 because this was the watershed year when the history of the break-up of the USSR begins. In the course of 1989 *perestroika* lost its momentum as the revolutions in Eastern Europe and the rise of nationalism within the USSR generated a sharp backlash which drove Gorbachev, no longer fully in control of events, towards though never quite into the arms of party conservatives. I have assumed some degree of prior knowledge of the earlier history on the part of the reader, since the first years of Gorbachev and *perestroika* have been adequately covered in a number of excellent studies, most recently and definitively in Archie Brown's *The Gorbachev Factor*.

For almost all the period covered in this history, I was involved in observing and analysing events day by day in Moscow or London and I have drawn on some of the first hand reports I wrote at the time. I have not however indulged in personal reminiscences although I witnessed many of the major political occasions and dramatic events and met, if in some cases only on formal occasions, nearly all the main Russian protagonists. The analytical introduction was largely written before the 1996 presidential elections the outcome of which might have led me to lighten a little its rather pessimistic tone. But I believe the analysis generally remains valid. Following Yeltsin's remarkable comeback, Russia's future direction is still far from clear and many difficulties and dangers lie ahead. But hopefully the point of no return may now have been passed.

I should emphasize that the judgements and comments in this book are my own and do not represent official FCO views. I have benefited a great deal from the collective wisdom of colleagues in the British Embassy in Moscow 1991–4, led successively by two exceptionally able and wise Ambassadors in Sir Rodric Braithwaite and Sir Brian Fall and in the Eastern Research Unit of the FCO's Research and Analysis Department, especially Tony Bishop, Kate Horner and Peter Roland who made valuable comments on the text. But they are not of course responsible for any errors of judgement or fact I may have made. Thanks to the assistance of my colleagues in the FCO I had the opportunity in May 1995, after my retirement from the Diplomatic Service, to visit Moscow and discuss some of the episodes and judgements in this book with among others Yegor Gaidar, Gennady Burbulis, Yegor Yakovlev and Otto Latsis. Among the hundreds of my Russian interlocutors over recent years I have derived enormous benefit especially from the many discussions and arguments but above all from the friendship I have enjoyed with Lev Razgon, Viktor Sheinis, Andranik Migranyan, Alexander Maksimovich Yakovlev, Nikolai Shmelev and Nikolai Andreev. Finally, I am extremely grateful for the remarkable skill, speed, accuracy and forbearance of Yvonne Anderson and Raina Graham who typed the manuscript.

G. D. G. Murrell CMG OBE
London, 8 August 1996

Russia's Transition: What Went Wrong?

BALANCE SHEET

The prevailing mood about Russia in the West is one of disillusion. The optimism aroused by the collapse of the USSR and the Communist system at the end of 1991 has largely evaporated. Heroic memories of Yeltsin's defence of the White House in August 1991 have been overlaid and tarnished by the pictures of the blackened façade of the same building, shelled on his instructions in October 1993. The economy is still struggling, crime and corruption are rife. The Communists and neo-Fascists were solidly represented in the new Duma and reinforced their position in the December 1995 elections. The democrats are in disarray, lacking cohesion or effective leadership and at loggerheads with Yeltsin. The honeymoon with the West is officially at an end. Russia is fighting a brutal, quasi-colonial war in the North Caucasus.

People remember their hopes but forget their fears. There has been no famine, large-scale civil war or collapse of the Federation; neither has there been severe industrial unrest, let alone the "social explosion" repeatedly predicted by the Russian opposition and seriously anticipated in the West. On the credit side of the balance sheet, free, multi-party elections, however disappointing the result, have taken place for the first time in Russian history. Russia has a market economy. There has been a revulsion against violence and arbitrary arrest; the basic democratic values of freedom of speech, assembly, association and travel, and respect for the rule of law, have taken root. Such principles now influence the behaviour even of those who do not really believe in them: the inhibitions of the leaders of the August putsch against more drastic action were a principal reason for its failure. A heavy political price has had to be paid for the violence of October 1993 and in Chechnya, witnessed by millions on their television screens. There is general acceptance of the inevitability of change and that there is no way back.

LEGACY

The problems of what I have optimistically called "Russia's transition to democracy" were underestimated. There is no precedent in world history for the peaceful transformation of a totalitarian system which was also a multi-national empire. Post-war Germany had the advantage that the Nazi system had been extirpated and it had some democratic traditions within recent memory on which to build as well as massive assistance from the Allies. It turned out to be an advantage that Germany had to rebuild its economy almost from scratch. Spain's totalitarian system was not all pervading; it retained institutions, the Monarchy and the Church, which provided a focus for new authority. Its economy did not depend on its ideology and political system. The Central and East European countries could discard comparatively painlessly the system regarded as an alien implant and appeal to national and democratic traditions. Their societies retained enough of their pre-communist shape to provide the basis for new or revived political parties. But even in East Germany, where circumstances were almost ideal, the path towards democracy has been difficult enough.

In Russia / USSR, the Soviet system was much more deeply embedded than in Eastern Europe. It had penetrated the whole of society for three or four generations. The entire economy was bound up with and inseparable from the political system and collapsed together with it. Russia faced the task of building democratic political institutions while transforming its economic system and trying to construct a new national identity. It had to do so while the old economic system was collapsing but its foundations still remained deeply entrenched. It would have been easier to reform an undeveloped economy or one in total ruins than an economy which was incorrigibly "misdeveloped". The social system had been completely transformed by 70 years of communism; nothing survived of pre-revolutionary society. There was no basis on which to build new democratic institutions. The dissident "movement", operating in a political vacuum, could never develop into an embryo opposition as Solidarity did in Poland. It was too fragmented and focused on human rights protest, rather than alternative political programmes which were inconceivable in the current political environment. Dissident figures, with the exception of Academician Sakharov, all too briefly, and Sergei Kovalev, were almost entirely excluded from post-communist politics. The old emigré political organizations had no relevance and disappeared without trace. There were no leaders available from outside the Soviet political system, comparable for example to Havel or Walesa.

The Soviet Communist Party not only destroyed and prohibited all other political parties; it was deliberately organized to exclude the possibility of any autonomous social unit, since it co-opted the ambitious in every walk of life and installed its cells in every enterprise, institution and social organization. It brought about the disintegration or atomization of society. As Richard Sakwa has put it, the State had to "act as the creator of the social basis on which democracy was to stand".[1] The CPSU so monopolized politics and power that nothing could grow in its shadow. Five years after the Party formally abandoned its leading role and despite the multi-party elections of December 1993 and December 1995, the reconstituted Russian Communist Party is still the largest and best organized nation-wide political party.

Russian society provided a peculiarly unresponsive environment for radical economic change. The Soviet system produced (as the sociologist, Victor Zaslavsky, has pointed out) a specific psychological and social type – the "State-dependent worker", whose main characteristics are: work avoidance; reluctance to accept risk or use initiative; preference for security over achievement.[2] "The idea of cradle-to-grave social justice, exercised by a paternalistic government that defends, educates and punishes its subjects, is deeply lodged in the popular consciousness."[3] This dependency and anti-work ethic affected not only workers and peasants but the greater part of the scientific and creative intelligentsia employed in heavily subsidized institutes, academies, journals, creative unions, etc. The intelligentsia produced by the Soviet system was highly educated and articulate. It responded with alacrity to *glasnost*, showed skill and sophistication in political argument, embraced with enthusiasm the principles of democracy and a civil society. But it manifested the traditional vices as well as virtues of the Russian intelligentsia, which made it almost as ill-prepared as the rest of society for normal democratic politics: a tendency to excess or "maximalism" in which freedom (*svoboda*) tended to become licence (*volya*); intolerance and a refusal to compromise; unwillingness or inability to communicate ideas intelligibly to the public at large (which has made the reformists highly vulnerable to populism: in the 1993 TV election campaign, Gaidar sat at a desk expounding benefits of economic reform in his slightly supercilious manner. Zhirinovsky was shown in the market-place arguing about high prices. Even the liberal and dissident intellectuals were (in George Schopflin's phrase) "negatively dependent" on the State. When the barriers came down and censorship was abolished they did not know what to write or which way to turn; there was little experience or capability for constructive political action.

The Soviet system to some extent reinforced traditional Russian characteristics, bred by serfdom and a rigidly hierarchical authoritarian society of envy, submissiveness, sloth, and collectivism. But as Gaidar argues forcefully in his recent book, *State and Evolution*, Russia has not only an authoritarian and conformist tradition but a strong reformist one (Peter the Great, Speransky, Alexander II, Witte and Stolypin). By the end of the nineteenth century, Russia had developed a strong entrepreneurial class, in the first decade of the twentieth century private investment was growing, agrarian reform had been begun by Stolypin ("Russian agriculture never developed as successfully as in the short interval between the commune and the kolkhoz" giving the lie to theories about the "ingrained collectivism of the Russian peasant and his hostility to private property"). On the eve of World War I, Russia had "secured the basis for steady capitalist growth".[4] Russia was also making gradual progress towards a civil society; but the Revolution and Soviet totalitarianism have left virtually no trace of the positive aspects of Russia's legacy.

FAILURES OF NEW INSTITUTIONS

The attempt to build new institutions or democratize existing ones, begun by Gorbachev in 1988, took place in the midst of political struggle and while the old system was being painfully dismantled. This led to distortions and compromises which remained to haunt the post-Communist political system. To fill the political vacuum left by the formal abolition of the CPSU's monopoly on power, Gorbachev tried to create a more or less genuine parliament. An immediate transition to open democratic elections was politically impossible. Gorbachev was obliged to try to legitimize the reform in the eyes of the Party by appealing to a Soviet precedent – a cumbersome two-tier legislature comprising the USSR Congress of People's Deputies and the Supreme Soviet; and to guarantee the Communist Party and the public organizations dominated by it a third of the seats through a quota system in the elections of May 1989.

Russian Congress

When the Russian (RSFSR) Congress was elected a year later in 1990 the quota system was abolished but the CPSU was still in control of the country and able to exert a dominant influence on the electoral process. A document from the Party archives, a verbatim record of a Politburo meeting chaired by Gorbachev which discussed the outcome of those elections (published by *Kuranty* 19 November 1993), reveals the satisfaction of Politburo members, notably Kryuchkov and Ryzhkov, with the high proportion of Party officials, KGB representatives, etc. They noted that:

- 86 per cent of the elected deputies were party members;
- 110 (11 per cent) were senior party officials including 19 regional First Party Secretaries;
- a high proportion of officials from the KGB, MVD and other law-enforcement agencies including more from the KGB than ever before;
- a strong representation of senior army officers;
- only 20 per cent of the deputies were supporters of the Democratic Platform and "70 per cent of the deputies stood firmly on the CPSU platform".

It was with this inherently un-parliamentary legislature, dominated by representatives of the old regime, that Russia had to begin its attempt to function as a parliamentary democracy following the collapse of the communist system.

Ideas of political reform were dominated by Western models, especially the separation of powers and checks and balances. This was natural in a country whose history had been dominated by authoritarian leaders and tyrants. In practice the new institutions, born in the midst of a power struggle, were infected by Soviet political and bureaucratic habits so that attempts to divide power between institutions led to a power struggle between them. In accordance with Soviet political instinct and tradition new institutions sought to achieve total power rather than a share of it. Even Academician Sakharov seemed to bow to this logic when he called for the first USSR Congress of People's Deputies to declare that it had assumed all political power (his intention was to consummate the end of Party rule). The same logic gave rise to Article 104 of the RSFSR Constitution which declared that the Congress held supreme political authority; and the revival of the slogan "all power to the Soviets" which the Communist Party had launched in 1917 to create a façade for the concentration of all power in its own hands.

Gorbachev instituted the USSR Presidency in 1990 in order to provide himself with a new power base independent of the Party. Yeltsin instituted the Russian Presidency the following year essentially as a move in the power game against Gorbachev, since his route to political influence of the Centre was blocked. (In the other republics incumbent party leaders followed suit in order to bolster their authority against the Centre.) Institutions imitated from Western models, partly shaped by the concurrent power struggle and co-existing with Soviet structures still in place, not surprisingly failed to function smoothly. They contained built-in flaws which were conducive to the political conflicts and eventual confrontation of 1992 / 3.

Separation of Powers

The failure to dismantle or adjust Soviet structures as new institutions were created, exacerbated the problem. When Yeltsin was elected President in June 1991 the post of chairman of the Supreme Soviet which he had occupied for the previous year was not abolished or reduced in scope. His eventual successor, Khasbulatov, inherited quasi-presidential powers. When the presidency was instituted with new powers, it was grafted on to the existing system with no corresponding reduction in the powers of parliament, thus setting the scene for the protracted argument over a presidential versus a parliamentary republic which was to degenerate into an outright power struggle between the legislature and executive. A senior Russian lawyer, Professor A. M. Yakovlev (recently the President's Representative in the Federal Assembly, from 1994–6), has lamented the failure of Russia either before or since the revolution to accept or understand the principle of division of powers.[5] The tsars treated the State as their patrimony and Nicholas II fiercely resisted any infringement of the principle of absolutism. Lenin rejected any separation of powers in favour of "all power to the Soviets" as a smoke-screen for the Party's monopoly of power. The crisis of 1992/3 was not just a struggle for dominance between the legislature and the executive but a struggle for total power: Khasbulatov wanted to add executive power to the legislative; Yeltsin tried to rule by decree so as to add legislative to executive power.

The real tragedy of this conflict was not just that it led to the violence of October 1993 but that it tended to discredit the very ideas of parliamentary democracy, respect for the Constitution and the rule of law, as all these came to be seen as instruments in a cynical power struggle. At the heart of the problem was the fact that the revolution which followed the attempted coup in August 1991 was not completed. The old institutions and the old Constitution were left in place when the USSR was dismantled, including the Congress rooted in the Communist era and enjoying almost unlimited power. Elections and a new parliament might have created a more solid institutional base for a new democratic political system. But, as discussed below, a clean break with the old regime in the political circumstances of the time was probably impracticable.

LACK OF A MULTI-PARTY SYSTEM

The inadequacies of Russian parliamentarism were closely linked to the failure to create political parties or coherent nation-wide movements to fill the vacuum when the CPSU collapsed. One of the reasons the Russian parliament ended up acting as a monolith in pursuit of institutional interests was the absence of real political parties contending for influence within it. The political environment did not favour the development of party politics. During *perestroika* the opposition was a broad coalition based on generalized ethical protest against the Soviet system: there were no social or ideological bases for new political parties with distinctive programmes and identifiable constituencies. The dozens of self-styled parties spawned by the October 1990 Law on Association never got beyond the tadpole stage (all head no tail). They were based on well-known personalities in the democratic movement who had talent and ambition but mostly lacked organizational experience or aptitude (and included a proportion of opportunists and malcontents). None was able to rally significant popular support. Although the Communist political super-structure collapsed in 1991, society, especially in the regions, had not changed; the population briefly and intensively politicized during *perestroika* became exhausted and apathetic and allergic to the idea of any political party (as the saying went: the country was barely able to feed one party, why do we need more?).

Democratic Movement

A split in the CPSU between reformist and conservative wings might have provided the basis for a multi-party system. But Gorbachev was obsessed to the end by the shibboleth of party unity and he clung to the illusion even after the August putsch that the Party as a whole could be reformed.

Yeltsin founded the Democratic Platform in the CPSU with the aim of leading a break-away reformist wing, but when the reformists were isolated at the Twenty-eighth Congress he abandoned the idea and walked out of the Party. Yeltsin was the leading figure in the first democratic opposition groups, the Inter-Regional Group (IRG) and Democratic Russia. But though he flirted with the idea of forming and leading a new democratic party, and was repeatedly urged to do so by some of his advisers, he always backed away. He preferred to remain a leader of "all the people" relying on popular appeal while preserving freedom of manoeuvre unrestricted by political programmes and un-beholden to anyone but "the People". Yeltsin formally ceased to be a member of Democratic Russia when elected Chairman of the Supreme Soviet of the RSFSR in 1990 and thereafter kept himself at a distance while appealing for and relying on its support in critical moments, when it repeatedly played a key role (the Presidential elections in June 1991; the August putsch; the Ninth Congress and April 1993 referendum campaign). Leaders of Democratic Russia were at odds with Yeltsin on important issues from an early stage. They were appalled by his choice of Rutskoi as running mate in the 1991 elections and criticized his decision in April 1991 to support Gorbachev in the Novo-Ogarevo process.

Yeltsin's failure to lead the democratic movement, while never entirely rejecting the possibility, deprived the democrats of effective leadership. With Yeltsin permanently in the wings no one else would venture centre stage. The more ambitious of the secondary figures formed their own parties and movements and split away; in the tradition of Russian politics they have tended to be more intolerant of their ideological allies than their enemies and the divisions in the democratic movement have grown wider. The absence of nation-wide political parties has also meant that regional interests, or more exactly the interests of regional elites, have continued to play an excessive and divisive role in Russian politics. Lacking organized political support at grass-roots level in the regions, Yeltsin has tended to rely on the support and promote the influence of regional leaders, who have rarely repaid him with political backing when he needed it. Regional leaders have also increased their authority in the absence of organized political opposition and with some significant exceptions have done little to encourage the cause of political and economic reform.

The electoral system adopted for the Duma at the end of 1993 was specifically designed to accelerate the formation of a multi-party system by allocating 50 per cent of the seats on a proportional representation/party list basis. However, it largely failed in its purpose. The political alliances were hastily concocted often by well-known individuals gathering under one banner in order to qualify in the PR section of the ballot but with little common cause and before discussing a political programme. Many electoral blocs split after the elections despite the constraints of fraction discipline in the Duma. The one "success" of the new electoral system was to give birth to the Liberal Democratic Party which had scarcely existed as a nation-wide party before the elections but has begun to organize seriously since. The votes received by the LDP in the party list contest depended almost exclusively on Zhirinovsky's personality as leader; the LDP elected only five candidates from the constituencies.

When Russia's Democratic Choice, Gaidar's new political party, was formally inaugurated in June 1994, it was the first serious nation-wide mainstream democratic political party to appear, five years after the first significant democratic association, the IRG, was formed at the First Congress of People's Deputies. But it achieved the necessary unity and cohesion at the price of the defection of the leadership of Democratic Russia, its increasingly estranged partner in the Russia's Choice electoral bloc, and the abstention of all the leading democratic figures except Chubais.

NATIONALISM VERSUS REFORM

The multi-national composition and structure of the Soviet Union proved the country's greatest weakness when it came under internal political pressure. It was nationalism rather than the reform movement which brought about the final destruction of the communist system; but it also severely hampered the attempt at an orderly democratic transformation.

The Bolsheviks reconstituted and reorganized the Russian empire administratively on a hierarchical, national-territorial basis, establishing frontiers and creating new national entities with little regard to history or geography. The Constituent Republics of the USSR were accorded all the trappings of statehood. This served various purposes: to conciliate national feelings which the communists had exploited to mobilize opposition to the Tsarist regime; to satisfy the national elites by providing the local intelligentsia with prestigious jobs; and perhaps to provide a structure which could conveniently accommodate the incorporation in due course of neighbouring independent countries. As long as the country was effectively run as a unitary state by the highly centralized Communist Party of the Soviet Union, the structures and the frontiers had no political significance. When the CPSU lost power the country broke up along the lines defined by the arbitrary borders bequeathed by Lenin and Stalin, and the artificial republic structures inherited real political power.

At first the Popular Front movements, notably in the Baltic republics, were discreetly welcomed by Gorbachev as allies against the party conservatives. They campaigned under the banner of *perestroika* avoiding nationalist slogans and were an integral part of the Soviet democratic movement. Once the collapse of communism in Eastern Europe in 1989 widened political horizons, the Popular Front movements distanced themselves from the reform process as such and focused their efforts on the struggle for independence. The democratic movement as a whole was consequently divided and weakened; at the Second Congress of People's Deputies in

December 1989, Baltic delegates boycotted the proceedings leaving the ranks of the Inter-Regional Group depleted. The cosmopolitan intellectuals who led the democratic movement could offer only generalizations about political and economic reform; they had nothing to compete with the attraction of nationalism as an effective mobilizing force, a complete political programme and a closed ideological system with answers for every question. Attempts by the democrats to construct a country-wide, all-Union reform movement came to nothing. As Andrei Grachev put it in *Kremlevskaya Khronika*:[6]

> It was nationalism, as subsequent events were to show, which both as a total ideological system and as a powerful mobilizing force was able to challenge communist totalitarianism, being at the same time its opposite and its blood brother.

As nationalism and separatism gathered force weakening and demoralizing the democratic movement, they also galvanized and enraged the conservatives at the centre (this in turn frightened and further stimulated the separatist movements). The party conservatives had been manoeuvred by Gorbachev into accepting hitherto unthinkable political changes including the loss of the Party's leading role; but the threat to the integrity of the country which became clear after 1989 stiffened their resolve and mobilized the whole bureaucracy of the central structures behind them. Support for the reformists in the new parliament rapidly eroded. At the Fourth Congress of People's Deputies in December 1990 the IRG had dwindled to 229 registered deputies, while the conservative bloc "Soyuz" (Union) claimed over 700 members.

Facing a losing struggle in the central political institutions, now reacting to a threat not only to the existing system but to their own survival, the democrats began to focus their efforts on gaining influence in the institutions of the Russian republic. This happened partly fortuitously since the elections in March 1990 for the Russian Congress were more democratic or less undemocratic than those to the USSR Congress because they took place a year later in the reform process. Candidates sponsored by the Democratic Russia movement achieved over 20 per cent of the seats. At this stage Yeltsin had no thought of breaking up the USSR or of promoting Russian sovereignty; he sought election as a Russian deputy and then as chairman of the Supreme Soviet, because with Gorbachev still in control at the centre where the odds were stacked heavily against him he needed a new power base. Once installed as chairman of the Supreme Soviet, and a year later when elected President, he followed the logic of the political struggle and attacked the Centre in order to weaken and ultimately destroy Gorbachev.

There appeared to be no limits to Gorbachev's ideological retreat in the face of the reform movement he no longer controlled; but preservation of the Union was his last ditch. He was forced further and further to the right, and by the winter of 1989–90 he (virtually) fell into the arms of his conservative enemies, who were concerned not just to prevent separatism but put an end to *perestroika*. The low point was January 1991 when Gorbachev failed to disavow the violence in Vilnius (evidently provoked by the KGB and part of the army leadership in the hope of forcing Gorbachev to declare presidential rule in Lithuania) and lost virtually all credibility with the democratic opposition.

Republics versus the Centre

By now the struggle for political and economic reform against conservatives at the centre and in the regions had been largely overtaken and submerged in the constitutional power struggle between the republics and the centre. The Russian Declaration of Sovereignty on 12 June 1990 was followed by a more substantial Declaration by Ukraine on 16 July and all the other republics had followed suit by the end of the year. The War of Laws ensued with republics claiming precedence for their legislation over that of the Union. As republics began to assert ownership of enterprises, resources and property, ideas of economic reform took second place to what amounted to a division of the spoils.

Yeltsin's espousal of Russian sovereignty did not correspond to anything previously discernible in his political philosophy and was essentially a move in his power struggle against Gorbachev. But he was closely identified with the cause of political and economic reform and continued to promote it. For other republic leaders, notably Kravchuk (former ideological secretary in the Ukrainian Central Committee primarily responsible for suppressing nationalism), the Central Asian leaders and "*nomenklatura* nationalists" everywhere, the fight for sovereignty and ultimately independence offered the opportunity to identify with a popular cause, insulate themselves from the reformist infection emanating from Moscow

and preserve their power and privileges. They joined in the struggle to destroy the communist system in order to preserve their
own bit of it intact. The national cause gave them a ready-made
alibi. Economic and social problems, due in significant measure
to their own incompetence and past complicity with the system,
could be blamed on exploitation by Russia and the Centre. As
Andrei Grachev complains, the independence movement was used
to defend the jobs and privileges of the *nomenklatura* and led "not to
progress of democracy on one-sixth of the earth but the appearance
of a dozen mini-empires of local apparat elite". Grachev is perhaps
right to suggest that the consequences for reform in Russia were
the most damaging of all, though he makes his point in bitterly
extravagant terms:

> The Russian neo-bureaucracy, hungry for supreme power, was ready
> to cook itself an omelette on the volcano of republican nationalism,
> heedless of the fact that this would end in tragedy for Russia
> above all.[7]

Sovereignization and the Russian Federation

The consequences for Russia were twofold: the trauma of the loss
of empire, coupled with the knock-on effect of "sovereignization"
which had dismantled the USSR and now threatened the integrity of the Russian Federation. Yeltsin had himself stimulated the
domino process by telling the Tatars in August 1990, in words
which have come back to haunt him ever since, that they should
"take as much sovereignty as they could swallow". He did so in
order to trump Gorbachev who had began playing the card of
enhanced status for the "autonomous" republics within Russia in
a tit-for-tat response to the campaign of the Union republics to take
powers away from the centre. Ever since Yeltsin has been trying to
contain the ambitions of the Russian republics, notably Chechnya,
which decided in November 1991 that it could "swallow" full
independence. In the course of the constitutional power struggle
of 1992–3 between the executive and the legislature, Yeltsin made
concessions to the republics in the hope of securing their support
against the parliament. In the event he obtained little effective
support but antagonized the more numerous and mostly more
populous ethnic Russian regions which demanded equal economic
and political status with the republics. There are significant exceptions but the overall effect of sovereignization has been to enhance

the political and economic power of regional elites at the expense
of the development of democracy and economic reform.

"Loss of Empire"

The "loss of empire" has had deeper and more traumatic consequences. In the other FSU republics the leaders and populations
had the moral-political boost of a recovered or newly-discovered
national identity following the collapse of the USSR. Russia in
contrast suffered a loss of identity. Leaders in the other republics
(including former party bosses deeply involved in the system) could
dissociate themselves from the communist legacy by treating it as an
alien imposition as the East Europeans had done. The Russians were
stuck with the fact that it was home grown (though Solzhenitsyn
regarded the Revolution as an alien phenomenon and hard-line
nationalists pointed to the preponderance of non-Russians and Jews
among the Bolsheviks). If the Soviet Union or Russia had been an
empire in the conventional and familiar sense, the effect would have
been less painful and profound. But the Russian State had never
existed as a separate entity within its present frontiers; there was
no clear dividing line between the metropolis and the periphery.
The Tsarist Empire was based on the principle of autocracy and
was not the "Russian Empire" at least until the reign of Alexander
III (1881–94), who began the policy of russification. In the USSR,
Russian language and culture was accorded a superior status and
the Russian people termed the "elder brother" of the other nations.
But Russians had no political or economic privileges. Russia, as
a general rule, was not so much exploiting as subsidizing its
"colonies" – a fact which, after all the statistical arguments during
perestroika, the economic realities of the post-Communist world have
now made clear. The imbalance in the economies of the FSU republics, the irrational location and ecologically harmful development of
industry, the influx of Russian and Ukrainian workers, were due
as much to intensive lobbying for central investments by republic
leaders (including those in the Baltic republics) as to the arbitrary
decisions of State planners in Moscow. Russian minorities felt more
like second-class citizens than colonial overlords. Solzhenitsyn's
Cancer Ward and Zhirinovsky's autobiography, *Last Push South*,
reflect in their different ways the resentment felt by Russians at
the positive discrimination in favour of local nationals in higher

education and senior professional employment. Zhirinovsky's political psychology is very much the product of this resentment.

The collapse of the USSR left most Russians, including democrats and liberals, feeling bereft rather than celebrating the birth of their new state, which most of them felt was misbegotten and malformed. In the perception of the political class, the separation of Ukraine and Belarus had shifted the centre of gravity of their country a thousand kilometres to the east further from Europe and returned it in geo-political terms to the end of the seventeenth century when Russia was seeking outlets to the Baltic and Black Seas. There was a sense of humiliation comparable to defeat in war. Indeed the belated World War II peace settlement, which has followed the fall of the Berlin Wall, left Russia rather than Germany looking like the main loser. Russia's identity crisis is the dominant political factor in its post-Communist history, overshadowing issues of economic or political reform and the constitutional struggle between the executive and the legislature. It took four months after the Russian State was born and several days acrimonious debate at the Sixth Congress to decide what the country should be called; and over a year to remove the final references in its constitution to the USSR. The sense of grievance at the loss of great power status and prestige animates and unites the nationalist and communist oppositions, which do not accept the legitimacy of the new State in its present frontiers and call, in effect, for the restoration in some form of the country which existed before. This accounts for much of their popular support. Few Russians want the Soviet system or the Communist ideology back; many resent the truncation of their country and its reduced status in the world.

Russian Nationalism

For many democrats, traditionally internationalist and cosmopolitan in outlook, the disintegration of the USSR was no less traumatic. Many prominent figures left the democratic movement and joined the opposition; this was a significant factor in the drift to the Right among deputies of the Congress of People's Deputies in 1992–3, which swelled the ranks of the opposition and brought the constitutional crisis to a head. The leader of the Democratic Party of Russia, Travkin, split from the Democratic Russia movement and led a demonstration against the break-up of the USSR in December 1991. Yury Vlasov, whose tirade against the KGB at the First USSR

Congress in 1989 was a dramatic highlight of *glasnost*, became a rabid nationalist. Baburin, a Democratic Russia candidate at the elections to the Russian Congress in 1990, became a leader of the nationalist opposition. Aksyuchits, leader of the Russian Christian Democratic Movement, and Alexander Tsipko, one of the most influential reformist intellectuals in the early period of *perestroika*, have associated themselves with movements akin to the National Salvation Front. Leading democrats who did not join the opposition have nonetheless expressed strongly nationalist views (Popov, Sobchak, Stankevich). It was only a small minority of pragmatic democrats or liberal nationalists like Gaidar who perceived that shedding the burden of empire could make Russia a much more secure and viable base for market reform, financial stabilization and democratic institutions.

The democrats, identified with the dismantling of the USSR and associated with economic reforms based on Western models and encouraged by the West, have increasingly been portrayed by the opposition as servile and unpatriotic. The Yeltsin administration has felt obliged to react by adopting a more robust posture in defence of the integrity of the State, the interests of Russia and of the 25 million Russians in the near abroad. In an attempt to resolve Russia's identity crisis, the assertion of Russian State interests has become an end in itself and the strengthening of Russia's statehood threatens to become more important as a political objective than building democratic institutions within the State. In part this is a traditional response intended to deflect discontent with economic hardship and social disorder, mobilize popular support, and try to instil a greater sense of national cohesion and international respect; in part it reflects a view that the priority now should be to shore up the authority of the State, restore social stability and discipline since democratic institutions and the legal system are not functioning effectively and enjoy little respect. Russia's statehood was the leitmotif of Yeltsin's "State of The Nation" address to parliament in February 1994. Against this background, Chechnya's defection and defiance came to seem increasingly intolerable.

FAILURE OF LEADERSHIP?: GORBACHEV

Throughout the last ten years of reform and transformation the Soviet Union and Russia have been led by two provincial party

leaders, in some ways exceptional men, but in others typical products of the Soviet system. There were no serious rivals as leaders
of reform who emerged either from within the system or outside it.
Gorbachev had the support of a few senior colleagues (Yakovlev,
Shevardnadze, Bakatin) and advisers from the party intelligentsia.
But no younger party officials of real ability came forward to
support him. Gorbachev purged the Central Committee several
times and manoeuvred it into acquiescence in his policies; but it
remained predominantly hostile to him and the reform process to
the end.

Those who reproach Gorbachev for his vacillation, compromises
and slow implementation of reform forget or ignore the political
realities he had to contend with, in particular the balance of forces
in the Party at every level from Politburo downwards. Much of
what his critics, domestic or foreign, suggested he should have
done was politically impossible in the prevailing circumstances.
To begin with reform in the economy, especially agriculture (as
in China) rather than in politics, was to enter a blind alley because
the Soviet economy was inextricably bound up with the political
system (especially agriculture where reform has still scarcely begun
five years after the collapse of the Communist system). It was
not so much ideological inhibition as political prudence which
made Gorbachev manoeuvre and compromise. In so doing he
protected not only his own position but the reform process and
the radical democrats who reviled him for his half-measures and
lack of principle. A Russian politologist wrote that "Gorbachev may
have had an internal ideological frontier which he could not cross
but if so neither he nor anyone else knows where it is".[8] In fact he
abandoned sacred cow after sacred cow, including the leading role
of the Party, and he embraced concepts totally alien to the Party
such as privatization. He knew better than the democrats egging
him on from the sidelines what the traffic could bear.

From about the end of 1989, with *glasnost* in full flood, separatist
movements gaining strength in the republics and "people power"
threatening to spread from Eastern Europe, the reform process was
running out of control and Gorbachev was reacting to events rather
than controlling them. He could have halted the process by resorting
to force and making his own position secure, but to his credit he
refused to do so; but his concessions to the democratic movement
were invariably too late for him to regain the initiative and the
leadership of the reform process. He believed that he must manage

the conservatives not confront them, for fear of provoking a backlash which he could not contain. The backlash eventually occurred; but he claimed in his memoir *The August Coup* that he had succeeded in steering Soviet society beyond a point of no return. "If the coup had taken place a year and a half or two years earlier it might have succeeded. But now society was completely changed". Andrei Grachev, addressing the question of whether Gorbachev should not have foreseen and prevented the coup, wrote that it would be better to ask how many coups Gorbachev managed to avert for five and a half years, each of which could have been successful and fatal because occurring in much more favourable circumstances.[9]

USSR Presidency

However, by 1990, under severe pressure from the conservatives, Gorbachev was losing momentum; he made three decisions which were fatal for *perestroika* and the prospects for a more civilized demise of the USSR. Once he had grasped the nettle of Article 6 of the Constitution and the Party had formally abandoned its monopoly of political power in March 1990 it was logical for Gorbachev to institute the Soviet presidency in order to provide a new focus of state authority and make himself formally independent of the Party. But he baulked at the risk of popular elections to the presidency and had himself elected, unopposed, by the Congress of People's Deputies (moreover having been nominated by the CPSU Central Committee). His chances of popular election at that time were good. His only credible opponent was Yeltsin, who would have had strong support in Russia but probably would not have achieved a majority in a majority of republics as prescribed in the draft constitution. Yeltsin, himself (admittedly not the most reliable witness when anything to do with Gorbachev is concerned) stated at the Eighth Congress in March 1993 that he was convinced Gorbachev would have won if he had taken the risk. Popular election would not only have immeasurably strengthened Gorbachev's authority (his lack of any popular mandate was always a fatal weakness), it would also have provided an authoritative centre which the USSR, already starting to come apart at the seams, so conspicuously lacked. As popularly elected USSR President, Gorbachev need not have been forced into the alliance with the central Soviet structures, the KGB,

MVD and the Army, which in the winter of 1990–1 fatally undermined the reform process and his credibility with the democratic movement.

Gorbachev has argued, probably sincerely, that it was the risk of political instability rather than to his own political future which persuaded him that it would be inopportune to hold presidential elections in the spring or summer of 1990. The dramatic events in Eastern Europe in 1989, followed by an upsurge of "people power" in the Soviet Union itself, culminating in the huge Moscow demonstration of 25 February, had produced something close to panic in the leadership. Gorbachev persuaded himself that a presidential election campaign could destabilize an already tense and potentially explosive situation.

Twenty-eighth Party Congress

It was evidently the loss of nerve engendered by the collapse of communism in Eastern Europe and the polarization of political forces in the Soviet Union which explains Gorbachev's second major mistake in 1990: his failure to make any serious effort to use the Twenty-eighth (and last) Congress of the CPSU in July 1990 to try to reform it or, as a last resort, divide it. He allowed the conservatives in the Party leadership to dictate a method of electing delegates, which ensured that the reformists were in a small minority. Yeltsin chose the right moment at the Congress itself to announce his departure from the Party and decisively reinforce his credentials with the democratic movement. Gorbachev resisted advice from his entourage to resign as Party leader or even leave the Party once he was elected President. It was partly a question of scruples: it would have been unseemly to abandon the Party which had brought him to power; partly a perhaps well-grounded fear that under different management the Party might prove dangerous. In his memoir, *December 1991*, Gorbachev wrote that that job of Party General-Secretary was "choking him", but he did not leave it for fear that the Party would then fall into the hands of his conservative opponents. By now, he was beginning to lose his illusions about the Party's reformist potential. Explaining his refusal to resign as Party leader after facing a storm of abuse at a meeting with middle-ranking Party officials during the July Congress, he remarked: "I musn't let that mangy enraged dog off the lead – if I do that the whole pack will be against me."[10]

500 Days

Lacking a popular mandate, Gorbachev was still beholden to the Party whose Central Committee had nominated him as President; and he still hoped that the Party could act as a unifying factor in a country whose central authority was crumbling. It was his concern for the cohesion of the Centre which led him to reject the chance to form an alliance with Yeltsin and the democratic camp and reassert leadership of the reform process. In the summer of 1990 he endorsed the "500 Days" programme for transition to a market economy, involving significant devolution of authority to the republics, devised by Shatalin and Yavlinsky and supported by his own economic adviser Petrakov. He discussed the programme with Yeltsin and a joint working group of their advisers was set up. A *Pravda* editorial of 7 August 1990 (by Yegor Gaidar) referred to a "political alliance" between Gorbachev and Yeltsin. But when the Prime Minister Ryzhkov stubbornly opposed the reform plan, Gorbachev retreated and attempted a compromise between the government's own proposals, the 500 Days Programme and a "presidential" variant of it. Yeltsin contemptuously dismissed the compromise as a marriage between a snake and a hedgehog. In the autumn there was again an atmosphere of crisis with rumours of plots to seize power and of military coups. Gorbachev was once more obsessed by fears of political instability. He feared that the resignation of the government at a time when central authority seemed to be fast evaporating would create a vacuum at the Centre, and he was worried that the 500 Days Programme yielded too much authority to the republics. Forced to choose, he preferred to keep Ryzhkov on board and reject the chance to form a timely alliance with Yeltsin and the republic leaders and regain leadership of the reform movement.

In the spring of the following year Gorbachev returned belatedly to the idea of such an alliance when he launched the Novo-Ogarevo process at the end of April 1991. Following the hard-line "winter offensive" culminating in the violence in Vilnius in January 1991, which virtually destroyed Gorbachev's credit with the democrats, Gorbachev had become almost a hostage of the reactionaries and at last began to perceive the serious threat from the Right. (By now he had alienated the power structures by his scruples and faced a 'pincer movement' from both flanks.) He evidently also believed that the results of the referendum on the preservation of the Union (March 1991) gave him a stronger hand in dealing with the republics. However, even if Gorbachev had moved earlier to support a radical, economic reform programme and devolution of significant power to the republics, the end result might still have been the same. The leaders of the central Soviet structures, as August 1991 showed, were not prepared to acquiesce in their own emasculation.

FAILURE OF LEADERSHIP?: YELTSIN

The Unfinished Revolution

In theory, the greatest missed opportunity in Russia's transition from communism is the failure to complete the democratic revolution which followed the defeat of the attempted coup in August 1991. The central pillars of the communist system had collapsed. The Party and KGB were discredited, only the army emerged relatively untainted but demoralized and deprived of political will. Organized opposition to political and economic reform had virtually disappeared. The crowds of Democratic Russia supporters who had rallied to the White House, cheered the dismantling of Dzerzhinsky's statue in front of the KGB headquarters and besieged the Central Committee building on Staraya Square, felt that the victory was theirs. Given any encouragement from Yeltsin they seemed capable of sweeping away the remnants of the communist system. In the post-putsch atmosphere, Yeltsin could have purged the Party and KGB apparatus and dismantled their organizations. He went no further than to suspend the Communist Party and confiscate its assets, ostentatiously signing a decree to that effect over the protests of Gorbachev at a session of the Russian parliament. Yeltsin, addressing the issue in his memoirs, claims that he was haunted by the spectre of October 1917: "pogroms, riots, looting, constant meetings, anarchy . . . I could have turned August into October 1917 with one gesture, one stroke of the pen. But I didn't do it. And I am not sorry".[11]

Gavriil Popov (Mayor of Moscow at the time of the coup), in an article in *Izvestiya* on the first anniversary of the putsch, gives credit to Yeltsin for the fact that the failure of the coup was not followed by anarchy and bloodshed at the hands of groups of zealous "democrats" who poured into Moscow on 22 August; and praises his decision to construct a coalition of democrats and members of the former *nomenklatura* prepared to implement reforms. There were pragmatic as well as moral reasons for Yeltsin's restraint. As Popov points out, Yeltsin had had to negotiate with sections of the army and the KGB during the coup to secure their neutrality or inaction; he had debts to pay. The White House had been defended not only by democrats but by deputies of different political persuasions and by members of Yeltsin's own team, former colleagues from the Communist Party apparatus (Yury Petrov, Oleg Lobov, Viktor Ilyushin *et al.*). In any case, there was no practical possibility for the democrats to "take power" after the putsch, since apart from Yeltsin they had no leadership, no programme and no organization.

To root out the communist system in Russia would have torn the country apart; the failure to do so has meant accepting a potentially fatal legacy, in the minds of some, leaving a cancer which had spread too far to be operable. But, as Gaidar pointed out in his essay "Building Russia", a lustration law, such as was adopted in Czechoslovakia, was not feasible in Russia where the intensity of the involvement of the Party in society and of society in the Party was of a quite different order.[12] A more limited ban on the state employment of former Central Committee, Regional and District Party officials would have been feasible; but this would have struck uncomfortably close to home – Yeltsin himself was a former senior Party official, as were many of his closest colleagues. In Gaidar's view, Yeltsin could and should have made more immediate cadre changes in the regions where the *nomenklatura* remained firmly entrenched.[13]

Not only was there no settling of accounts, there has been no real coming to terms with the communist past. The *glasnost* revelations about repression and abuse led to no trials or retribution against those responsible who are still alive (in contrast to the Soviet regime's relentless pursuit and punishment of ageing war criminals). Those whose crimes were exposed in the media remained aggressively unrepentant. *Glasnost* on Soviet history was intense but too short-lived perhaps for the message to sink fully home; and once all the barriers came down it was soon overtaken by the flood of cheap detective fiction, pornography and mysticism. "Camp literature" is no longer read and after Abuladze's *Repentance*, which made a huge impression when it was released in 1986, there has been no other major feature film to make a real impact on the public consciousness. Solzhenitsyn, when he returned to Russia in the summer of 1994, was shocked that so few had read or even heard of *Gulag Archipelago*.

The historical lesson was not fully learned, there was no repentance and nostalgia for the USSR soon re-emerged. The Russian Communist Party, with hundreds of thousands of members and millions of voters, makes no apology at all for the past. The Russian equivalent of Nuremberg might have been the Constitutional Court hearings on the CPSU and the Russian Communist Party. But the communists appeared as plaintiffs as well as accused, demanding the lifting of Yeltsin's ban on the Party's activities and the restoration of its property. At first on the defensive, it soon began to use the case as a propaganda platform. The Constitutional Court delivered equivocal verdicts in November 1992 and the summer of 1993 upholding the ban on the CPSU's leading organs but allowing the Communist Party to resume legal activities. The failure to bring to account anyone responsible for Stalinist repressions, the persecution of dissidents, the August putsch and the insurrection of October 1993 (whose leaders were released in the political amnesty of February 1994) is sometimes attributed by Russian liberals to a new tolerance and humanity, a reluctance to seek revenge or perpetuate old hatreds. But the effect has been to create an impression of powerlessness and lawlessness and feed the sense of impunity of reactionary politicians who make no secret of their intention to bring the democrats to account should they return to power.

New Elections

If a revolutionary settling of accounts with the old system was neither practicable nor desirable, there was a democratic, peaceful alternative: new elections under a new constitution to provide a democratic base for the post-communist order. Yeltsin acknowledges in his memoirs that the main lost opportunity of the post-putsch period was the chance for a radical change of the parliamentary system.[14] He writes that the idea of dissolving the Congress and calling elections and perhaps raising the issue of a new constitution for the new country was mooted but not taken up. It may have been wrong, he writes, to advance on the economic front, leaving the reform of the political system for later. But he felt that the painful measures proposed by Gaidar required calm, not new, social upheavals. Talking informally to foreign diplomats in

Moscow in April 1993, Yeltsin put it more bluntly: he had spent sleepless nights reproaching himself for not having taken action immediately after the collapse of the August coup to get a new constitution approved and provide a democratically legitimate base for the three branches of power. But at the time he had shared the general sense of euphoria and the opportunity had been missed.

There were political and practical arguments against new elections. (According to Gaidar, in the political circumstances of the time they were out of question.)[15] The Russian Supreme Soviet had been the centre of resistance to the putsch and deputies, with few exceptions, had supported Yeltsin; a number of local Soviets had also declared for Yeltsin, although probably more had sat on the fence or supported the putsch. To dissolve the parliament in its hour of triumph would have seemed unjust and ungrateful. (Technically, Yeltsin did not have the Constitutional power to call elections but his right to do so would probably not have been challenged.) It was too soon to attempt to hold multi-party elections and it was also argued that elections would not have produced a parliament much different in political complexion. (As Yeltsin put it: "Was society ready to put forward other, better deputies?") In fact the change in the political balance would probably have been small but significant. The communists were chastened in the aftermath of the putsch – deputies from the old *nomenklatura* would probably not have been re-elected if they had ventured to stand. (In the event, they were able to sit tight and resume their true colours when the political climate changed.) A list of candidates endorsed by Yeltsin in new elections could have produced a majority of deputies committed to his support. Above all, elections could have produced some kind of popular mandate for radical, economic reform and at the least a parliament not determined from the outset to frustrate them.

The practical arguments against elections are perhaps more convincing. Events moved too fast. In the four months following the coup, the Russian leadership was preoccupied with the renewed power struggle to gain control of what remained of the central apparatus, while negotiating first to produce an adulterated version of the Union Treaty and then the Belovezhsky Agreement, which destroyed the Union. To hold elections in this turbulent transitional period would have been extremely difficult. Immediately following the collapse of the USSR, the Gaidar government launched its radical reform programme, which in view of the collapse of the economy could not have been further delayed. Elections in the aftermath of the price liberalization of 2 January 1992 would have been a risky undertaking. Yeltsin evidently saw no need to take risks. His own position was secure. His standing was high and he had obtained special powers from the Fifth Congress for one year to introduce economic reform measures and make changes in the government without consulting parliament. He did not anticipate serious problems with the parliament and thought he could rely on his personal prestige and popularity. He felt under no obligation to bring to power the democrats, who were under the illusion that it was they who had won the victory in August. (Like Gorbachev, he had never entirely trusted them and felt more comfortable with reform-minded apparatchiki than with radical intellectuals.) As a result, the emerging Russian state was stuck half-way in the Soviet era; its parliament and courts, rooted in the communist system, the KGB only superficially reformed. This was a very fragile political base for launching radical economic reforms, the rationale for which was incomprehensible alike to the majority of deputies and the mass of the population. It set the scene for the protracted bitter and pernicious constitutional crisis of 1992 to 1993.

Another possible option for Yeltsin after the putsch was to seek to replace Gorbachev as President of the USSR, while remaining Russian President. This course was advocated by Gavriil Popov, who argued that the Russian leadership should have convened the USSR Congress and had Yeltsin elected Soviet President.[16] This would have made it possible to dismantle the USSR without totally destroying it and while preserving "much of what was useful in the USSR". According to Popov, Yeltsin did not want to be Soviet President; but the Democrats should have insisted. In fact Yeltsin's subsequent memoirs suggest that he did toy with the idea but not very seriously (as Burbulis has confirmed). Yeltsin had fought too long against the bogey of the "Centre" for this to be a credible move. And for the non-Russian republics, already reacting nervously to the upsurge of Russian triumphalism following the defeat of the coup, it would have been totally unacceptable – especially for Ukraine whose involvement in any future form of Union was regarded by the Russian leadership as absolutely essential.

Constitutional Crisis: Delayed Dissolution

If Yeltsin had any illusions about the nature of the Russian parliament in late 1991, they must have largely vanished by Spring of

1992 when at the Sixth Congress, Gaidar's government was almost forced into resignation. Yeltsin hinted at the possible dissolution of the parliament during the Congress and afterwards called for a million signatures to be collected for a referendum on the issue. But he drew back. In 1992, between the Sixth and Seventh Congresses, he failed to decide between a policy of compromise or confrontation and repeatedly fell between two stools. A concerted effort to lobby fractions in 1992 might have won enough deputies to his side to have at least neutralized Khasbulatov, who was making himself increasingly unpopular with much of the opposition. But Yeltsin was still vacillating when the Seventh Congress began in December. The result was his mistimed challenge to the Congress which went off at half-cock and led to a serious political reverse. The referendum he had demanded in his challenge to the Congress was included in adulterated form in the Seventh Congress Compromise Agreement; but in the early months of 1993 he again backed away from the idea until, following a further serious set-back at the Eighth Congress in March, which amended the Constitution to further reduce presidential powers, he attempted to impose a referendum on the Congress by a decree which introduced a period of special rule. The Ninth Congress later the same month, having failed in an attempt to impeach him, finally agreed to a referendum in April but rigged the terms and the questions to ensure that the parliament could suffer no political consequences whatever the outcome.

Yeltsin won a clear vote of confidence and support for his economic policies in the referendum and was in a strong moral position to dissolve Congress and call early parliamentary elections, although the referendum did not provide him with constitutional authority to do so. He could with little risk have taken the high moral ground by agreeing to simultaneous presidential and parliamentary elections. Once again he let the opportunity slip, preferring a strategy of outflanking the parliament by promoting his own constitution for a presidential republic via a specially convened constitutional conference. This initiative was pursued with too little energy or urgency and predictably ran into the sand. Had Yeltsin taken in April, in the wake of his referendum success, the action he eventually resorted to in September, a demoralized parliament would have offered little resistance; and the support of the security forces and military for a President who had just renewed his mandate would scarcely have been in doubt. The risk of conflict and bloodshed would have been correspondingly small.

December 1993 Elections

After the event there was a tendency to regard the outcome of the 1993 Duma elections as the inevitable or logical result of popular resentment at economic hardship and the perceived failure of economic reform, and revulsion at the assault on the parliament building. However, widespread expectations of success for the democrats were not entirely ill-founded and appeared to be supported by the early opinion polls. If the democratic parties had formed a coalition instead of attacking each other – if they had run an effective television campaign – the result might have been different. Yeltsin's refusal to endorse Russia's Choice or do more than indicate general sympathy for the democratic parties was unfortunate. It could be argued that Yeltsin's name would have been more of a liability than an asset after the October violence for which many held him responsible. But the pattern of the elections in the constituencies showed a preference for familiar and strong personalities, including Russia's Choice ministers, e.g. Kozyrev, Shumeiko, Pamfilova, who all won healthy majorities. This throws doubt on the theory that the voters were registering a protest against the reforms and the democrats. Yeltsin's name at the head of a Russia's Choice list, or his clear endorsement of Gaidar's electoral bloc, might have made a significant difference. In the event only the Liberal Democratic Party list was headed by a charismatic figure who made a direct personal appeal to the electorate. But Yeltsin's refusal to commit himself to the democrats was entirely consistent with the attitude he had taken since he first achieved an independent political power base as Chairman of the Russian Supreme Soviet.

TRANSITIONAL CRISIS

Different policies or decisions by Gorbachev or Yeltsin might have made the transitional process less painful in some respects, but a transitional crisis was inevitable. The gradual or partial dismantling of the Soviet system would have failed like all previous attempts at reform in Russia and the Soviet Union. The system was monolithic and deeply entrenched: change in one element of the system (political, ideological, economic) affected all others. The system had to be effectively smashed to allow serious reform to proceed. The Chinese option was not available to the Soviet leadership, i.e. the imposition of market reform combined with the preservation of tight political control. The economic and political systems in the Soviet Union were totally integrated; moreover Gorbachev did not have sufficient political power, as did the Chinese leadership, to force the Party apparat to accept reforms affecting its own interests.

The total incapacitation of the Communist system was, therefore, an essential pre-requisite for reform; but it entailed heavy costs since it led to the breakdown of necessary and normal functions of the State and no new institutions could be immediately developed to replace them. The deterioration of the social infrastructure, the growth of crime and corruption, indiscipline and instability, coupled with the economic hardship of the reforms, became associated in the Russian public mind with four years of the "Democrats", rather than the legacy of 74 years of Communism. The low political culture of Russian society, with its instincts of dependency, security and egalitarianism, provided an intolerant environment for radical and sudden economic and political change.

Losers

The losers from the collapse of the old political system inevitably outnumbered the winners. Every section of Soviet society was heavily dependent on the State. Even those not materially worse off have suffered some loss of status, security or self-esteem:

- *Industrial workers*. There is still no mass unemployment, but millions of workers are on short-time or only nominally employed; they have suffered a reduction of both status and security. Those in defence industry "company towns" have almost no prospects of alternative employment.
- *Public sector workers*. Under the Soviet system they suffered low pay and low prestige, but their earnings are now one-half the national average, and reductions of government expenditure on health, education, etc., have severely affected morale.
- *Peasants*. Slow progress in land privatization is one of the main failures of the economic reforms. This is due not only to the resistance of the agrarian lobby – collective and State farm bureaucrats in alliance with former Party officials are still firmly entrenched in the countryside – but the lack of response to new opportunities from farm workers themselves.

Russian sociologists claim that the Soviet system destroyed the Russian peasantry as a class, reducing them to hired workers dependent on alcohol and the state. Support for democratic reform in the countryside, drained of the young and able for decades, is minimal.

- *Pensioners.* Approaching 25 per cent of the population, almost by definition they had little or nothing to gain from the collapse of the USSR and the reforms. They saw their savings severely eroded by inflation in 1992 and, above all, lost status and self-esteem having worked all their lives for a system and a cause now despised and rejected in a country which no longer exists. They are politically active: the majority turn out more conscientiously than any other section of the population to vote in elections; the most militant are regularly visible as the hard-faced, bemedalled veterans waving red flags in opposition demonstrations. (There were many victims of Stalinism and the Soviet system among the older generation, but fewer survived than among those who supported or accepted it.)

- *Military.* Army officers suffered severe blows to their morale and material circumstances as well as a loss of status, security and public esteem. They are too lacking in cohesion to be a political force in their own right but tend to support nationalists and communists at elections (according to Yeltsin, one-third of the Army voted for Zhirinovsky in the December 1993 Duma elections). They present no direct threat to democracy but they are unreliable props for it in the last resort as the hesitations and ambiguities of August 1991 and October 1993 showed.

Intelligentsia

The creative and scientific intelligentsia, the traditional bulwark of liberal and democratic values, was also heavily dependent on the State and has suffered accordingly as subsidies for the vast network of feather-bedded institutes, academies, unions, publications, etc., have been drastically reduced. The most enterprising scientists have prospered or joined the brain-drain, but many, and not only the undeserving, have gone to the wall. Those left in reduced circumstances have become embittered and some accuse the democrats of destroying Russia's science with Western help. Dispossessed scientists, especially from the military industrial complex, provide much of the ideological leadership for the nationalist and hard-line communist movements, as do "establishment" writers, actors, film directors, etc., and the army of former cultural bureaucrats. Even creative intellectuals who retain their liberal values and democratic ideals have become dismayed and disillusioned by the effects on Russian culture of rampant commercialization and the flooding of the cultural "market" with the cheapest and nastiest of Western products.

The mass support for the democrats during *perestroika* was provided by a coalition, mostly based on ethical protest against the Soviet system. In the light of post-Communist realities, with the democrats nominally in power, it inevitably broke up, leaving a dwindling minority of those ideologically committed to reforms and a small, though growing, minority of those who stand to benefit from them. Few in the population understood the rationale for the alleged "shock therapy" or the extent of the economic collapse which preceded it. (In truth, little effort was made to explain either.) Gaidar was attempting to create the social base for his reforms in the process of implementing them. Progress was bound to be slow and the number of winners small. There are new businessmen, traders and entrepreneurs; professional people, intellectuals with the initiative to profit from their skills; the beginnings of a middle-class which has never existed in Russia. There is support, if not for democrats and reform, then for the status quo, from bureaucrats, industrial managers, Party officials who have adjusted to the new system having been well-placed in the old one to benefit from "*nomenklatura* privatization" (the misappropriation of State property which took place in the main during the last two years before the collapse of the USSR). A growing number of people in the rest of society are learning to adjust and adapt and, especially among the younger generation, to perceive the widening of their horizons as compensation for present insecurity and disruption.

Danger of a Backlash

But it is questionable whether this amounts to an adequate political base to contain the backlash against economic hardship, loss of national self-esteem and revulsion against the breakdown of law and order and the prevalence of corruption and privilege. (Corruption and privilege are no greater than under the Soviet system but they are more blatant and in forms psychologically alien to Russians and, therefore, unacceptable.) Russians are in fact better off than the statistics suggest and the social costs of reform have been exaggerated; but the "feel-bad factor" is still dominant. A public opinion survey carried out in the spring of 1994 found that a majority, 51 per cent, of the population gave a positive rating to the former communist regime and only 36 per cent had a positive view of the current regime. A larger majority, 61 per cent, had a positive view of the former economic system with only 7 per cent in favour of the market. 65 per cent stated that their families were better off five years ago (i.e. 1989).[17] However, the younger the age group questioned the more positive was the view about the new system; and only 23 per cent of the total said they would welcome a restoration of the communist system, which suggests that nostalgia about the past does not necessarily imply a desire to turn the clock back.

It is a moot point whether regardless of the negative attitude of the population and the intentions of any future reactionary government the economic changes of the past four years could now be reversed. Chubais announced already in March 1994 that over half the country's GDP was produced by the private sector, and, by the end of 1994, 60 per cent of the labour force was employed outside the State sector.[18] More and more citizens have a stake in the market economy as owners of flats, dachas, shares, etc. New commercial structures and banks with growing political influence represent important vested interests. In two or three years' time the private sector could become self-sustaining and a significant political force but at present much of it still consists of ephemeral profiteering, "feeding off the corpse of the decaying command economy". The mainstream Russian communists (and their Agrarian clones) pay lip-service to economic reform and accept in principle privatization in some forms and the "social market". If they were to achieve power (e.g. in a coalition with nationalists) they would probably not set out to restore the central planning system or re-nationalize all privatized firms. The prospect is rather that their policies would be destabilizing (e.g. subsidies to industry and agriculture, wages and prices controls, allocation of key commodities) and would cause serious loss of confidence and disruption to the still immature private sector; and that their instinctive remedies for the chaos they would cause would lead step by step to the reimposition of more and more State controls. One thing leads to another.

Fears of instability and the possible reversal of the "democratic gains" of the last ten years has reopened a debate among Russian politologists on whether Russia was capable of a direct transition to democracy or needed an intermediate period of enlightened authoritarianism. In mid-*perestroika*, 1988–9, scholars and commentators (e.g. Migranyan and Klyamkin) argued that the problems and costs entailed by radical economic reform would lead to its failure unless it was imposed by a strong political authority. It is now argued (e.g. by Gordon and Pliskevich)[19] that a staged transition from totalitarianism through authoritarianism to democracy was not in fact feasible. While it remained intact, the system would not have tolerated and would have rejected partial and gradual reform. The smashing of the system and a democratic breakthrough were essential. But the "great leap forward to democracy" was doomed to failure because of the inevitable reaction of an ill-prepared society to economic and social hardship and political responsibility. The situation now requires some "restoration" of the State authority involving strengthening the executive, limiting parliamentary powers and partially curtailing civil liberties to enable the State to deal with organized crime and restore stability. A period of semi-authoritarianism, it is argued, may therefore be necessary to guard against a political reversal and prepare the way for an eventual resumption of progress towards full democracy.

Comparisons have been made with the reaction against reform and the democrats in Eastern and Central Europe and the Baltic Republics where reformed and renamed communist parties have enjoyed some electoral success and / or a return to power, for example in Poland, Hungary and Lithuania. The economic and political problems of transition from Communism are such that some retrenchment is hardly surprising or necessarily a dangerous development. The difficulty for Russia is that there is no acceptable alternative to the present administration in the shape for example of some centrist, social democratic or reformed communist party which might set acceptable limits to the retreat from political and economic reform. In Russia the reverse swing of the pendulum could go a long way towards right- or left-wing authoritarianism.

The communist and nationalist oppositions, including their representatives in parliament, have not accepted the new rules of the game, though prepared for the time being to observe them because they think they can win. But they will follow the parliamentary path only while it leads to power. And if they win by the rules there is every possibility that they could change them or throw away the rule book. There is no evidence for the widespread assumption among Western observers and even in Russia that the Russian Communists have changed their spots and turned into budding social democrats. As Gaidar notes in *Building Russia*: "The trouble is our Communist Party has by no means rejected the past, its contempt for law and the Constitution, or non-parliamentary methods of struggle, including armed revolt."

Viktor Sheinis, a moderate democratic deputy and a politologist respected for his judicious views on Russian politics, has suggested that an opposition victory would spell the end of democracy:

> in Russia the coming of the opposition to power can only be a recipe for disaster because there are not many responsible politicians among its ranks and the positive changes which have been taking place since 1985 are not irreversible.

The restoration of Stalinism would not be possible but a "feast of the victors" would be very costly.[20] The fact that democratic principles and freedom of speech are now widely accepted as normal in Russia is a serious obstacle to a return to authoritarianism but not a guarantee against it. The political struggle is still centred on the Constitutional order itself and the legitimacy of the new Russian State. It is about the system rather than within the system.

HAS THE WEST GOT IT RIGHT?

Financial Support

Russian reformists and some Western economists have argued that the West missed an historic opportunity to underpin Russia's economic and democratic reform by failing to provide rapid, large-scale financial assistance when it was most needed during the crucial early months of 1992. Gaidar's reform, launched on 2 January 1992, involved a programme of price liberalization and macroeconomic stabilization precisely on the lines which the West had been urging on the Soviet and Russian governments. The reform ran into heavy and mounting domestic political opposition from a combination of communist and nationalist deputies and the industrial lobby, spearheaded by state enterprise directors. *Izvestiya*, on 7 February, called in alarmist terms for Western aid to be expedited. In delaying, "the

West was committing one of the most tragic mistakes of the 20th Century". Former President Nixon, in an article in the *Wall Street Journal* of 12 March, wrote of the "potentially dangerous delay" in providing large-scale financial assistance. The UK favoured a stabilization fund but President Bush, in part because of the US elections, was reluctant to promote early assistance for one.

According to Gaidar (in a conversation in May 1995), he had full freedom of manoeuvre in economic decision-making only up to April 1992. In May to June, the reformers were already on the defensive and by July the window of opportunity had closed. The announcement by President Bush on the eve of the Sixth Congress in April of the G7 $24 billion financial assistance package had been politically helpful (as was the admission of Russia and other FSU countries to membership of the IMF on 27 April), but there was no follow-up. The stabilization fund and other elements in the package were contingent on agreement on an IMF programme which took a long time to negotiate. According to Gaidar, IMF decisions were taken too slowly – in months when, for the survival of the reform policy, "it was a matter of days or even hours".

In face of a fierce, domestic political onslaught on the reform policy, and in the absence of a clear and major commitment by Western governments for financial support, Yeltsin lost his nerve, sacked the Fuel and Energy Minister, Lopukhin (who wanted to liberalize energy prices), and brought representatives of the industrial lobby into the cabinet. By the time the granting of the IMF stand-by arrangement was announced in July the government had unleashed a flood of subsidized credits to industry and agriculture and was in full retreat from the policy of stabilization. The reforms and the reformists suffered a set-back from which they have struggled to recover ever since, and which had serious political as well as economic consequences.

In early 1992, Western governments appeared to focus their efforts principally on humanitarian aid and the debt question, leaving the negotiation of vital credits and financial support to the IMF, which applied rigidly its normal terms and conditions, despite some pressure from the G7 for greater speed and flexibility. At one of the main historical turning points in this century a broader political approach, on the lines or at least in the spirit of the Marshall Plan (with due allowance for the very different post-war situation), was surely called for. According to Anders Aslund, in 1948–9 the US contributed 2.1 per cent of its GDP to European recovery, compared to a budget request for 1995 for aid to the whole FSU of 0.01 per cent.[21] The Russian perception, however unfair, across the political spectrum has been that the West promised much and delivered little, a perception which has contributed to growing cynicism and resentment towards the West.

NATO Expansion

There is no historical precedent for an imperial power abandoning so much territory and control, if not exactly voluntarily then without much resistance and with remarkably good grace, while accepting the terms and embracing the ideals of its adversaries. The hard-nosed Western view is that Moscow deserved no prizes for yielding up its ill-gotten gains and acknowledging at last that the West was right about democracy, capitalism and human rights. This is perhaps true, but Russia at least asked little in return but speedy acceptance into the various clubs of civilized Western nations and respect for a country which had managed to salvage its great power status and desperately wanted a seat at the top table. The Russian perception is that neither acceptance nor respect have been granted in full measure: indeed Russians feel, understandably, that for all the West's economic and political support they have been treated as a defeated country – the loser moreover not only in the Cold War but in World War II as well.

Given Russia's legacy from the collapse of communism of economic, social and ethnic problems, the emergence of a Versailles complex would be no surprise. It would be made much more likely by implementation of the policy of NATO enlargement eastwards, which, viewed from Moscow, represents a move by the West to take advantage of Russia's weakness to establish a new military balance in Europe. It would, moreover, involve the incorporation into a military alliance, regarded by Russians for decades as hostile, of a group of countries, former allies, with deep historical grievances and accounts to settle with Russia; and a vested interest in highlighting a threat from Moscow since this provides both the rationale for their NATO membership and a lever for obtaining political and economic support from the West.

The assumption of a Russian threat, which is now widespread in the West, could prove to be self-fulfilling since the effect of the domestic political repercussions would be to undermine the democrats and provide grist to the mill of the Reds / Browns. Wherever the line was finally drawn between NATO and Russia (assuming that it is not on the frontiers of Russia itself) the countries in between would be exposed and vulnerable and there would be enormous pressure on any Russian leadership to draw them into a military alliance or special security arrangements.

At present, no real Russian threat exists. There is certainly widespread support in Russia for the idea that Russia should have a dominant influence in the FSU and for some measure of economic and political reintegration. But no-one outside the hard-line fringe believes for all their rhetoric that the reconstitution of the USSR or the Russian Empire is practicable or desirable. And not even the hard-line fringe believes that Russia has the will, resources or desire to re-establish hegemony in Eastern Europe.

Yeltsin's victory in the June/July 1996 Presidential elections, and his subsequent appointment of the leading reformer Chubais as his Head of Administration, could open a new and hopeful chapter in Russia's turbulent transition to democracy, and improve prospects for genuine partnership with the West. But Russia's democratic and economic reforms still rest on fragile foundations, and the West's patient support and understanding for a country striving to overcome a uniquely traumatic historical legacy will be of vital importance.

Notes

1 Richard Sakwa, *Russian Politics and Society*, Routledge, 1992, p. 32.
2 Article in *The New Russia*, edited by G. Lapidus, Westview Press, 1995, p. 122.
3 Viktor Yaroshenko, *Novy Mir* no. 3, 1993 (quoted by Zaslavsky).
4 Ye. Gaidar, *Gosudarstvo i Evolyutsia*, Moscow, 1995.
5 A. M. Yakovlev. Private conversation, Moscow, January 1993.
6 A. Grachev, *Kremlevskaya Khronika*, Moscow, 1994.
7 *Ibid.*
8 I. Klyamkin, *Literaturnaya Gazeta*, 16 August 1989.
9 Grachev, *Kremlevskaya Khronika*, p. 280.
10 A. Chernyaev, *6 let s Gorbachevym*, Moscow, 1994, p. 356.
11 *Zapiski Prezidenta*, Moscow, 1994, p. 166.
12 Ye. Gaidar, *Otkrytaya Politika*, May 1994.
13 Gaidar. Private conversation, Moscow, May 1995.
14 *Zapiski Prezidenta*, Moscow, 1994, p. 165.
15 Gaidar. Private conversation, Moscow, May 1995.
16 G. Popov, *Izvestiya*, 24 August 1992.

17　*New Russia Barometer III*, Richard Rose and Christian Haerpfer. *Studies in Public Policy*, no. 228, University of Strathclyde.

18　A. Aslund, *How Russia Became a Market Economy*, Brookings Institution, 1995.

19　A. Migranyan, *Novy Mir* no. 7, 1989; L. Gordon, N. Pliskevich, *Razvilki i Lovushki perekhodnogo perioda. Polis*, no. 3, 1994.

20　V. Sheinis, *Political Interlude: Russia Between Two Elections*, July 1994.

21　A. Aslund, *How Russia Became a Market Economy*, Brookings Institution, 1995.

Part I

The End of Perestroika: 1989–1991

1

End of the Party's Leading Role

DEBATE ON PARTY REFORM: NOVEMBER 1989–FEBRUARY 1990

By the end of 1989 the reform process was encountering severe turbulence, with the party conservatives dismayed and rebellious in face of the collapse of communism in Eastern Europe, the growing independence movement in the Baltic Republics, ethnic unrest elsewhere in the USSR and continuing economic decline. The frontiers of *glasnost* had expanded to the point where the history debate was beginning to call in question the role of Lenin and the values of the October Revolution and thus the legitimacy of the existing political system. Gorbachev was under pressure from two directions: increasingly disillusioned radicals urged him to come off the fence and opt for radical reform of the Party and the economy; Party conservatives more and more stridently called on him to stop the rot and preserve the Union and the Party from disintegration.

The issue of Party reform was coming to a head. Gorbachev had first broached the question of political reform at the January 1987 CPSU Central Committee Plenum, when he admitted that the problems which had accumulated in the Soviet Union were in significant measure linked to defects in the Party itself and he spoke of the need to democratize the Party and society. Originally conceived as a way to weaken resistance from the entrenched Party apparat to economic reform which had made little progress, political reform soon developed a rationale and momentum of its own. At the 19th Party Conference in June 1988 and the subsequent Central Committee Plenum in July, the concept was broadened to include the idea of the "socialist legal state" and major Constitutional changes designed to achieve what Gorbachev called a "socialist system of checks and balances". A new "highest organ of state power", the Congress of People's Deputies had been elected in

April 1989, which in turn elected a new Supreme Soviet as a standing Parliament in session for up to 8 months each year rather than a few days like its rubber stamp predecessor; the centre of political gravity was beginning to shift away from the Party. At the same time the unitary nature of the Party, the glue which held the USSR together, was under threat from the growth of national communism in the Baltic Republics and the Transcaucusus. Growing alarm in the Party was beginning to generate a backlash. At the July 1989 CPSU Central Committee Conference, Prime Minister Ryzhkov had lamented bitterly that the Party no longer held the levers of control.

A plenum of the Party Central Committee met on 9 December amid widespread reports that a group of Regional Party Secretaries spearheaded by the Leningrad Party organization were planning to demand Gorbachev's removal. In a break with recent practice the speeches at the plenum were not published. On 19th and 20 December *Pravda* carried denials by Politburo members of rumours of a split in the Politburo and moves against Gorbachev. At the Second Congress of People's Deputies in December, Gorbachev made an angry and emotional intervention to reject accusations that he was promoting the disintegration of the USSR and the Communist Party, and the burial of socialism. He said he remained a "convinced communist" and hinted at his readiness to resign.

The Central Committee met again on 25–26 December in the wake of the decision of the Lithuanian Communist Party announced on 20 December to leave the CPSU. In his opening address, the only part of the proceedings to be published, Gorbachev declared that the present Party and State leadership would not permit the dissolution of the union. He also spoke of the need to accelerate *perestroika* and reform of the Party. The Resolution of the Plenum called for Gorbachev to visit Lithuania.

Article 6

The debate on reform in the CPSU intensified in the run-up to the Central Committee plenum scheduled for early February which was to discuss the platform for the Twenty-eighth Party Congress. The key issues were demands for the revision or abolition of Article 6 of the Constitution, which enshrined the leading role of the Party in State and society, and for the lifting of the ban on the fractions within the Party. (The radicals had tried but failed to put Article 6 onto the agenda of the Second Congress in December.) *Pravda* was now publishing weekly features on Party reform which began in lively and radical fashion though later adopting a more cautious line. It published one letter from a worker who compared the Party leadership to a bad chess player who in losing a piece has lost the match but does not realize it. Gorbachev was already beginning to shift his ground. During his visit to Vilnius in January, he retreated from his previous robust opposition to the multi-party system, remarking that he saw "no tragedy in the multi-party system" and no need to fear it "as the devil fears incense".

Democratic Platform

An All-Union Conference of Party Reformists took place at the Moscow Aviation Institute on 20–21 January 1990 at which the principal figures were Yeltsin, Yury Afanasiev, Gavriil Popov, Murashev, Burbulis, Stankevich and Shostakovsky (the rector of the Higher Party School). The conference adopted a platform for the forthcoming Twenty-eighth Party Congress, the main points of which were:

- abolition of Article 6;
- introduction of the multi-party system;
- transformation of the CPSU into a parliamentary type of political party.

The basic aim of the Party reformists was to gain a majority at the Twenty-eighth Congress and/or prepare the ground for a split and the founding of a new Social Democratic Party. The reformists formed what was in effect a party fraction under the title "Democratic Platform in the CPSU". At this stage reforming the Party was still a key political objective for Yeltsin. At the 19th Party Conference in June 1988 he had asked for rehabilitation in the Party; at the inaugural conference in July 1989 of the Inter-Regional Group (the opposition group of Congress Deputies), his speech had focused almost exclusively on the need to reform the Party.

February 1990 Plenum

Gorbachev moved the Party further towards reform at the Central

Committee plenum on 5–7 February 1990. It adopted a platform for the Twenty-eighth Congress which called for the revision of Article 6 of the Constitution and in effect accepted the eventual emergence of other political parties. The end of Article 6 had enormous implications for the political system since it referred not only to the Party's leading role but to the CPSU as "the nucleus of the political system and of all State and public organizations". The abolition of the article in effect meant the withdrawal of the Party from its ubiquitous controlling presence within all public and State organizations; the withering away of the *nomenklatura* system and the end of Marxism-Leninism as the State ideology, i.e. the unravelling of the Party from the fabric of the whole system. The Democratic Platform was already campaigning for the withdrawal of Party organs from the army, the KGB and the MVD. Gorbachev himself seemed reluctant to accept the implications. Even after conceding the removal of Article 6, he continued to refer to the CPSU as the ruling Party responsible for the state and the economy and declared it should not become involved in "frivolous parliamentary games." (Some people in the Party took the line that the removal of Article 6 had no practical significance since before 1977 the CPSU had not even been mentioned in the Constitution.)

The February plenum also endorsed Gorbachev's proposal for the introduction of the presidential system in the USSR which implied the transfer of real political power from the Party leadership to elective State institutions. But the draft platform was much more cautious on reform within the Party than on the relationship between the CPSU and the State, and retained the sacred cows of democratic centralism and the ban on fractions. The Party thus appeared in principle ready to loosen its grip on power and allow the emergence of other parties while refusing to accept the practical implications and adapt itself so that it could compete in a multi-party system. On these grounds Yeltsin voted against the platform, the only Central Committee member to do so. Yeltsin had argued that the best way to transfer to the multi-party system was to lift the ban on fractions. Otherwise there would be a mass exodus of Party members to join new parties. Yeltsin no doubt had in mind the possibility of a split in the CPSU but one which would leave a reformist wing with organizations intact and material resources at its disposal. Yeltsin said in an interview on Hungarian television in February 1990[1] that changes could still be made to the draft and he indicated that he would campaign to radicalize it.

People Power

In pressing ahead with a measure of Party reform in the teeth of a hostile majority in the Politburo and the Central Committee, Gorbachev had to some extent benefited from an upsurge of popular radical feeling. In January and February a series of demonstrations, disturbances and local protests in major provincial cities in Russia and the Ukraine led to the resignation of upwards of a dozen hard-line regional Party Secretaries. The official media, especially the main evening news programme, *Vremya*, at first gave positive coverage to these developments, and the demonstrations, culminating in the huge Moscow manifestation of 4 February seemed to have a measure of official support. But as it began to appear that the revolutionary fever which had swept Eastern Europe was beginning to affect provincial Party strongholds in Russia and the Ukraine, the official attitude changed. The Party press took a much more cautious line on attempts to remove Party leaders in Ulyanovsk and Donetsk, and *Pravda* criticized the First Party Secretary in Voroshilovgrad for resigning too readily under local pressure. Gorbachev attacked the radicals in his speech to the Supreme Soviet on 14 February and *Pravda* published an editorial in almost hysterical tones referring to orators who called for the storming of the Kremlin and the Lubyanka.[2] Fears that the radical tide was getting out of hand and the alarmist tone in the official media increased sharply on the eve of the demonstration in Moscow on 25 February, (the anniversary of the February revolution), which attracted about a quarter of a million people despite a very heavy militia and army presence. But people power which Gorbachev had initially discreetly encouraged in order to intimidate the conservatives was now beginning to frighten him. This was a significant factor in his subsequent drift to the right. Gorbachev's close adviser Chernyaev wrote that the 25 February demonstration pushed Gorbachev back into the arms of the "dear Party"; he added that "the events of February and the reaction of those at the top put a sharp brake on *perestroika*".[3]

INSTITUTION OF THE USSR PRESIDENCY: MARCH 1990

The institution of the USSR Presidency was a logical corollary to the abandonment of the Party's leading role which left a political vacuum and required a new centre of executive authority at the

State level. It also enabled Gorbachev to acquire a new, independent and more stable power base, though despite repeated urging by some of his closest advisers he refused to abandon the bridge of the sinking Party ship. There were sound constitutional and political reasons for the move but it had all the hallmarks of hasty improvisation by Gorbachev.

Gorbachev had hitherto always resisted the idea of a presidential system, including as recently as October 1989 at the Supreme Soviet debate on constitutional amendments when the Presidency had been advocated by the Inter-Regional Group. Gorbachev put forward the proposals for the Executive Presidency in his report to the Central Committee plenum on 5 February and it was duly endorsed in the CPSU draft platform for the Twenty-eighth Congress. Gorbachev attempted to railroad through the institution of the Presidency in record time. The presidium of the Supreme Soviet, at his behest, proposed an Extraordinary Session of the People's Congress on 27 February to elect a USSR President. In the event the Congress took place on 12 March. Gorbachev justified the proposal on constitutional grounds but also argued that a strong State authority and a firm hand were required in view of growing ethnic and political unrest. In an intemperate speech in the Supreme Soviet on 27 February, he claimed that the Inter-Regional Group was seeking to block the Presidency because it hoped to profit from political instability. Gorbachev had evidently decided there was a crisis of authority and genuinely feared the possibility that he would be swept away by the radical tide. Controversy over the dubious legality of the emergency powers under which Soviet troops were moved into Baku in January may also have played a part in Gorbachev's decision to seek a new base of authority and additional executive powers.

The institution of the Presidency aroused opposition and misgivings in various political quarters. There were a number of controversial aspects:

- election of the first USSR President by the Congress instead of in a popular election;
- the combination of the Presidency and the post of Party General-Secretary;
- objections to the extent of the proposed Presidential powers, especially when combined with the party leadership;
- misgivings in the Republics about the strengthening of central

power, especially if it involved new powers to declare states of emergency (Lithuania brought forward its formal Declaration of Independence on 11 March in order to pre-empt a possible move by the new President).

Third USSR Congress: March 1990

At the Third Extraordinary Congress of People's Deputies, 12–15 March 1990, there was a contentious debate on Presidential powers and the procedure for the election of the President. Gorbachev in the Chair pushed through his proposals using dubious procedural tactics but obtained only a narrow constitutional (two-thirds) majority for election by the Congress. Gorbachev argued (supported by the influential academician Likhachev) that presidential elections in the current political unrest could be dangerously destabilizing.

Congress voted against the President remaining also leader of the CPSU but failed to achieve the necessary two-thirds majority. Gorbachev argued that it was essential to avoid creating two centres of political power. He clearly feared that the Party no longer under his control would undermine his own authority. (In his memoir, *December 1991 My Position*, Gorbachev claims that the job of General-Secretary was "choking him" but he did not leave it for fear that the Party would fall into the hands of his conservative opponents). He may also have calculated that his position as President would become less secure – the Central Committee had nominated him for the post and many deputies may have supported him reluctantly, from the habit of Party discipline.

The institution of the Presidency was nonetheless a major step to separate Party and State, and establish for the first time in Soviet history a legal constitutional basis for political power. The Politburo was thereby deprived of its ultimate political and juridical power; it was further sidelined by the creation of a Presidential Council, formally an advisory rather than a decision-making body, but including the occupants of the senior offices of State, and a Federation Council comprising the chairmen of Republic parliaments. But although Gorbachev acquired a certain independence from the Party and more formal power, the lack of a popular mandate meant that he did not increase his authority. He now held all the levers of power but less and less seemed to happen when he pulled them.

COUNTER-ATTACK BY PARTY HARD-LINERS: APRIL–JUNE 1990

The overall political trend was one of accelerating polarization of political forces with the radicals on the "left" and the Russian nationalists and Party conservatives on the "right" increasingly alienated from Gorbachev and the middle ground rapidly eroding. Right-wing Russian nationalists, led by the Russian Writers Union, were becoming increasingly vocal and extreme. In the first issue of *Literary Russia* for 1990, Prokhanov, derided by radicals as "the Nightingale of the General Staff", published an article which epitomized the apocalyptic gloom and strident hostility to the reforms of the right-wing nationalists. It represented *perestroika* as a seven-point programme for the destruction of the Soviet State which would culminate in a nuclear civil war. Later a group of 74 Russian writers published an appeal calling for support from the army and KGB to protect the state and prevent the corruption of Russian morals by political and economic reform.

Central Committee "Open Letter"

In a significant and aggressive move, the Party Central Committee issued an open letter of 10 April attacking the Democratic Platform and authorizing local party organizations to expel its members. A number of DP leaders (including Yury Afanasiev, Nikolai Travkin and Igor Chubais) resigned though Yeltsin remained in the Party. The purpose of the letter was to isolate the radicals in the Party and ensure that as few members of the Democratic Platform as possible were elected delegates to the Twenty-eighth Party Congress. In endorsing this letter and also authorizing Regional Party Committees to adopt undemocratic procedures for electing delegates to the Congress (now brought forward to July) Gorbachev destroyed the last possibility for creating a reformed Party which would support, or at least no longer obstruct his policies.

Russian Communist Party

Party hard-liners opened a new front by setting up at a meeting in Leningrad on 21–22 April a "Russian CP in the CPSU." Gorbachev was opposed to the creation of a separate Russian Communist Party which he argued would either dominate the CPSU (since it would comprise nearly 60 per cent of its membership) or lead to its "federalization". Gorbachev also realized that it would represent a powerful reactionary political force outside his control, even if he remained leader of the CPSU. He had attempted to ward off such a development by creating a "Russian Buro" of the Central Committee headed by himself in December 1989. But he was obliged to concede the holding of an All-Union Conference of Russian communists, scheduled for June 1990 at which the creation of a separate RCP was to be discussed. In June, the Russian Communist Party Conference saw a victory of the hard-liners, who transformed the Conference into a Congress and elected Ivan Polozkov, First Secretary (Oleg Lobov came second in the first round of voting); Gennady Zyuganov was elected a Party Secretary.

TWENTY-EIGHTH CPSU CONGRESS: JULY 1990

At the Twenty-eighth and last CPSU Congress from 2–13 July, Gorbachev outmanoeuvred the hostile and resentful majority of delegates to secure his own re-election as General-Secretary, a revamped "federalized" and ineffectual party presidium and even the election of his own short list of nominees to the Central Committee. His leading hard-line opponent, Ligachev, was easily defeated by Ivashko in the vote for Deputy Leader of the Party. But this was an empty victory. The Congress marked the beginning of the end for the Party and the failure of Gorbachev's lengthy but ultimately half-hearted endeavour to make it the motor of the reform process, or at least preserve it as the glue for an increasingly fragmented state and society. The last hope of salvaging a viable and relevant Communist Party was a split which would leave a sizeable reformist wing with organization and resources in place. According to Otto Latsis (elected a member of the Central Committee at the Congress) Gorbachev might have had the support of 40 per cent of the delegates in the event of a split.[4] But in the event it was the Democratic Platform reformists among the delegates who split: some, including Sobchak and Popov, followed Yeltsin who demonstratively resigned from the Party at the Congress, while others remained in the CPSU to "continue the fight". The idea of a Social Democratic wing came to nothing. In effect the reformists had done what Stankevich had warned them not to do at the Democratic Platform Founding Congress – they "walked away from the Party with empty hands and bare bottoms".

The CPSU, largely neutralized as an effective political force, was in terminal decline, though still dangerous. It did not give birth to a viable Social Democratic Party but it spawned the Russian Communist Party which jumped aboard the nationalist bandwagon, survived the collapse of the USSR, inherited the Party structures and continues to exert a significant and reactionary influence. Rank and file party members left in droves (370,000 left the Party in the first six months of 1990 and a further 311,000 in July and August); those with political ambitions joined new democratic movements which were already proliferating but which lacked any solid ideological or social base.

Gorbachev made two fatal mistakes in the early part of 1990:

1   He overreacted to the radical upsurge and the threat of "people power", apparently fearing that the East European scenario was about to be re-enacted in the Soviet Union (anxieties reinforced by the May Day Parade when the tail end of the demonstrators on Red Square jeered and insulted him). He concluded that the situation was too unstable to risk a popular election for the Presidency of the USSR and had himself elected by the Congress instead. At that stage he might well have won a nation-wide election which would have strengthened immeasurably not only his personal authority but that of the Centre.

2   He torpedoed any final hope of reforming the CPSU and tilted the Party sharply to the right by authorizing the CPSU Central Committee Open Letter in April attacking the Democratic Platform. He mistakenly believed that the real threat was from the radical left while he could always handle the Party conservatives.

Gorbachev had apparently made himself secure from the hostile majority in the Central Committee by securing election as General-Secretary from the Congress itself. But one consequence of the end of the Party's ruling role, was that its officials no longer felt constrained by the traditional discipline and conformism and began to take a more openly aggressive stance. Although the Party was formally disconnected from the levers of power at the Centre, its structures and apparatus remained in place and, especially in the regions, retained considerable strength and power. It was also still exerting a pernicious influence through its structures within the army, the ministerial bureaucracy and the KGB.

the political spectrum, he lost more credibility. The bitter personal rivalry with Yeltsin who had now acquired his own power base in the Russian parliament was to vitiate any attempt by Gorbachev to move to the left decisively. He never lost his visceral distrust of the radicals; while the radicals were increasingly reluctant to work with and thus help to bolster USSR authorities already on the skids as power seeped away to the Republics.

Autumn Crisis

By the Autumn of 1990 there was a growing sense of crisis, almost panic. The media were full of predictions of nation-wide strikes, uprisings, coups and civil war; comparisons were made with the situation between February and October 1917.[7] Gorbachev was receiving floods of letters (organized and supplied by Kryuchkov) demanding that he impose law and order. During the second stage of the Russian Communist Party Congress, there were vicious attacks on the 500 Days Programme (which had been published in *Izvestiya* in early September) as anti-Soviet and a betrayal of socialism. In the liberal press Gorbachev was being spoken of as a prisoner of conservative forces or of his own stereotypes and limitations; he had "exhausted his reformist potential". Gorbachev ignored repeated demands for Ryzhkov's dismissal: from members of the Presidential Council, from Yeltsin at a press conference and from his own advisers.

Gorbachev's Additional Powers

The demonstration on 16 September organized by the Moscow Soviet to demand the resignation of the Ryzhkov government appeared to revive real or contrived fears in high places that the democrats were plotting to seize power (a re-run of the panic over the 25 February demonstration). Precautionary military deployments were apparently made on 10–11 September which leaked out and gave rise to fears in the democratic camp of a military coup. Such rumours were still rife during the Supreme Soviet debate (21–24 September) on the economic reform at which Gorbachev asked for and obtained additional powers including the right to institute emergency measures to stabilize "socio-political life". Gorbachev reacted angrily to opposition by the IRG to his request for additional powers and accused them of exploiting instability for their own political ends.

"Action Programme Ninety"

The atmosphere of mutual suspicion was intensified when the hard-liners began a Party press campaign beginning with *Pravda* of 26 September which published a TASS article linking the Moscow Soviet, the Russian parliament and the Inter-Regional Group with a "subversive document" called *Action Programme Ninety*, alleged to be a plot for the seizure of power.

This flimsy provocation was probably designed to play upon Gorbachev's almost paranoid fear that the radicals were planning to mobilize popular discontent in order to overthrow him (one of Gorbachev's first decrees after he became President in March was to remove the right to authorize demonstrations from the Moscow Soviet to the Council of Ministers, a decree which was overturned by the Constitutional Supervision Committee). It was a provocation in the worst traditions of the Communist Party and the KGB but it was a measure of the changes in Soviet society that in the harsh light of *glasnost* it provoked only ridicule. The sinister possibility remains, however, that it was part of a contingency plan to justify a crack-down or even an eventual coup. Gorbachev, at a time when he was ostensibly trying to promote a left–centre alliance, may not have authorized the affair but did nothing to disavow it.

But Gorbachev's overtures towards the centre–left proved half-hearted and short-lived. He soon began to take a tougher line in defence of central authority and, in a reversal of far reaching significance, he reneged on his joint sponsorship of the 500 Days economic reform programme.

500 DAYS: SEPTEMBER–OCTOBER 1990

In the face of Prime Minister Ryzhkov's stubborn opposition, backed by threats to resign, to the presidential variant of the 500 Days Programme, Gorbachev retreated and failed to support the draft he had himself sponsored. At the Supreme Soviet session in September, he temporized, trying to preserve both the alliance with Yeltsin and the Ryzhkov government, eventually producing a compromise programme, the "Basic Guidelines", to be implemented by the Conservative Ryzhkov government and with the assistance of his own enhanced presidential powers. This was adopted by the Supreme Soviet on 19 October. Yeltsin contemptuously described it as a marriage between a snake and a hedgehog. When it came to the crunch, Gorbachev preferred to keep Ryzhkov on board rather than Yeltsin. He declared that the country could not afford a shake-up in the central leadership in the current unstable situation; he feared that the resignation of the government, when central authority was already fast evaporating, would create a vacuum (the Council of Ministers was almost the only administrative structure still functioning throughout the USSR).

The Gorbachev / Yeltsin alliance was now extremely fragile with no agreement in sight on economic reform or the Union Treaty. Gorbachev seemed to have embarked on a last ditch attempt to uphold the authority of the Presidency and the other central institutions of power in a reformed Federal Union. (The term "confederation" appeared briefly in Gorbachev's vocabulary only to disappear.) On 16 October Yeltsin responded in a speech in the Russian Supreme Soviet to Gorbachev's abandonment of the 500 Days Programme by putting forward three options:

- Russia would go it alone with the 500 Days Programme;
- there would be a "real coalition" in which Yeltsin would nominate key ministers in the USSR government;
- Russia would stand aside and wait for the Gorbachev programme to fail.

Although the RSFSR announced that it would implement the 500 Days Programme as from 1 November, this was largely bluff and the third option was the only realistic one.

Notes

1 BBC Summary of World Broadcasts (SWB), Part 1, 14 February 1990.
2 *Pravda*, 17 February 1990.
3 A. Chernyaev: *"6 let s Gorbachevym"*, pp. 334–6.
4 Private conversation, May 1995.
5 A. Chernyaev: *"6 let s Gorbachevym"*, pp. 365.
6 Article by Ye. Gaidar, *Pravda*, 7 August 1990.
7 N. Mikhailov, *Izvestiya*, 8 September 1990; Academician, P. Volobuyev, *Sovetskaya Kultura*, 8 September 1990.

2

Hard-line Backlash

MORE POWERS LESS AUTHORITY: OCTOBER–NOVEMBER 1990

Gorbachev's priority now was to shore up the crumbling authority of the Centre and he again distanced himself from the radical left. A series of presidential decrees were issued in October and November, the main thrust of which was to reassert central authority – for example:

- powers for the government to impose controlled prices;
- orders to hold military parades on the occasion of the October Revolution anniversary in capitals and other major cities;
- measures to prevent outrages against Lenin monuments, war memorials, state symbols, etc.

Gorbachev was again under increasing right-wing pressure; there was a massive Party press campaign to discredit the democratic camp, especially the Moscow and Leningrad Soviets, the Democratic Platform and the Russian parliament.

Gorbachev's public standing had by now reached a record low ebb. An opinion poll published in mid-November showed his approval rating had slumped month by month from 52 per cent in December 1989 to 21 per cent in October 1990. The right wing was again mobilizing for a no-confidence vote at the Fourth Congress of People's Deputies. He was also under pressure from the opposite wing; a letter from prominent intellectuals, his erstwhile supporters, called on him to take action for radical reform or resign.[1] For a time Gorbachev seemed to be losing his grip. He made two disastrously rambling and ineffective speeches – to army deputies on 13 November (when the reactionary Soyuz leader, Alksnis declared that he had "lost the army"), and on 16 November to the Supreme Soviet when having totally misjudged the occasion and the mood of the deputies he nearly "lost the parliament". He spoke again on the second day of the Supreme Soviet debate, briefly and trenchantly, and addressing this time the issues the parliament and public wanted to hear about – the constitutional crisis, the food situation and law and order – somewhat retrieved the situation. But Gorbachev's reaction to the crisis of authority and his diminishing control was to seek yet another increase in his powers, the third in the space of eight months (following the institution of the Executive Presidency in March and Law on Additional Powers adopted in September). But each increase in Gorbachev's powers was accompanied by a corresponding decrease in his authority. There was no point in his accumulating new formal powers when he had no means to implement his decisions, since real political authority, insofar as it existed anywhere, was drifting to the Republics.

However, Gorbachev again demonstrated his skill in manipulation by bouncing the Supreme Soviet into approving sweeping constitutional changes, produced out of a hat, which they had no opportunity to consider or discuss. The main changes involved:

- a Cabinet of Ministers subordinated directly to the President;
- a National Security Council which eventually replaced the Presidential Council (abolished by the Congress in December);
- a Council of the Federation with new powers to co-ordinate the Centre and the Republics;
- a Vice-Presidency.

The main effect of the constitutional changes was to increase Gorbachev's powers at the expense of the Council of Ministers transformed into a smaller Cabinet under his direct control.

Gorbachev was angered by Yeltsin's speech of 16 October and only with difficulty dissuaded by his advisers from a televised retort to it. Gorbachev and Yeltsin walked side by side across Red Square in the last November 7 demonstration and stood together on the Mausoleum; and they had another meeting on 11 November at which they discussed the Union Treaty. But when Yeltsin reported their conversation to the Russian parliament in a tendentious and confrontational manner, Gorbachev was infuriated and told his entourage he was "declaring war". Yeltsin, in a speech on 19 November to the Ukrainian Supreme Soviet, was highly critical of Gorbachev's latest constitutional changes, which he said reflected the urge to make the Centre all powerful again. And he complained that there had been no consultation with the Republics.

HARD-LINE WINTER OFFENSIVE: NOVEMBER 1990–JANUARY 1991

Gorbachev was now taking measures to try to reassert central authority while his rhetoric reverted to old style emphasis on the leading role of the Party, the principles of socialism, opposition to private ownership of land. The appointment of Kravchenko to head Gostelradio on 14 November signalled the intention to tighten control of the media. In a televised statement on 27 November, the Minister of Defence, Yazov, announced an instruction to military units to use weapons if military installations came under attack; and take over power stations, water supplies etc. if garrisons were blockaded (as had been threatened in Latvia); and to protect military cemeteries and monuments, and remove memorials to fascists. Gorbachev appeared to be reverting to outmoded ideas and methods rather than as hitherto, swimming with the tide of reform. He referred repeatedly to "the last ditch" and his dedication to the socialist choice. He appeared to be digging in in an untenable position.

Democratic Movement

The political tide had swung against the democrats who were in increasing disarray:

- the death of Sakharov in December 1989 had deprived the movement of a leader of real moral stature;
- there was evidence of falling popular support. At by-elections in Moscow and Leningrad, the prominent democrats Murashev and Boldyrev had failed to gain election because of a low turnout;
- at the Congress of People's Deputies in December only 229 Deputies registered as members of the IRG (compared to 360 in 1989); while Soyuz claimed 720 registered members by the end of the Congress;
- the democratic Mayors of Leningrad and Moscow were increasingly unpopular as the economic situation worsened;

- Yeltsin was in tenuous control of his own power base with no solid or reliable majority in the Russian parliament. At the RSFSR Congress he narrowly won the crucial vote on private ownership of land but was defeated on several important issues in relation to the RSFSR Constitution and the Union Treaty, notably the institution of an RSFSR Presidency. The cohesion of the RSFSR government was under strain with the resignation of key economic reformers – Deputy Prime Minister Yavlinsky and the Finance Minister Boris Fedorov.

But Yeltsin's rating in the polls was still of the order of 70 per cent and although there was increasing discontent with the economic situation, the change in the popular mood did not match the political swing to the right. The public at large did not appear to share the Right's concerns and grievances about the loss of empire. Attempts to create a hard-line Labour movement, the OFT, did not get far nor did the proposal to turn "Soyuz" into a nation-wide political movement.

Fourth USSR Congress: December 1990

The Fourth Congress of USSR People's Deputies met in December 1990 amid rumours that Gorbachev might declare a state of emergency and calls from the right wing for the establishment of a Committee of National Salvation. The right wing was in an assertive mood while the democrats appeared demoralized and fearful. The Congress began with a near-hysterical speech by the Chechen reactionary Umalatova demanding Gorbachev's resignation. In his dramatic resignation speech the Foreign Minister Shevardnadze declared that "the Democrats have scattered and the reformists disappeared into the bushes" and he warned of impending dictatorship and the growing influence of reactionaries. Aleksandr Yakovlev spoke of a "wave of vengeful conservatism". Shevardnadze's resignation more or less completed the rout of leading reformers and liberals in prominent political positions. Bakatin had been dismissed earlier in December as Minister for Internal Affairs; Yakovlev already marginalized, lost any formal political status with the abolition of the Presidential Council, as did Shatalin, author of the 500 Days Programme. Gorbachev's economic adviser, Petrakov, had resigned over his rejection of the 500 Days

Programme. The new appointees were old-style party bureaucrats like Vice-President Yanaev and Minister of the Interior Pugo, or functionaries with no real political clout such as Foreign Minister Bessmertnykh and Prime Minister Pavlov.

Vilnius: January 1991

The hard-line winter offensive reached its climax with the attack on 13 January by USSR special police forces with the assistance of the local Soviet army garrison on the television station in Vilnius. The assault, in which 14 people were killed, was ostensibly in response to demands by a self appointed Lithuanian National Salvation Committee of unknown membership; but it was probably engineered by the KGB and military leadership in the hope of prompting Gorbachev to declare Presidential Rule in the Republic. Gorbachev denied any foreknowledge of the events and did not clearly endorse the police and army action but nor did he disavow it. The affair severely damaged Gorbachev's reputation in the West and further discredited him in the eyes of the radicals. He was virulently condemned in the liberal press and made matters worse by proposing in the Supreme Soviet the suspension of the Press Law (the proposal was voted down). In a television broadcast a week after the event, Gorbachev belatedly made some effort to distance himself and express regret for the violence. Yeltsin's robust reaction to the events in Vilnius (and a further incident a week later in Riga when the Latvian MVD building was attacked) further widened the gulf between him and Gorbachev. Yeltsin provocatively called on Russian troops to disobey orders to act against civilians; he proposed setting up a separate Russian army to defend RSFSR sovereignty; and suggested that Russia, Ukraine, Kazakhstan and Belorussia might draft their own four power Union Treaty.

Gorbachev was under intense pressure from the right wing in a mood of aggressive resentment at what they saw as Gorbachev's sell-out to the West, his readiness to accept foreign handouts, the persecution of communists, the monopoly of the media by the radicals, the "mafia" takeover of the economy, the loss of empire, the disintegration of the Party and the threat to the integrity of the State itself. But Gorbachev's lurch to the right in the winter of 1990–1 would not have occurred if the pressures and complaints had not struck chords in Gorbachev's own deepest political instincts.

It appeared that at last he had reached his ideological and political limits, the "last ditch" beyond which lay the break-up of the Soviet Union and the abandonment of the last vestiges of socialism. If he was to preserve the Union and the "socialist choice" he could rely only on the existing central power structures still functioning more or less throughout the country: the army, the KGB, the ministerial bureaucracy (especially the military industrial complex) and to some extent the CPSU.

POLITICAL ROLE OF THE POWER STRUCTURES

Armed Forces

By 1989 the army's prestige and influence had reached a low ebb. In July the Defence Minister Yazov was only barely confirmed by the Supreme Soviet at the ministerial confirmation hearings (while Shevardnadze was confirmed unanimously). A Supreme Soviet resolution releasing students from military service was adopted despite strong military opposition. There were frequent press attacks on the military and the defence sector for consuming the lion's share of the nation's resources. The army was reviled for its part in the Tbilisi massacre in April 1989 and the intervention in Baku in January 1990. With the practical and psychological problems resulting from the withdrawal of Soviet forces from Eastern Europe, the resentment of the army hierarchy grew and began to be expressed publicly for the first time. In July 1990 at the Russian and CPSU Party Congresses, there were outspoken speeches by officers who complained about the "anti-army press" and the capitulationist "new thinking" in foreign policy. In November Gorbachev was heckled at his meeting with military Supreme Soviet deputies.

The army began to adopt a more overt political role. Gorbachev attended (for the first time) the traditional meeting on 22 February for Armed Forces Day and a mass demonstration to support the army which took place in Moscow on the following day. The February Central Committee plenum was attended in force by military commanders and the Chief of the General Staff, Moiseev sharply attacked Yeltsin. In December a statement was published by 53 prominent personalities calling for a state of emergency and presidential rule in conflict zones if constitutional methods proved ineffective. Among the signatories were Generals Varennikov, Moiseev,

Kulikov and Shatalin and Admiral Chernavin. The appointment of General Gromov as First Deputy Minister for Internal Affairs and the joint decree by the MVD and Ministry of Defence of 29 December 1990 on joint patrols in cities to maintain law and order appeared to institutionalize the army's involvement in policing functions.

The KGB

The KGB was also under severe political pressure having been discredited as an institution by the flood of revelations about its past crimes and abuses. There were calls for its abolition or the curtailment of its powers and at the least for its accountability under the rule of law. The KGB responded with a PR campaign stressing its role in foreign intelligence (less tainted in public eyes) from which most of its new leadership had been recruited. It shifted the emphasis, at least in public, of its internal activities from countering dissidents to the fight against organized crime and corruption. To justify its role, the KGB now began to acquire new functions and rights in effect to interfere in the economy (to check on food distribution; monitor monetary exchange; to enter and investigate enterprises suspected of involvement in corruption;) which it used to influence the political struggle. The radical press suggested that the KGB was deliberately exaggerating the crime-wave and inflating its own role for fear of "losing its place at the trough or sharing the fate of its East European colleagues";[2] and that its concern for fighting economic sabotage might well be used as a pretext for attacking market relations.[3] A series of commercial scandals was exploited, perhaps even promoted by the KGB precisely to that end.

The Head of the KGB, Kryuchkov, was adopting an increasingly high profile while stirring up hostility both to the West and to economic reform. In a television statement of 12 December 1990, and in his speech to the Congress on 22 December, Kryuchkov made use of the vocabulary of the Cold War and even Stalinism with references to subversion by Western Special Services; contaminated grain deliveries; economic sabotage; encouragement by the West of ethnic unrest and separatism; the political and social dangers of the market. The KGB had a vested interest in the worsening of East–West relations and in pandering to right-wing xenophobia. The KGB were certainly involved in the Action Programme 90 provocation, an evidently successful attempt to exploit Gorbachev's paranoid distrust of the "Democrats". It was also involved in promoting the "Centrist Bloc" of obscure and tiny political parties, including one headed by Vladimir Zhirinovsky who had already been denounced in the press as a KGB stooge.

The CPSU

The Communist Party began to reassert itself as the political pendulum swung back to the right. Gorbachev, who had been distancing himself, once again identified himself with the CPSU as the "ruling party". Party officials were assigned to key posts (Yanaev, Pugo and several new Gorbachev aides). The Politburo and Secretariat no longer confined their agenda to purely internal party matters. The Russian Communist Party's increasingly aggressive line was demonstrated at its Central Committee Plenum on 31 January and in an article in Sovetskaya Rossiya of 5 February by Polozkov who spoke of communists "emerging from the trenches" and "going onto the offensive".

The resurgence of right-wing forces at the Centre and the growing role of its power structures was in part due to the failure of the new State structures which Gorbachev had set up between 1988 and 1990 with the object of outflanking conservative opposition to reform in the Party, to function effectively and create a legitimate democratic basis for political power. The new structures lacked cohesion or any mechanism for implementing decisions. Moreover following their successes in the Spring of 1990 local and republic elections, the radicals tended to give up the serious attempt to gain influence at the centre as it came to be increasingly dominated by the right. Republic institutions, with the RSFSR setting the pace, focused on increasing their own power at the expense of the centre. As the process of "sovereignization" and the "war of laws" got underway, the cause of political and economic reform in the RSFSR and other republics began to take second place to this constitutional power struggle. The Centre had the moral disadvantage of enjoying less legitimacy in public eyes. Gorbachev had no popular mandate and the USSR parliament had been elected under less democratic rules (because earlier in the reform process) than the Republic bodies. Gorbachev, trying to preserve the authority of the Centre, found himself forced into the arms of the conservatives.

Notes

1 *Moscow News* no. 46, 1990.
2 *Tass*, 19 December 1990.
3 *Vechernyaya Moskva*, 24 October 1990; *Izvestiya*, 31 January 1991.

3

Gorbachev's Last Gambit

GORBACHEV TRIES "CENTRISM": FEBRUARY–MARCH 1991

In the Spring of 1991, Gorbachev again started to shift his ground and he made tentative overtures towards the "left". His tendency to vacillation was typified by two contrasting speeches during a visit to Belorussia, 26–28 February. In the first he broached the possibility of a truce with the radicals and spoke of the need to strengthen the political centre; but this overture figured as the tail-piece to the most intemperate attack he had yet made on the democratic opposition. He described it as power seeking, ambitious, destructive, allied with separatists, nationalists and semi-fascists; it used unconstitutional methods and "neo-Bolshevik" tactics; it was inspired or controlled from abroad. He scorned the offer of a left–centre bloc (apparently forgetting that only the previous August he had described himself as a member of the centre-left). And he made a personal attack on Yeltsin (who the week before had called on television for his resignation) and Popov. The overall tone of the speech, which drowned out his hints of a truce, deeply alarmed his liberal supporters.

Two days later he made another speech in Mogilev which was effectively a corrective to the first. He criticized the right as well as the left (in more restrained terms) and called for a "stable political coalition of centrist forces" although still with a "socialist orienta-tion". He also tentatively began to distance himself from the Party conservatives, saying that the CPSU should define its position *vis-à-vis* both dogmatic conservative forces advocating socialism without democracy and liberal bourgeois forces proposing democracy with-out socialism. However, Gorbachev gave no hint of apology or retreat over the events in Vilnius and Riga, increasing hard-line pressure on the media or his law and order decrees. Gorbachev used the word "centre" or "centrism" about 20 times in this speech but by now the right and left were so polarized and radicalized that there was no centre ground left and certainly no centrist political force on which he could rely. In a slight gesture to the democrats, he confirmed during his visit to Belorussia that Yakovlev remained one of his advisers and said that he would propose Bakatin as a member of the new Security Council.

Gorbachev continued to develop the theme of centrism in a series of interviews and speeches; but centrism appeared to involve compromise with the right rather than the left – he continued his sharp criticism of the "destructive" opposition. In a television interview on 26 March he said "the political Centre should include all the best active forces from right and left; it should exclude adventurers and reactionaries both from right and left". But he followed this up by another intemperate attack on the Opposition which he said had no programme, was irresponsible, seeking to destabilize society, etc. Chernyaev notes Gorbachev always reacted very differently to attacks from the right and the left. He responded angrily and emotionally to criticism from the democratic opposition but appeared to have infinite patience with the increasingly insulting and hostile rhetoric from the Party conservatives. Gorbachev did not like Polozkov and company but "they are somehow his sort of people, understandable, predictable and, as he reckons, manageable". Chernyaev also records that in March 1991 Gorbachev was meeting almost daily the "power mastodons", Kryuchkov, Yazov and Pugo.

COMPROMISE WITH YELTSIN AND THE REPUBLICS

March Referendum: Third RSFSR Congress

At this point Yeltsin was riding high and pursuing a rhetorical onslaught against Gorbachev. In a TV interview on 19 February he made scathing criticisms of Gorbachev and demanded his resignation. He spoke in similar terms at a meeting of left parties in the Dom Kino and at the Putilov factory in Leningrad on 20 March. Chernyaev described the speech as "a glove thrown in Gorbachev's face".[1] The results of the All-Union Referendum of 17 March (in which six Republics refused to participate) were interpreted as a victory by both Gorbachev and Yeltsin: over 76 per cent of the 80 per cent turn-out assented to the complex formulation in favour of preserving the Union; while almost 70 per cent voted "yes" to an additional question in the RSFSR ballot on instituting a Russian Presidency. The confrontation reached its height when Gorbachev banned a pro-Yeltsin demonstration in Moscow on 28 March on the eve of the third RSFSR Congress which had been called by Yeltsin's opponents in the hope of overthrowing him. As Chernyaev put it, Gorbachev provoked an open trial of strength which he lost: despite a heavy police show of force, more than two hundred thousand Yeltsin supporters turned out. In the event, the Congress was swung in favour of Yeltsin by the defection of a group of Communists led by Rutskoi and ended by fixing a date for presidential elections and giving Yeltsin emergency powers to reform the Russian economy by decree.

Nine plus One at Novo-Ogarevo: April 1991

The meeting between Gorbachev and Yeltsin and eight other Republic leaders at Novo-Ogarevo outside Moscow on 23 April took Gorbachev's hard-line opponents by surprise. It was his last major political gambit. The meeting produced a Joint Statement which covered measures to deal with the economic and political crisis and it set a new political agenda. Gorbachev was in need of a strong move on the eve of the Central Committee plenum of 25 April which was taking place against the background of growing social unrest, food shortages including bread queues and anti-government strikes, and was expected to mount a new assault on his policies and leadership.

Novo-Ogarevo was welcomed by moderate democrats. Stankevich (Deputy Mayor of Moscow), said that for the first time the Centre had chosen in favour of political stability by means of a compromise with the Republics and the beginning of a dialogue with the Opposition. He spoke of a possible coalition in a "government of national confidence". However, there was a mixed reaction from the democratic movement as a whole with sharp criticism of Yeltsin by the radicals for selling-out to the Centre.

The text appeared at first sight an unequal compromise, somewhat favourable to the Centre. It involved undertakings by the Republics to:

- observe Union laws and respect central institutions during the transition to a new Union;
- take joint economic anti-crisis measures (this did not however imply support for the Pavlov Anti-Crisis Programme approved by the USSR Supreme Soviet on the same day);
- support special regimes in key industries and transport;
- appeal to halt political strikes.

In return the Republics obtained:

- the acceptance of the "sovereign" status of the Republics;
- recognition of their pre-eminent role *vis-à-vis* autonomous republics (the Centre for tactical reasons had tended to encourage the ambitions of the latter);
- the promise of a new constitution and elections to new central institutions within six months of the conclusion of the Union Treaty.

There was speculation about a hidden agenda including an agreement to set aside the draft Union Treaty now on the table and consider a new draft from the bottom up. In a speech to miners in the Kuzbass on 29 April, Yeltsin adopted a somewhat truculent tone stating that five Republics would sign their own Union Treaty if the Centre were to renege on the new agreement. He appeared to indicate that concessions had been made which had not been spelled out in the published Joint Statement.

The Novo-Ogarevo Agreement was an unexpected development, perhaps reflecting greater economic and political realism in the Republics as well as the Centre. Gorbachev, under very heavy pressure from the right, turned to an alliance with the Republics as a counter-balance. He may have decided that he was now under greater threat from the right than from the democratic opposition. The eight non-Russian Republic leaders evidently wanted to preserve some credible Centre in order to contain the influence of a potentially overpowerful and ambitious Russia; the Kazakh leader, Nazarbaev, in particular, given the very large Russian minority in Kazakhstan, felt the need for the Centre as buffer and mediator. Yeltsin's motivation was less clear and many of his supporters felt that he had for once been outmanoeuvred by Gorbachev. Probably for Yeltsin the most important aspect of the agreement was that the early conclusion of a new Union Treaty would spell the end of the central power structures and therefore of Gorbachev's pre-eminent political role. The Republic leaders may have been more concerned than they professed to be by the results of the All-Union Referendum in favour of preserving the Union. They may have shared the apprehensions of Yeltsin, who claimed subsequently that the Referendum was designed to give legitimacy to a nation-wide state of emergency and a legal right to fight against Russian independence.[2]

Gorbachev was now showing signs of moving towards more radical ideas of economic reform and distancing himself from the right. In a speech in Alma Ata on 30 May, he described the 9 + 1 Agreement as a turning point from confrontation to co-operation, referred to the improvement in the political situation following the upheavals of spring and called for the synchronization of radical reform with Western co-operation. He approved, if he did not sponsor, the visit to Washington by Yavlinsky and Primakov at the end of May to explain the economic reform programme known as the "Grand Bargain".

Truce with Yeltsin

By June 1991 there was a realignment of political forces and the possibility of a new consensus. Gorbachev's position had been bolstered by the 9 + 1 Agreement and the hard-line threat at the April plenum had collapsed when he had threatened to resign and the liberal minority of Central Committee members (including Bakatin, Nazarbaev, Volsky, Latsis et al.) had said they would follow suit.[3] At a meeting with Mrs Thatcher on 27 May, Gorbachev spoke of a "second wind for reform". Soyuz had failed to collect sufficient signatures to convene an Extraordinary Congress; and the campaign on the other flank by Yeltsin and the democratic opposition, with the support of the miners' strike, to force the resignation of Gorbachev and the government and the dissolution of the Congress had also fizzled out.

Yeltsin and the Republic leaders had given some ground to avert the danger of Gorbachev's overthrow by the right; and were evidently ready to co-operate on a joint economic programme both in view of the severity of the current crisis and of the possibil-ity of a western economic assistance package linked to internal reform, which had been mooted in Yavlinsky's "Grand Bargain". For Gorbachev it was a reprise of the situation of the autumn of 1990 when he had baulked at the 500 Days Programme under pressure from the right and because of his misgivings that it gave too much power to the Republics. Now he appeared to have grasped the nettle but doubts remained about his real commitment to economic reform and his readiness to accept a much weaker centre. Yeltsin was to claim later that Gorbachev was simply playing for time.

Yeltsin Elected President of Russia: June 1991

The Fourth RSFSR Congress on 24 May had finally adopted the law on the RSFSR presidency and, on 12 June, Yeltsin was elected President of Russia with 58 per cent of the votes; Ryzhkov, who had received massive Party backing, received 16 per cent and Zhirinovsky unexpectedly came third with 8 per cent . Overall the results were a striking success for the radicals with Popov and Sobchak elected mayors of Moscow and Leningrad respectively. Gorbachev's reaction was much less grudging than on the occasion of Yeltsin's election as Chairman of the RSFSR Supreme Soviet a year before. Yeltsin's election was helpful for Gorbachev, at least in respect of his short-term aims of a successful meeting with the G7 in London the following month and rapid progress towards a Union Treaty. For his part, Yeltsin had moderated his political line and his criticism of Gorbachev. In his election programme he called for State regulation of the transfer to the market, and the rapid conclusion of a Union Treaty. He had chosen Rutskoi, a reform Communist, as his running-mate. Gorbachev seemed close to an alliance with Yeltsin against the hard-liners at the centre though he was still weighed down by the remnants of his ideological baggage and distrust of the radicals.

STORM WARNINGS? THE CENTRE'S LAST STAND: JUNE–AUGUST 1991

"Constitutional Coup"

At the USSR Supreme Soviet session in mid-June the Prime Minister, Pavlov, called for special additional powers to take action to deal with the economic crisis without having to consult parliament or president. A few days later at a closed session of parliament there was a series of hard-line speeches by the Minister for the Interior

Pugo, the head of the KGB Kryuchkov and the Minister of Defence Yazov, which portrayed the current situation in the blackest terms and were implicitly critical of Gorbachev himself. The two events were almost certainly uncoordinated and unconnected (Pavlov has strenuously denied any connection)[4] but they were represented in the media and by the radicals as an "attempted constitutional coup". For once there was a strong reaction to criticism from the right by Gorbachev who responded on 21 June with an effective speech which seemed to have put the Prime Minister and the "power ministers" firmly in their place. Gorbachev was generally seen as having scored a resounding victory. The liberal former editor of *Izvestiya* and deputy chairman of the Supreme Soviet, Laptev, stated that Gorbachev had seen off the Pavlov challenge and the "hard men" had been brought to heel. There was a widespread feeling that the hard-line threat had receded and moreover that the scope for unconstitutional action had in any case been much reduced by Yeltsin's popular election as President of the Russian Federation.

On 19 June the US Ambassador had conveyed personally to Gorbachev a warning from Bush that the US agencies had information that a coup against him was planned for the following day. (The warning had come to the Americans from the Mayor of Moscow Popov). According to Chernyaev, Gorbachev had laughed and dismissed the reports as "100 per cent improbable", but thanked the President for his concern. Afterwards Gorbachev told Chernyaev that Primakov (then a member of the Security Council) had rung him the day before warning him not to trust the KGB. Gorbachev had again reacted dismissively but, according to Chernyaev, these warnings had left their traces and were reflected in his tough speech in the Supreme Soviet in response to the statements of Kryuchkov, Pugo and Yazov.[5]

Party Plot

Prior to the July Central Committee Plenum and at the Plenum itself preparations were set in train by a group of influential Party Secretaries, headed by Prokofiev, the Moscow Party leader, to convene an Extraordinary Party Congress with the aim of removing Gorbachev as General Secretary. The draft "social-democratic" Party Programme, which Gorbachev planned to have adopted by the 29th Party Congress, scheduled for the end of the year, was not formally approved by the Plenum (which approved it only "for publication");

and his opponents insisted over Gorbachev's objections that the Congress should be an Extraordinary one because the rules in that case would give them better chances of ousting him. According to Otto Latsis, Gorbachev's removal as Party leader was intended as the prelude for a coup which would have had a quasi-constitutional character.[6]

"Word to the People"

On 23 July, *Sovetskaya Rossiya* published a statement entitled "Word to the People", signed by 12 prominent hard-liners, including the Deputy Minister of Defence, Varennikov, the Deputy Minister for the Interior, Gromov, the Secretary of the Russian Communist Party, Zyuganov, and Tizyakov and Starodubtsev (like Varennikov, future leaders of the August putsch attempt). The statement called for the setting up of a national patriotic movement to save the Soviet Union and contained scathing criticism of the Soviet leadership and implicitly of Gorbachev personally. The statement was probably conceived as a riposte to recent appeals by groups of prominent democrats and intended to rally hard-line forces on the eve of the Central Committee Party plenum of 25 July. The radical press reacted to the statement with an uneasy mixture of mockery and alarm, focusing in particular on the signature of two senior generals on a statement effectively attacking the President and his policies. This statement, and the "constitutional coup" in June, appear in retrospect to be clear warning signals of the impending coup attempt. At the time, and in the context of constant alarms and excursions, dire warnings and threats, it did not seem so – least of all to Gorbachev himself. It seemed then more like the final convulsions of a doomed system, almost the last nail in whose coffin would be the signature on 20 August by six Republics of the Union Treaty.

Notes

1   A. Chernyaev: *"6 let s Gorbachevym"*, pp. 431.
2   *Zapiski Prezidenta*, Moscow, 1994, p. 37.
3   Volsky told the Plenum 72 would resign, but, according to Latsis (in private conversation May 1995), this figure was only a guess.
4   V. Pavlov, *Avgust iznutri*, Moscow, 1993.
5   A. Chernyaev: *"6 let s Gorbachevym"*, Moscow, 1994.
6   Private conversation, May 1995.

Part II

———

End of the USSR:
August–December 1991

4

August 1991

AUGUST 1991 COUP ATTEMPT

Summary of Events

On Saturday, 17 August, the Head of the KGB, Kryuchkov, convened at a KGB "safe house" in the south-west district of Moscow a meeting of his fellow conspirators (including Prime Minister Pavlov, Defence Minister Yazov and senior Party officials Baklanov and Shenin) which decided to send a delegation on the following day to Foros in the Crimea, where Gorbachev was on holiday. Preparations had already been made by the KGB to cut-off Gorbachev's communications and this was done as the delegation, headed by Baklanov and General Varennikov, arrived. Gorbachev rejected their demands to agree to a state of emergency or resign, and the plotters returned to Moscow (Varennikov went to Kiev to confront Kravchuk). A declaration by a so-called State Committee for the State of Emergency was issued at 6.00 a.m. the following morning, 19 August, by Vice-President Yanaev, calling himself Acting President. The statement alleged that Gorbachev was ill and unable to carry out his duties. Troops, tanks and APCs were moved into Moscow and by midday had established a heavy presence in the centre of the city.

Although a KGB unit was sent to his dacha, Yeltsin was not arrested or isolated and eventually made his way to the Russian parliament building where he addressed the demonstrators who were already gathering. The Russian leadership established their headquarters in the White House and began issuing a series of Decrees and Appeals denouncing the coup and calling for resistance. The members of the State of Emergency Committee, headed by Vice-President Yanaev but without Kryuchkov or Prime Minister

Pavlov, who was prostrated by drink and / or nervous exhaustion, gave an unconvincing performance at a press conference in the early evening of 19 August.

Plans were being made to storm the White House, which was now defended by upwards of 100,000 demonstrators, who had built makeshift barricades, and a unit of the Taman Tank Division which had defected to Yeltsin. Military leaders were now beginning to have doubts and took refuge in evasion and inaction. There was a serious clash on an underpass of the Moscow Ring Road 200 yards from the White House late on 20 August and three White House defenders were killed. Preparations for the attack were beginning to stall and the coup leaders were losing their nerve one by one.

At 2.00 a.m. on 21 August Kryuchkov telephoned the White House to say there would be no attack that day. The coup began to unravel fast. Yeltsin told the Russian parliament, which assembled in Emergency Session on the morning of 21 August, that Kryuchkov had proposed that they go together to Foros to see Gorbachev. The parliament, fearing a trap, decided that Vice-President Rutskoi and Prime Minister Silaev should go instead. By mid-day on 21 August columns of tanks were withdrawing from Moscow. Kryuchkov, Yazov, Baklanov and Lukyanov flew to Foros evidently hoping they could still come to some arrangement with Gorbachev, who refused to see them. Rutskoi and the Russian delegation arrived soon afterwards and brought Gorbachev back to Moscow. Kryuchkov and the others were sent back separately and arrested on arrival in the capital.

Purpose of the Coup

The attempted coup in August 1991 was carried out by and on behalf of the leadership of the central structures for whom the signature of the Union Treaty, scheduled for 20 August, was in effect a death sentence. Gorbachev had finally allied himself with Yeltsin and the Republic leaders to achieve the best deal he could obtain to preserve some form of Union at the price of a much weakened USSR presidency and the dismantling or emasculation of the Centre. The main purpose of the coup organizers was to preserve the USSR and the power and privileges of its establishment; and to halt, and as far as possible reverse the political and economic reform process which had developed an uncontrollable and threatening momentum. The coup leaders evidently realized that some things had changed irreversibly. They did not call for or probably intend the restoration of Communism or Party rule. There was no mention of the Party or Socialism in their statements and decrees; and they paid lip service to continuing political and economic reform. The main themes of their pronouncements were law and order, the depredations of the shadow economy (the "chaotic, uncontrolled, slide to the market") and the need to restore the prestige of the Soviet Union, humiliated by Western condescension and "handouts from abroad".

Although senior Party officials were heavily involved in the coup, the CPSU organs per se took no direct part. The Central Committee Headquarters on Staraya Square appeared deserted during the first day. But the Central Committee Secretariat issued a coded instruction in the morning of 19 August to regional Party organizations to render all assistance to the Emergency Committee. There is little doubt that had the coup succeeded the Party would have risen rapidly from the dead and started to reclaim its former role.

The Plotters

The head of the KGB, Kryuchkov, was the prime mover. According to Yeltsin's memoirs he began detailed planning in early August involving a group of KGB experts and General Grachev from the Ministry of Defence. He talked at an early stage to representatives of the CPSU, Baklanov and Shenin, and later, on the eve of the coup, brought in the head of Gorbachev's own Secretariat, Boldin. According to Yeltsin, the inner group who took the main decisions were Kryuchkov, Baklanov, Shenin and the Prime Minister Pavlov and the Minister of Defence Yazov, with the latter playing a largely passive role.[1] The chairman of the USSR Supreme Soviet, Lukyanov, later to be publicly described by Yeltsin as the "chief ideologist of the putsch" declined to be a member of the Emergency Committee because of his role as a representative of the legislative power; but he supported the coup and played a key part. The Vice-President, Yanaev, was an indecisive and ineffectual figurehead who hesitated before finally signing the State of Emergency documents.

Why the Coup Failed

Though hastily and poorly planned, the coup was not as farcically inept as it has sometimes been portrayed; it was not bound to fail and, in fact, came very close to success. Its organizers believed not unreasonably that a massive show of force, backed by a united front of the leadership of the KGB, MVD and the Army, supported by the Vice-President and Prime Minister, would be sufficient to produce the traditional reflex of fear and obedience, without the need for widespread arrests or other draconian measures. (Their model was probably the declaration of martial law in Poland in 1981.) This was not a complete misjudgement. The reaction was passive or even positive throughout most of the country and local state of emergency committees sprang up in nearly every town and district. There were no demonstrations, except in Moscow and Leningrad, and no national strike. The failure to arrest Yeltsin and the Russian leadership was not so much incompetence as a calculated risk by Kryuchkov, who wanted to preserve an appearance of legality and avoid violence. He assumed that with no armed force at his disposal, Yeltsin would be impotent and his popular support rapidly evaporate.

But vital loopholes were left by the failure to establish total control of communications and the media. The Russian leadership was able to organize by telephone (communications from the White House were cut off but one recently installed line survived) and the main television news on the evening of 19 August, amid all the pronouncements of the State of Emergency Committee, carried a brief shot of Yeltsin addressing the crowd from an APC and an interview with a defiant defender on the barricades, which boosted the morale of the democrats and possibly helped to swell the numbers outside the White House. But their numbers never exceeded 100,000 dwindling to 20,000 during the night; the barricades were inadequate, the defenders mostly unarmed and the White House could have been seized without great difficulty or very great bloodshed.

The key factors in the failure of the coup were lack of cohesion among the organizers and their lack of a leader or even, as Yeltsin has commented, a presentable figurehead (in contrast to the democratic resistance which had a decisive leader with the advantage of constitutional authority). There was no one to resolve the differences between Kryuchkov, anxious to avoid force, and Baklanov and Varennikov, arguing for tough measures; or to impose the will of the plotters on the Army leaders who preferred to do as little as possible or, like General Grachev, temporized before finally supporting Yeltsin.

Ultimately the coup was defeated by the courage of a minority of Moscovites who went on to the streets to defend the democratic reforms and the scruples and / or lack of resolution of its organizers who acted weakly while trying to avoid force and preserve a veneer of legality and constitutionality. Both can be attributed to the enormous changes in Soviet society which the reforms had brought. Enough of the people refused to be intimidated; and the reactionaries had lost their will to behave in the traditional ruthless way. The failure of the coup was the greatest success for democracy so far in Russian history.

AFTERMATH OF THE COUP

The failure of the coup resulted in the collapse of the USSR Central power structures. Virtually all the ministers in the Cabinet had supported the coup or acquiesced in it and the government was dismissed in toto by Gorbachev soon after his return to Moscow. The KGB and the MVD were discredited; of the USSR institutions only the Army remained in place and retained some credibility. On 22 August the statue of Dzerzhinsky on the square in front of the KGB headquarters was dismantled in front of a jeering crowd; the Party Central Committee Headquarters on Staraya Square was attacked by demonstrators on the same evening; it was evacuated and, in due course, the Russian government took over the premises.

Russian Take-Over

The Russian authorities lost no time in filling the vacuum at the Centre. A Yeltsin decree established Russian jurisdiction over Union assets on RSFSR territory. The Russian Prime Minister, Silaev, asserted control over Union ministries as long as there was no effective Union government. Union communications on Russian territory were brought under the control of the Russian KGB; and the KGB's archives were transferred to Russian custody. Yeltsin claimed that Russia had "saved the Union" and demanded that Russia should nominate the key ministers in the Union government.

The coup leaders had thus accomplished the final destruction of what they had gambled desperately to preserve. The defeat of the coup was followed by a democratic revolution, which smashed the system; and this double shock accelerated the break-up of the

empire. The central pillars of the Soviet system were destroyed:
the CPSU effectively dissolved; its property to be confiscated; the
KGB to be dismantled; the Army general staff to be purged. The
media was dominated by liberals with Party publications, including
Pravda, briefly suspended.

Gorbachev had returned to Moscow, his reputation damaged
and his power undermined. Yeltsin was in the driving seat
dictating terms and key appointments to Gorbachev while the
RSFSR take-over of the centre proceeded. The surge of Russian
nationalism and the perception that the RSFSR was swallowing up
the centre conjured up visions of a restored Russian empire and
prompted the other Republics to make rapid moves to distance
themselves. Latvia and Estonia declared independence during the
coup; Ukraine, Belorussia and Moldova within a few days; and
Azerbaijan, Uzbekistan and Kirgizia by the end of the month.

Reactions in the Other Republics

The Republic leaders might have reacted to the perceived threat of
Russian dominance at the Centre by seeking to prop up Gorbachev
as a counter-weight. But the experience of the coup evidently
persuaded them that the Centre was irredeemably dangerous,
Gorbachev unreliable and by now a lost cause. Moreover some
of the Republic leaders were seeking to protect themselves not
so much from a reactionary or Russian nationalist Centre as from
the consequences of the democratic revolution in Moscow. With
the exception of the Baltic States and Moldova, whose leaderships
saw a direct threat to themselves via their Russian minorities and
knew they would not survive a successful coup, the Republic leaders
adopted a wait and see attitude during the events of 19–20 August.
President Kravchuk of Ukraine and Nazarbaev of Kazakhstan issued
non-committal statements. Kravchuk appeared to be expressing
acquiescence, if not approval, of the coup when he said in an
interview on *Vremya* on 19 August that "what has happened was
bound to happen. Things could not go on as they were". (Yeltsin
commented ironically in *View from the Kremlin* that western
leaders had defined their position more quickly than Nazarbaev
and Kravchuk who "conducted careful negotiations with the State
of Emergency Committee and responded to my exclamations in an
embarrassed and guilty way saying that everything is calm here

and we will make our position clear soon".) The Republic leaders duly followed Moscow's example and left the CPSU, banning its activities in the army, state apparatus etc. But their internal politics were barely affected by either the coup or the post-coup revolution. It was a Russian coup and a Russian revolution (moreover one which had relatively little impact outside Moscow and St Petersburg).

Russian politicians accused the Republic leaders of seeking to grab the spoils from a victory in which they had no part and argued bitterly that the rush to independence was the work of coalitions of nationalists seeking independence at any price and Party bureaucrats desperate to preserve their own power. In this atmosphere Yeltsin issued a statement on 27 August through his Press Secretary that the RSFSR accepted the right of each State to self-determination but reserved the right to raise a review of their borders with Russia (except in the case of the Baltic States). On the following day the Mayor of Moscow, Popov, stated that Russia had serious claims on parts of Ukraine and Kazakhstan.

Gorbachev

Gorbachev returned from his traumatic three-day incarceration in Foros to find his authority largely evaporated and to face accusations of responsibility for the coup and even complicity in it. At his first press conference on 22 August he appeared badly out of touch with events and the popular mood; he was still calling on communists to rally round the new Party programme and make the Party "a vital force for *perestroika*". As an *Izvestiya* headline put it, he had "returned to a different country" but did not seem to realize this.[2] Gorbachev's first provisional appointments as Minister of Defence and head of the KGB were effectively countermanded by Yeltsin who in future had to be consulted about all key posts. Gorbachev was subjected to public humiliation by Yeltsin and abusive heckling by RSFSR deputies at the Supreme Soviet Session in the White House on 23 August when Yeltsin demonstratively signed a decree banning the CPSU on Russian territory, ignoring protests from Gorbachev who had just reiterated his belief that the Party could still be reformed. There was little sign of public sympathy for Gorbachev in his ordeal or that of his family, or admiration for his courage under intense mental pressure which had been an essential factor in the defeat of the coup.

Gorbachev had shown culpable ill-judgement in appointing Kryuchkov, Yanaev, Pugo and Yazov, sometimes in the teeth of advice from his own entourage, and in sticking to them despite clear evidence of their disloyalty. But he had performed a difficult and dangerous balancing act for the past two years, dragging and cajoling the hard-liners in the old power structures towards a democratic society. It could be argued that had he tried to remove or confront them, the coup might have taken place earlier in different and more favourable circumstances for the plotters, and would then have succeeded. The failure of the coup was the greatest testament to his achievement. Gorbachev himself argued in *December 1991* that he was forced to manoeuvre and delay in order to preserve the reform process: "18 months or 2 years ago the Party could have taken everything back into its hands without any argument. It had the army, the military industrial complex, the cadres, everything on its side".

Notes

1 *Zapiski Prezidenta*, p. 77.
2 *Izvestiya* (no. 201) of 23 August.

5

The Rise of Russia/End of the USSR

ATTEMPT TO SALVAGE THE UNION: SEPTEMBER 1991

Gorbachev now began a hopeless but determined effort to claw back some of his own authority and salvage the Union. In a strong performance at the USSR Supreme Soviet on 26 August, he admitted partial responsibility for the fact that the coup had happened but said that events had changed him. "He had arrived back in a different country but was himself a different man". In future there would be no compromises in pursuit of democratic goals. He called for the immediate signing of a Union Treaty with those Republics willing to do so; an economic agreement with all 15 Republics; and the setting up of a Security Council to include all Republic leaders. He said there must be political control over the army and the KGB, and real moves towards the market system. A new Vice-President and a new government should be appointed.

Last USSR Congress

The Congress of USSR People's Deputies, now effectively redundant but still formally the highest authority in the country, met in Extraordinary session 2–5 September. Its agenda and proceedings were dictated by 10 Republic leaders and Gorbachev who met on the eve of the Session and made it clear that they intended to marginalize the Congress prior to its dissolution. A statement read out at the opening of the Congress by the Kazakh President, Nazarbaev, called for:

- preparations for a new Union of Soviet states in which each republic would chose its own form of association;

- an economic union in which all republics would participate;
- the setting up of a State Council consisting of the USSR and the Republic Presidents;
- support by the Congress for membership of all the Republics in the UN;
- a new two chamber Supreme Soviet in which the Republics would delegate deputies and have the dominant voice.

Yeltsin called for a new Union with the preservation of Union armed forces and a Centre controlling nuclear weapons and guaranteeing human rights. He said Russia would never be an empire or an elder brother but an equal among equals. He criticized Gorbachev for vacillation and inconsistent support for reforms and said that he had brought the coup upon himself. But he added that Gorbachev had changed like the whole country and deserved confidence.

Gorbachev, in the chair, manipulated the proceedings in his old familiar style, pushing through proposals which had been worked out in advance with the Republic leaders. Although the Congress was clearly at its last gasp, some sense of authority and control at the Centre was briefly restored by the Session. Gorbachev recovered a semblance of authority and influence but only by keeping strictly in step with the Republic leaders. The whole proceedings were constitutionally dubious but appeared the only feasible way to bridge the gap between the old system and the new interim structures which it created to run the country: a State Council (Gorbachev and the Republic Presidents), a Supreme Soviet with enhanced Republic influence and an Inter-Republican Economic Committee headed by the Russian Prime Minister Silaev.

YELTSIN AND THE "RUSSIA FIRST" DEBATE: SEPTEMBER–OCTOBER 1991

After his initial euphoria and muscle-flexing in the wake of the coup, Yeltsin began to adopt a more restrained and statesman- like position offering a measure of support and co-operation for Gorbachev (they sat side by side at the USSR Congress), and toning down the note of Russian triumphalism which had so alarmed the Republics. Yeltsin at this stage still favoured preserving the Union in some form and evidently realized this would not be possible if Russia became indistinguishable from the Centre. His statements on frontiers had evidently been intended as a shot across the bows of the Republics rushing to abandon the Union.

But by now a dispute had arisen among his advisers and the Russian leadership over whether in the new situation Russia should continue to support the preservation of a Union in some form or "go it alone". The "Russia First" camp was led by the State Secretary, Gennady Burbulis, with the support of a group of economists headed by Gaidar. The pro-Union group included the Prime Minister, Silaev, Yavlinsky, Deputy Prime Minister Saburov. Burbulis, who as early as September had published a memorandum taking the line that Russia should be the legal successor of the Union, professed to support a "soft" Union based on temporary agreements, but was prepared for full separation. The "Russia First" camp believed that the empire was a political liability and an economic burden: a strong economic community with central institutions was not in the economic interests of Russia; the Republics were trying to have it both ways: retain the benefits of economic union while asserting full political independence. Silaev and other Russian ministers in the transitional Union structures, soon found themselves in conflict with their Russian colleagues and Silaev eventually resigned as Russian Prime Minister when the post became incompatible with his responsibilities as Chairman of the Inter-Republican Economic Committee. Deputy Prime Minister Saburov resigned after his initials on the draft Economic Community Treaty were disavowed by the Russian Government. Yeltsin, who had always publicly supported the preservation of the Union, was at first hesitant and undecided. But eventually he came down on the side of the "Russia First" camp and this, together with the result of the Ukrainian referendum on independence of 1 December, led him to Belaya Vezha and sealed the fate of the Union.

Yeltsin

Yeltsin's performance in the August coup had given an enormous boost to his popularity and credit at home and abroad. It left him the dominant political personality in the country and the undisputed leader of reform in Russia. But in the wake of his triumph, Yeltsin relatively soon began to lose momentum and direction. When his first 100 days as President of Russia were marked by the domestic and foreign media (on 17 October), there was considerable gloom about Yeltsin's health, his alleged dictatorial tendencies, doubts about his commitment to reform, and even whether he would stay long in office. A prolonged absence on holiday in Sochi had given rise to rumours about his health and drinking habits; he was said to have been inaccessible to members of the Russian leadership at a time when it was in considerable disarray over policy on the economy and the Union Treaty.

The political situation had become less favourable for Yeltsin. The Russian Supreme Soviet still contained a large proportion of hard-liners, who had now recovered from the shock of the coup and were increasingly critical of Yeltsin. Parliament refused to put the adoption of a new Russian constitution on the agenda of the Fifth RSFSR Congress; it insisted on elections of provincial Governors which Yeltsin had wished to postpone. There was unease in the liberal media at the rapid build-up of the Russian bureaucracy; new State organs proliferated including the State Council, the Presidential Administration and numerous groups of experts whose structures had quickly taken over all and more of the office space vacated by the CPSU and redundant USSR ministries. The Council of Ministers was confusingly subordinated partly to the State Council and partly to the Presidency. The autonomous Republics, at first cowed by Yeltsin's victory and in some cases their complicity or passivity during the coup, were again becoming assertive, complaining that they had been ignored in negotiations over the new Union Treaty. There was no visible progress on economic reform and fears were being expressed of a winter of discontent with strikes and hunger, and even a second coup. On the eve of the Fifth RSFSR Congress, which resumed in October, there was a sense of drift and uncertainty.

DECISION FOR RADICAL ECONOMIC REFORM: OCTOBER 1991

Fifth RSFSR Congress

In what was to become a familiar pattern, Yeltsin emerged from a period of inactivity and confusion to make a decisive move. At the Fifth Congress of the RSFSR People's Deputies, he grasped the nettle of radical economic reform in what he said was "the most important decision of my life". The key elements in the measures he outlined in his major speech on 28 October were the liberalization of prices, financial stabilization and the acceleration of privatization and land reform. He warned that the measures would prove painful and tough, but incautiously promised the beginning of recovery by the autumn of 1992. (At the First Congress he had called for reform without lowering living standards.) Yeltsin unexpectedly took over the post of Prime Minister, assuming direct responsibility for the economic situation, and asked for and obtained additional powers for one year to change executive structures and appoint ministers without parliamentary approval, and to introduce economic reform measures by decree. The reform plan was effectively an ultimatum to the Republics to join Russia or Russia would go it alone. Given the position the Ukraine had taken, it signalled that Yeltsin had virtually given up hope of preserving the Union and accepted the "Russia First" line of Burbulis, although publicly he continued to profess support for the Union. Yeltsin also delivered an ultimatum to the Centre. On 15 October he had spoken of the need to "complete the destruction of the Centre"; and at the Congress he stated that "Russia was prepared to take responsibility as the legal successor of the Soviet Union", echoing Burbulis. He also declared that from November, Russia would cease all budget contributions to central institutions, except those few approved in the Economic Treaty of 18 October. In November, Yeltsin appointed Burbulis First Deputy and Gaidar and Shokhin Deputy Prime Ministers, the latter two with specific responsibility for reform. The Congress took two decisions which cast a long shadow: it finally elected Khasbulatov, Chairman of the Supreme Soviet of the RSFSR; and it voted to reject a proposal to end the ten-year moratorium on the sale and purchase of land.

It appears from the account in Yeltsin's memoirs that the decision to appoint Burbulis' protégé Gaidar and back a radical reform programme was a matter of instinct rather than mature judgement.[1] Yeltsin did not study economic programmes or understand the economic issues involved (according to Boris Fedorov he, unlike Gorbachev, never read the "500 Days"). But Gaidar's youth, self-assurance and obvious competence appealed to him, and the idea of taking the plunge after years of teetering on the brink suited his temperament. Yeltsin had also considered Yavlinsky but noted (shrewdly) that the frustrations Yavlinsky had experienced had left him morbidly over-sensitive; however, his leading role in the attempt to conclude an Economic Community Treaty would in any case have disqualified him in the eyes of the "Russia First" lobby, now in the ascendant.

NOVO-OGAREVO: END OF THE ROAD

In the wake of the coup, Gorbachev had tried to put the signature of the Union Treaty back at the top of the agenda but the collapse of the Centre and the rush to independence of the Republics had created an entirely new situation and it was clear that the text due to be signed on 20 August would have to be radically revised. The Resolution of the USSR Congress, dictated by the ten Republic leaders and Gorbachev, had called for the rapid conclusion of a new Treaty, but the Republic leaders showed little urgency or enthusiasm, preoccupied as they were with presidential elections, acquiring flags and other attributes of statehood, and seeking seats at the UN. Only seven Republics (not including Ukraine) chose to participate in the new USSR Supreme Soviet which met on 21 October; and the Ukrainian Supreme Soviet had forbidden any participation by a Ukrainian delegation in discussions of a new draft Union Treaty. As the Novo-Ogarevo process resumed, Gorbachev, as Yeltsin put it, was always lagging a little bit behind the game, although he made concessions which would have been unthinkable before August, including the idea of a confederation rather than a federation. At the State Council meeting at Novo-Ogarevo of 14 November, seven Republics agreed to create a new Union now to be known as the Union of Sovereign States (SSG). A draft text was prepared and ready to be initialled by Republic leaders at a State Council Meeting on 25 November. But Ukraine and Azerbaijan leaders did not turn up; and when Yeltsin and the others began to demand more and more changes in the draft to further weaken the Centre and increase the powers of the Republics, Gorbachev walked out in disgust. Agreement was eventually reached to revise the text and then remit it to Republic Supreme Soviets for approval (which would have been an interminable and ultimately fruitless procedure). After the meeting Gorbachev walked slowly upstairs in front of the TV cameras, to meet the press, pausing to allow the Republic leaders to join him. They deliberately lagged behind and left him to give the press conference alone.

Following the Ukrainian referendum a week later which produced a 90 per cent vote in favour of independence, President

Kravchuk stated that Ukraine would take no part in the Novo-Ogarevo process. Both Gorbachev and Yeltsin had declared that a Union without Ukraine would be unthinkable and the last hopes of preserving a Union were now virtually gone.

MINSK AGREEMENT: 7–8 DECEMBER 1991

On 7 December, within less than a week of the Ukrainian referendum, the leaders of Russia, Ukraine and Belorussia met at Belaya Vezha in Western Belorussia to negotiate an agreement which they signed the following day in Minsk, establishing a commonwealth of the three Slav Republics to be known as the Commonwealth of Independent States (CIS). The text of the agreement stated that the USSR "As a subject of international law and geopolitical reality was ceasing its existence", and its laws and institutions no longer had force on their territories. The agreement spoke of co-ordinating foreign policy and the creation of a common economic space. Joint command over a common military strategic space and nuclear arms would be preserved. The Commonwealth was open to all members of the former Union and other States; its institutions would be located in Minsk. The participants recognized existing frontiers "within the framework of the Commonwealth".

When the documents were ready for signature the President of Kazakhstan, Nazarbaev, was belatedly invited to join the three Slav leaders, but in the event did not do so. Gorbachev had not been forewarned; Yeltsin telephoned President Bush about the agreement before Gorbachev heard of it from Shushkevich. After a meeting with Yeltsin and Nazarbaev on 9 December, Gorbachev issued a restrained statement in which he complained that neither the citizens nor the Parliaments of the Republics had been consulted about the agreement; "the fate of a multi-national country could not be determined by the will of the leaders of three Republics" but should be resolved constitutionally. There were protests within Russia about the Minsk agreement including from the democratic camp. Mayor Popov called for a referendum; Travkin's Democratic Party of Russia organized a rally in central Moscow against the break-up of the Union which, however, attracted a fairly small turnout including hard-line communists and Zhirinovsky's LDP. Rutskoi criticized the "impermissible haste" with which the agreement had been concluded but eventually supported its ratification.

According to his then Press Secretary, Andrei Grachev, Gorbachev was hoping for a more significant public reaction against the Minsk Agreement but once again "the people were silent". Gorbachev and Yeltsin both addressed Army leaders within 24 hours on 10–11 December to gauge their reactions and engage their sympathies. It was Yeltsin, who *inter alia* promised improved pay and conditions, who gained their support rather than Gorbachev, who appealed in general terms for the preservation of the Union. Grachev believes that Gorbachev, having regained confidence after the Putsch as a result of his frequent appearances on the international stage and talks with Western leaders who seemed to support the preservation of the USSR, over-reached himself by insisting on preserving a single State, when agreement on a Confederation might have been attainable.[2]

The Minsk Agreement was ratified on 10 December by the Belorussian and Ukrainian parliaments with large majorities but both parliaments added amendments and conditions to the text. The Russian Supreme Soviet ratified the agreement on 12 December by 188 votes to 6 with 7 abstentions (i.e. with the support of the great majority of communists and present and future "national patriots").

The Minsk Agreement showed every sign of having been concocted hastily in the wake of the Ukrainian referendum with virtually no advance discussion or preparation. Evidently the size of the majority for independence, including in the Russified east and south of Ukraine, persuaded Yeltsin finally to abandon his ambivalent support for the Union and accept the line of the "Russia First" lobby (the Russian team at Belaya Vezha included Burbulis, Gaidar, Shakhrai and Kozyrev). The objectives of the three signatories were different and not fully compatible. Yeltsin was concerned to keep Ukraine within Russia's political orbit in the hope of eventually drawing her back into a closer association. Yeltsin stated in his memoirs that "The CIS was the only possibility at that moment to preserve a single geopolitical space".[3] The Ukraine's main objective was an association with the RSFSR which involved minimal political obligations but safeguarded Ukraine's economic interests and defused frontier and minority issues. For Ukraine and Belorussia, the final elimination of the Centre was a vital purpose. As for Yeltsin, he specifically denied in his memoirs that he saw the separate agreement as a way of settling accounts with Gorbachev and removing him from power, but given the bitter rivalry between them, this personal motive cannot be entirely discounted.

END OF THE SOVIET UNION: DECEMBER 1991

CIS Conference in Alma Ata

On 12–13 December the leaders of Kazakhstan and the four Central Asian Republics met in Ashkhabad to discuss the CIS. They were seriously offended at having been ignored by the Minsk Three but they had little alternative but to acquiesce and seek to join them. The five Presidents issued a joint Declaration welcoming the CIS and calling on the Slav Republics to recognize the five as co-founders and equal participants. Gorbachev with the Centre removed from under him now had no ground left to stand on. At a meeting with Yeltsin on 17 December, he agreed on a transition from Union structures to those of the CIS to proceed within the framework of the constitution and to be completed by the end of December or early January. Gorbachev issued a final appeal to Republic leaders who gathered in Alma Ata on 21 December to preserve international representation for the Commonwealth and a unified strategic command, and establish Commonwealth citizenship. It was ignored. Eleven Republic leaders signed a Protocol to the Minsk agreement recording their membership on an equal basis in the CIS and issued the Alma Ata Declaration. They proposed setting up a Council of Heads of State as the supreme CIS body.

End of the USSR: 31 December 1991

After final haggling with Yeltsin on 23 and 24 December over the terms of his retirement and the handover of power (including the nuclear button) Gorbachev announced his resignation in a brief television statement on 25 December. On the evening of that day the red flag on the Kremlin was lowered. The USSR officially came to an end on 31 December.

Notes

1   *Zapiski Prezidenta*, pp. 163–5.
2   A. Grachev, *Kremlevskaya Khronika EKSMO*, Moscow, 1994.
3   *Zapiski Prezidenta*, p. 152.

Part III

Russia 1992: Economic Reform and Constitutional Power Struggle

6

Economic Reform and Political Backlash: Sixth Congress

PRICE LIBERALIZATION

The radical Economic Reform programme was launched on 2 January with the removal of price control from all but a few basic items (some staple foods, vodka, energy, transport, rents) for which State prices were raised by 200 per cent or more; the exchange rate was floated. The stated aim was to cut the budget deficit from 20 per cent of GNP in 1991 to close to zero in the first quarter of 1992. Expenditure cuts were planned in subsidies, defence, investment foreign aid and the bureaucracy. To cushion the impact a minimum wage was established, benefits and pensions were raised; and wages increased twofold. But savings were effectively devalued and this was especially damaging politically. Prices rose at once by about 250 per cent.

It was a deliberately high risk strategy and Gaidar had no illusions about the short-term political consequences. He said privately in January 1992 that even if successful he would become so unpopular that only his successor would reap the fruits. He therefore had no long-term political ambitions. His government was popularly known among liberals as the "Kamikaze government".

Backlash

The reforms produced a rapid improvement in supplies of food and consumer goods, but the public soon forgot that only weeks before the shops had been empty and even staples such as bread, salt and sugar had been unobtainable. There was a shocked reaction to the price rises and the political backlash was almost instantaneous.

Within two weeks Khasbulatov had attacked the "uncontrolled anarchic price rises" and called for the dismissal of the "poorly qualified and incompetent" Russian government, otherwise Parliament would use its constitutional authority to change the cabinet. Khasbulatov began every session of the Supreme Soviet Presidium with a diatribe against the government. Vice-President Rutskoi's rhetoric was more extreme. He derided Gaidar's team as "little boys in pink trousers", described the government as a "wrecking team" carrying out a policy of "economic genocide". The government was "criminal and should be brought to trial". The opposition press, notably *Pravda*, *Rabochaya Tribuna* and *Sovetskaya Rossiya* joined in with dire warnings of economic collapse and social unrest. Before long there was fierce criticism of the reforms also from formerly influential reform-minded economists, now on the shelf notably Shatalin and Petrakov. The latter declared in a series of press articles[1] that the combination of price liberalization, cuts in expenditure and the rouble/dollar exchange rate was bringing whole sectors of the economy to a halt and producing a "catastrophic economic situation".

Opposition Demonstrations

The hard-line opposition sought to exploit the public discontent over price rises to mobilize support on the streets. A demonstration on 12 January in Moscow attracted some 10,000–15,000 Communist sympathisers; on 9 February 20,000 demonstrated on Manege Square – slightly more than Yeltsin's supporters could muster for a rally on the same day at the White House. The right wing was beginning to organize politically. On 8–9 February a "Congress of Civil and Patriotic Russia" was attended by various centre and right political groups including the Christian Democrats and the Republican Party, as well as an uninvited contingent from the extremist and anti-Semitic Pamyat Society. On 9 February the Congress established the Russian Popular Assembly, an opposition movement with the declared aims of bringing down the government and in the longer term restoring Russia within its historical boundaries; and on 23 February another hard-line demonstration in Moscow numbering about 10,000 was involved in violent clashes with a strong force of police which blockaded all streets leading to the centre.

But as a whole the public mood was relatively calm and there was no serious violence or unrest. The Moscow demonstrations were not on the scale of those mounted by the democratic opposition a year earlier. The impact of the price rises was softened to some extent by private food stocks and a large rouble surplus. Opinion polls showed that, despite public discontent over prices, which Yeltsin experienced at first hand during a tour of cities on the Volga in January, his popular support was holding up with over 50 per cent expressing complete or qualified confidence in him. Despite rumours that he was about to resign as Prime Minister in order to distance himself from the government and the reforms, he continued to defend them, notably in a robust speech in the Supreme Soviet on 16 January.

LEADERSHIP DIVISIONS: JANUARY–FEBRUARY 1992

However, although Yeltsin's stock of public confidence was still high and eroding only slowly, there were still worrying signs. Questions were again asked about his health or drinking habits when he disappeared suddenly from Moscow at the end of the month (to pay a brief visit to the Black Sea Fleet at Novorossiisk). And he found shortly afterwards that, as for Gorbachev, "successful" trips to the West cut no ice at home: a cartoon in the tabloid, *Kommersant* showed a poster with Yeltsin's head surrounded by Doves of Peace while Gorbachev's birthmark was being painted on his forehead. Yeltsin seemed isolated and lacking a political base apart from his popularity; there were no senior colleagues in his team who were political figures in their own right; and there was no political party or movement behind him. Democratic Russia, alienated by Yeltsin's neglect, had been weakened by the departure of a group of right wing parties including Travkin's DPR at the end of 1991 and then the resignation of Yury Afanasiev and a group of prominent left wing radicals. Deprived of its opposition role and now lacking nationally known dynamic figures in its leadership, the rump of Democratic Russia appeared marginalized.

The economic reforms had opened up the fissures in the Russian leadership and the Yeltsin administration was already looking disjointed and incoherent. The President, Vice-President, Parliament and government seemed estranged, pursuing separate political agendas with minimal co-ordination or even meaningful contact.

Rutskoi

Vice-President Rutskoi, already on his way to becoming leader of the opposition, was promoting a political platform which had little or nothing in common with Yeltsin's policies. He made frequent speeches and published a series of articles, including two major ones, on 30 and 31 January in *Pravda* and *Izvestiya*, while Yeltsin was abroad, in which he not only attacked Yeltsin's economic policies but implicitly criticized his failure to defend Russia's state interests against the provocations of Ukraine and the pretensions of minorities within the Russian Federation. He called the CIS a "ramshackle structure" which had accelerated instead of halting the break-up of the State. He also expressed resentment at Western economic and cultural influence which he saw as damaging to Russia's pride and spirituality. His platform of nostalgia for discipline, social justice, patriotism and super-power status, was strikingly reminiscent of the pronouncements of the August putsch leaders and the rhetoric of the hard-line communist and nationalist opposition to Gorbachev (Rutskoi was already calling for the release of the August coup leaders).

Rutskoi had by now been stripped of most of his responsibilities in the administration. A decree of 19 December had removed five economic committees from his supervision including the Committee for Defence Conversion which was his priority interest. His commission to take charge of agricultural reform, following a meeting with Yeltsin on 12 February, was regarded by the democrats as a joke and by Rutskoi himself reportedly as a humiliation (the agricultural portfolio in recent Soviet times had been traditionally regarded as a poisoned chalice offered to troublesome rivals). Rutskoi complained in a *Pravda* article that Yeltsin's entourage was preventing any contact between him and the President. His powers and influence were very limited but as a popularly elected Vice-President, albeit on Yeltsin's coat-tails, his own position was secure and he was already staking out a political position whose combination of Russian nationalism and social conservatism seemed likely to attract growing support. He had his own political party, the Popular Party "Free Russia" although his relations with it were becoming strained (it had boycotted the February Congress of Patriots). His constituency included former communists, from whom his attitudes were now indistinguishable, military officers and Russian nationalists. However, at this stage Rutskoi was still professing to support the

President. He said in a television interview on 15 February: "I will never be in opposition to the President because . . . there is such a concept as the word of an officer. When Boris Nikolaevich and I were elected, I gave him my word that I would stand by him to the end, come what may." Yeltsin was later to remind Rutskoi of those words.

Khasbulatov

Rutskoi was moving towards an alliance with Khasbulatov, the ambitious and unscrupulous Chairman of the Supreme Soviet. Khasbulatov's Chechen nationality seemed to limit his popular appeal and prospects, and he had no political base other than the Russian parliament. But though he antagonized many deputies by his high-handed and manipulative chairmanship, Khasbulatov skilfully exploited the frustration and resentment of the Congress and Supreme Soviet at their failure to convert Constitutional supremacy into real political power. Most political decisions were now emerging from Yeltsin's labyrinthine administration, without clear authorship or prior discussion and publicity. Parliament's relationship with both President and Government became increasingly difficult and acrimonious.

EVE OF THE SIXTH CONGRESS: MARCH 1992

As the Sixth Congress approached, Yeltsin and the Government were coming under severe pressure. The efforts of the hard-line opposition to mobilize public support on the streets reached a climax with the demonstration on 17 March, the anniversary of the All-Union referendum, to demand the restoration of the USSR and the removal of Yeltsin. Despite claims of much higher figures the turnout was no more than 20,000–25,000 and the predominantly elderly demonstrators, the remnants and the dispossessed of the old regime, looked more pitiful than threatening. An attempt on the same day to convene the "Sixth Congress of USSR Deputies" ended in near farce.

Mood in Congress

However, the Russian Congress was a more serious threat. The majority of deputies were in hostile mood. Their anger at the economic reforms had been stoked by fears that the next round of price increases (bread prices had been de-controlled on 1 April) could lead to widespread unrest. There was also a mood of resentment that Russia had been cheated of its inheritance after the collapse of the USSR: the ineffectual CIS was no substitute for the loss of Ukraine and there were fears for the integrity of Russia itself following the defection of Chechnya and the independence vote in Tatarstan. The political balance in the parliament had changed and become more complex. There were no longer two broadly conservative and democratic camps but 14 fractions whose attitudes overlapped and were largely unpredictable. Many former democrats were hostile to the economic reform and increasingly prone to nationalistic attitudes. The core of the opposition was now composed of an alliance of communists and nationalists. Former opponents in the Parliament were making common cause in defence of the institutional interests of the Congress in its struggle for power and influence against the government and what they saw as Yeltsin's bloated and secretive administration.

Government Changes

On the eve of the Congress, the West sent a strong signal of support with the announcement of a US$ 24 billion aid package put together by the G7, while Yeltsin made a number of tactical moves to deflect the expected onslaught on his government. Deputy Prime Minister Shakhrai resigned, ostensibly so that he could act as the President's representative on the floor of the Congress. Gaidar was replaced as Minister of Finance by his first deputy (he had ceased to be Minister for the Economy when promoted First Deputy Prime Minister on 1 March); First Deputy Prime Minister Burbulis was relieved of his duties as from 14 April (while remaining State Secretary); Deputy Prime Minister Shokhin was also relieved of a part of his portfolio. As *Nezavisimaya Gazeta* put it, Yeltsin had removed his principal allies from the firing line in order to protect the government and strengthen his own position. Yeltsin also announced "partial correctives" to his economic reform policy at an eve of Congress rally of his supporters who met in the guise of an "Assembly of the Citizens of Russia". These involved tax breaks for industry and subsidies for agriculture, as well as an indication that he intended to bring experienced industrial managers into the government. However, Yeltsin staked out a strong position on the other main issue which divided him and the Congress: the constitutional powers of the President and the Parliament.

Yeltsin's Additional Powers

Two closely linked issues were to dominate the agenda of the Congress: the Government reform policy which the opposition majority in Congress wanted to slow down, dilute and control; and the President's additional powers to issue binding decrees on economic reform and exercise full control over Ministerial and other executive appointments granted for one year by the Fifth Congress which the Sixth Congress was now determined to curtail. Khasbulatov's overall objective was to detach the Government from the President, eliminate from it the chief reformers and make it directly answerable to Parliament. To this end, he sought to oblige Yeltsin to step down as Prime Minister and nominate a successor, whose appointment would require the approval of the Congress. It was the first round in a bitter constitutional power struggle and the prelude to a determined and sustained campaign by the Congress to restrict Yeltsin's powers and establish Parliamentary control over the Government. There was a respectable case to be made especially given the history of the country for wishing to limit Presidential power and make the Government accountable to Parliament. But this parliament lacked democratic credentials; and in any case as Yeltsin argued in his speech on the eve of the Congress, a move to parliamentary democracy in the absence of a multi-party system and in the midst of an economic crisis would be unworkable.

Yeltsin's main political objective was to accelerate the adoption of the new Constitution in place of the existing RSFSR Constitution adopted in the Soviet era in 1978 and now undergoing a constant process of revision to try to bring it into line with current realities. A draft of the new Constitution existed, the work of a Parliamentary Commission formally headed by Yeltsin, which had been meeting since the summer of 1990. But the majority of deputies preferred to cling to the old text since the adoption of a new Constitution would entail the dissolution of Congress and the end of their deputies' mandates. Moreover the current Constitution conferred enormous power on deputies (especially given that they could amend it at will by a two-thirds majority vote). The Congress had been elected in 1990, when the Party was still in power and able to exert a considerable measure of control over the electoral process. A significant number of deputies belonged squarely in the Soviet era and were determined to restore or preserve as much of it as possible. During the Congress they repeatedly blocked attempts to remove from the text of the existing Constitution articles referring to the USSR.

SIXTH RUSSIAN CONGRESS, 6–21 APRIL

The opening phase of the Congress proved less difficult for the government than had been expected. A proposal on the first day to include on the agenda a no-confidence vote in the government was narrowly rejected by 447 votes to 412. Yeltsin gave a robust defence of the government's economic programme offering his "correctives" but telling the Congress that its support for economic reform would be the best answer to arguments that it should be done away with. (A barbed comment hinting at his ultimate weapon, a referendum to dissolve the Congress.) Gaidar was given a fairly easy ride and the session was chaired by Khasbulatov in a way which was unexpectedly helpful to the President and Gaidar. The press reported that "the first attack on the government had been repulsed".

Gaidar Offers Resignation

However, a hard-line resolution had been tabled which referred to the "catastrophic situation" brought about by the reformist Government, proposed to strip the President of his additional powers and called on him to step down as Prime Minister and name a successor during the Congress. When Yeltsin spoke for the second time he took a conciliatory line, promising that 3–5 Ministers would be replaced by experienced industrialists and proposing what appeared to be an acceptable compromise amendment on the issue of his additional powers. But on the following day the Congress rejected the President's amendment; it then adopted a resolution containing wholesale criticism of the government's economic policies and demanding a series of inflationary measures which, if implemented, would have wrecked the entire reform strategy. Gaidar described it as "a total revision of the economic reform course". Ministers walked out of the Congress and Gaidar offered the government's resignation to the President. Yeltsin made no public response and did not reappear at the Congress until its final day on 21 April.

Yeltsin's absence and silence left the government floundering, locked in bitter conflict with the Parliament and with no visible support from the President. His words before the Congress about "A young bold, united team which must not be sacrificed to the Congress" now appeared somewhat hollow and the Russian press started talking about the "Gorbachev syndrome", ie an addiction to manoeuvre and compromise and readiness to sacrifice allies for the sake of an illusory consensus with the opposition. A compromise solution was eventually patched up between the Presidium of the Supreme Soviet and the government: the Congress's hostile Resolution would be balanced by a Declaration offering general support for the President's reform policies. The compromise was almost scotched by Khasbulatov who, in a near-hysterical outburst, accused the government of trying to blackmail the Congress. Government ministers again walked out and the session ended in uproar. Eventually both Resolution and Declaration were adopted and the government remained in place.

New Constitution

The Congress spent five days laboriously discussing amendments to the existing 1978 Constitution; the main focus of the debate was the battle by Shakhrai as Presidential representative to fend off amendments designed to curb the powers of the President. When the Congress finally came to consider the new draft Constitution the debate was inconclusive. It failed to adopt the draft even as a basis for discussion but merely approved its "general concept". The Congress refused to discuss alternative drafts including a so-called "Presidential draft" prepared by Shakhrai at the behest of Yeltsin who was concerned that the official draft gave too much power to the legislature.

"Fragile Compromise"

When Yeltsin made his concluding speech at the Congress on the

21 April, he referred to "a continuing constitutional crisis" which "had not been resolved and was increasingly acquiring a chronic character". Only "a fragile compromise" had been reached between the government and the deputies. He criticized the Congress for its constant attacks on the mass media and the aggressive tone of the debate on the CIS. But the overall tone of his speech was conciliatory and Yeltsin withdrew his threat to hold a referendum on the fate of the Congress or in order to by-pass its decisions.

However, Yeltsin left the Congress with pent-up feelings of resentment and hostility which were reflected in his outburst in Cheropovets in North Russia at the end of April, when he called for a million signatures to be collected for a referendum on a draft Constitution which he would put forward himself and which would have no place for the redundant Congress.

Yeltsin described the outcome of the Congress as "a draw" with the opposition or "possibly a victory for the reformers". Certainly the government and, at least in principle, the reform policy had survived more or less intact. Gaidar's personal standing was enhanced by his vigorous and cogent defence of his policies: he had won his political spurs. The government's leading critics did not emerge so well. Khasbulatov compromised himself by some outrageous and mendacious interventions (he was twice caught out lying to the Congress); and Vice-President Rutskoi after a typically intemperate statement on the situation in Moldova in which he called for the recognition of Transdniestria, played no further part in the proceedings.

In an interview a week after the Congress,[2] Shakhrai said it was "a dangerous illusion" to think the President and Government had won a victory at the Congress. The Government was now effectively "provisional". The powers of the President to control the composition of the Cabinet would cease when the Supreme Soviet adopted a law on the government. Shakhrai (like Burbulis) had advised Yeltsin to confront the Congress by demanding a vote of confidence in the government and the confirmation of Gaidar as Prime Minister. But others in his entourage had persuaded him to stand aloof and act as a detached arbiter. In the event Yeltsin's irresolute performance and prolonged absence raised doubts about his commitment to the government and to the reforms. The confrontation with the Congress had only been postponed; and it was to be renewed at the end of the year in much less favourable circumstances for him.

Notes

1 For example, *Nezavisimaya Gazeta*, 6 March 1992; *Izvestiya*, 18 March 1992.
2 *Izvestiya*, 29 April 1992.

7

Aftermath of the April Congress

CABINET CHANGES

After some delay Yeltsin implemented his undertaking to "strengthen" the government by the inclusion of new men with direct experience of industry. Shumeiko, a Deputy Chairman of the Supreme Soviet and former enterprise manager, was appointed First Deputy Prime Minister, ie on the same level as Gaidar. Khizha, a plant manager from the military industrial complex, and Chernomyrdin, former Soviet Minister for the gas industry, became Deputy Prime Ministers. Lopukhin, who had fought for full liberalization of energy prices, was dismissed as Minister for Fuel and Energy. Yeltsin spoke of a "bloc of ministers responsible for industry working alongside a bloc responsible for economic reform". This implausible concept raised doubts about the cohesion of the government and its ability or willingness to maintain the economic reforms on course. These doubts were increased by Yeltsin's decision to overrule Gaidar and hold off the freeing of energy prices. Yeltsin's "victory" proved costly for the cause of economic reform: monetary discipline had been relaxed and the government retreated from the attempt at macro-economic stabilization.

Pressures on Yeltsin had been building up since the Congress. The opposition groups had now broadened and diversified their campaign, shifting the focus of their attack from Gaidar and the government to Yeltsin himself. There had been attempts to discredit him personally through public accusations of drunkenness at the Tashkent CIS Summit; a move by a group of deputies to impeach him; and a campaign to collect signatures for a referendum to call for his removal. Meanwhile parliamentary obstruction of legislation on economic reform introduced by the government continued; and there were increasingly aggressive street demonstrations and picketing by hard-line political groups; and opposition instigation and support for public sector strikes.

Yeltsin had promised publicly several times that by the end of the year, prices would stabilize and the economic situation begin to improve. Against the background of general expectations now that the economic situation would further deteriorate by autumn or early winter with a possibility of serious social unrest and political turbulence, Yeltsin evidently decided to avoid a head-on confrontation with his opponents which might have produced political instability in very unfavourable economic circumstances. His tactics were therefore to conciliate opponents inside and outside parliament, and to broaden the base of the government in order to make it and himself less vulnerable. He was trying to preserve a difficult balance between pushing through the economic reforms to which he remained committed and safeguarding his political position. It was clear, however, that there were limits to the political risks he was prepared to take for the sake of economic virtue in the eyes of the IMF. He made the revealing comment on one occasion that you do not close down large factories or they might close you down. However, despite his compromises and tactical shifts, he remained committed to key elements of the reform policy – privatization, land reform, co-operation with the West.

Alarm in the Democratic Camp

Yeltsin tried to reassure the democratic camp where increasing concern was being expressed, that the post-Congress Cabinet changes, followed by the appointment of Gerashchenko as Chairman of the Russian Central Bank, and the resignations of Popov as Mayor of Moscow and Shakhrai as State Counsellor, showed that the reform was in retreat. Yeltsin told deputies of the parliamentary "reform" coalition that "the limits of compromise had been exhausted". In a television interview on 10 June, shortly before the first anniversary of his election as President of Russia, Yeltsin described the "correctives" he had introduced to the reform programme as a tactical shift not a change of direction. He denied that the Gaidar team was breaking up or the reform slowing down; he would allow no stepping back nor his own removal as President and would continue as Prime Minister for a few months more. (But he backed off from his threat in Cheropovets to call a referendum, explaining, rather lamely, that this had been an improvisation in front of a large crowd not an official statement.) He made some balancing appointments: the Chairman of the Privatization Committee, Chubais, was promoted Deputy Prime Minister and Yeltsin theatrically announced the promotion of Gaidar to Acting Prime Minister at the airport when about to depart for the United States on 15 June. In Washington he further redressed the balance with a resounding re-affirmation of his commitment to reform and he assured President Bush that "tactical adjustments" should not be mistaken for retreat.

Yeltsin had earlier responded to speculation about his own political future by stating during a visit to Barnaul in May that he would not resign before the expiry of his term (in June 1996) but would not seek a second term. He also declared in Washington that he would not resign and could not be removed until the end of his current term. His preoccupation with this theme and repeated changes of tack, suggested a sense of insecurity about his political position which appeared somewhat exaggerated. But his political strength derived almost exclusively from popular support and personal prestige, and his approval rating in the opinion polls had recently fallen to below 30 per cent for the first time. He had no political party, having rejected advice to form one, no majority in parliament, no social base in the population. He had refused to put himself at the head of the Democratic Russia movement which had campaigned for his election and mounted huge demonstrations in his support at critical moments.

The sense of alarm among the democrats continued to grow, fuelled by the aggressive picketing of the Ostankino television station by the hard-line "Labour Russia" movement which eventually led to violent clashes on 22 June when the pickets were dispersed. Shakhrai gave an interview about his resignation to *Komsomolskaya Pravda* on 18 June in which he warned of a possible coup against Yeltsin and the threat of fascist dictatorship, drawing the familiar analogy with Weimar Germany. He complained that his advice to take firmer executive action to implement reform had been rejected because of the influence of a group around the President in favour of delaying reforms.

Kozyrev Article

On 26 June the Constitutional Court issued a statement, couched in alarmist terms, which referred to calls by political leaders for the overthrow of the constitutional organs of state. The statement, which declared that the Constitutional Order was under threat and spoke of the danger of social explosion and anarchy, appeared to be directed against the President for threatening an unconstitutional referendum, the government for its social and economic policies and the opposition leaders for their aggressive rhetoric. It was the first clear indication that the Constitutional Court was taking upon itself a political role. Two weeks later the Foreign Minister Kozyrev published a sensational article in *Izvestiya* (1 July) in which he warned that the "war party" the "party of neo-bolshevism" was exerting growing influence. He alleged that the army and the former KGB were supporting separatists in Moldova and the Transcaucasus. Kozyrev expressed alarm at the extent of support in the media for the communists and nationalists, and hostility to NATO and the United States, and spoke about the danger of a coup against the President. He warned that democracy could not co-exist with a hard-line nationalist foreign policy. There were inevitably comparisons with the dramatic resignation speech of the then Foreign Minister Shevardnadze at the USSR Congress in December 1990, and it was widely expected that Kozyrev would resign or be dismissed.

On 4 July Yeltsin gave a press conference in which he sharply rebuked Kozyrev for the "harmful" statement he had published and ruled out the possibility of a coup. Yeltsin said that the Ministers of Defence, Security and Internal Affairs were loyal and the army was "ours". There was no popular support for the opposition. Yeltsin took the opportunity at the same press conference, which took place on the eve of the G7 Summit in Munich, to take a robust line on Western advice about Russia's economic policies. He said that Russia would not free fuel prices or freeze wages as required by the IMF, because this would trigger a ten-fold general price rise. Russia, if necessary, would do without the $24 billion.

THE OPPOSITION REGROUPS

In the interval between the Sixth and Seventh Congresses, the opposition regrouped and mobilized, while the democratic support and confidence continued to ebb. The hard-line opposition was still a motley un-co-ordinated collection of quasi-communist and nationalist groups and parties, with no coherent alternative policies and no convincing leaders, with the possible exception of Rutskoi. They had significant support in parliament but little among the population. However, their appeal to fear of economic hardship and nationalist resentment over Russia's declining status and the plight of its minorities in the former Soviet Republics was inherently potent. The crises in South Ossetia and Transdniestria had given a further boost to the nationalist cause and had also enabled Yeltsin's only credible rival for the leadership, Vice-President Rutskoi, to seize the limelight with a dramatic television speech to the nation during Yeltsin's absence in North America.

Civic Alliance

On 21 June the first meeting or "forum" of the new centrist coalition the Civic Alliance was held in Moscow, bringing together Rutskoi's Popular Party "Free Russia" (NPSR), Travkin's Democratic Party of Russia (DPR) and Volsky's Renewal (*Obnovlenie*) movement which was linked to the Union of Industrialists and Entrepreneurs. The new movement presented itself as a moderate and constructive opposition. Its leaders professed to support market reforms but slowed down and modified to avoid the danger of a social explosion; they called for state intervention and regulation of the economy to support industry and halt the fall in production, instead of the current focus on macro-economic stabilization. They also called for closer integration of the CIS and a more robust defence of Russia's national interests in foreign policy.

The leaders and their movements, however, made uneasy bedfellows. The maverick democratic leader Travkin had left Democratic Russia in December 1991 in protest at its acquiescence in the disintegration of the Union. But the majority of his party members remained much closer than he did to the democrats and had little in common with Rutskoi's party of reformed communists / social democrats which in turn was becoming estranged from the Vice-President and his increasingly reactionary and nationalist views; or Volsky's industrialists' union, widely regarded as representing the interests of "red directors" and the former *nomenklatura*. However, the Civic Alliance seeking to occupy advantageous ground in the centre of the political spectrum and claiming the support of up to 40 per cent of the deputies in parliament, was for a time taken very seriously including by President Yeltsin. Its leaders behaved like a shadow cabinet or government in waiting and the movement became a significant actor on the political scene in the run up to the Seventh Congress; although commentators were already pointing out that its leaders' political views were incompatible and its claims for significant support and influence in parliament, industry and the population at large mostly bluff.

National Salvation Front

In the autumn the growing unity of the hard left communist and hard right nationalist opposition, already manifested on the streets, took shape in a political coalition. A Political Declaration by the left and right opposition published in *Sovetskaya Rossiya* of 22 September heralded the inaugural congress of the National Salvation Front which was held in the Russian Parliamentary Centre in Moscow on 24 October. The congress attracted nearly 1,500 representatives from a motley collection of hard left and right parties and splinter groups, plus 18 People's Deputies including Isakov, Baburin and Astafiev, a number of retired right-wing generals, including Sterligov (KGB), and Makashov (who stood in the presidential elections against Yeltsin in 1991), communists including Zyuganov and Chikin, and nationalist and anti-semitic writers and academics including Prokhanov and Shafarevich. The hall where the congress took place was decorated with a nauseous mixture of communist, nationalist and religious symbolism featuring a monarchist black, yellow and white flag on one side of the platform and the red flag with hammer and sickle on the other. The manifesto of the NSF called in effect for the restoration of the USSR in a Russian nationalist guise; state control of the economy; restoration of military-strategic parity with the United States; and ruthless measures to establish law and order. The immediate aim of the movement was the removal of the government and the President. However, the NSF never functioned effectively as a united, political organization. Its leaders had little in common but their hatred for Yeltsin and the democrats, and their nostalgia for the USSR. The ambitions of its extremist leaders soon began to drive them apart.

Democratic Movement

The Democratic movement meanwhile did not have unity even on paper and continued to drift, in increasing disarray. It suffered from its indeterminate situation, neither in power nor in opposition, and failed to produce any credible new leadership, in part because of its ambivalent relationship with Yeltsin. The President mostly ignored the democrats while appealing (successfully) for their support in times of crisis. He occasionally talked of the need for a new Democratic movement or party but refused to tie his hands by deciding to lead or even join one. His position was constantly shifting. At a press conference in November, he again rejected the idea of creating his own party. As popularly elected President he represented all parties and the entire Russian people: "the main social base of the President is the Russian people". But a few weeks later, at the end of November, he again spoke of the need to organize a pro-reform movement and said that he as President should be "with it and in it".[1]

PARLIAMENTARY OFFENSIVE: JULY–OCTOBER 1992

At the summer and autumn sessions of the Supreme Soviet the opposition majority continued their offensive against the government's economic and foreign policies and support for Khasbulatov's campaign to increase the power of the parliament at the expense of the government and President. Relations between the legislature and the executive became increasingly acrimonious.

In June, Yeltsin submitted his draft law on the government as he had undertaken to do at the Sixth Congress but withdrew it after fierce criticism of the text by the Supreme Soviet's Legislation Committee. The Supreme Soviet voted to lift sanctions against Serbia following a debate which Kozyrev condemned as a throw-back to the 1970s with its stereotypes of NATO and the USA as enemies. Its resolution declaring invalid the transfer of Crimea from Russia to the Ukraine in 1954, produced a crisis in relations with Ukraine. At the end of August, Khasbulatov signed documents arrogating new powers to himself, his hard-line Deputy Chairman and his apparatus, and reducing those of his liberal First Deputy Chairman Filatov. There were protests by members of the Supreme Soviet Presidium and demands by democratic deputies for Khasbulatov's resignation.

The democratic camp and the liberal media reacted angrily to a Supreme Soviet resolution of 17 July, the last day of its summer session, resubordinating the leading democratic newspaper *Izvestiya* to parliamentary control. (*Izvestiya*, formerly the official organ of the USSR Supreme Soviet, had been converted to an independent paper by its editorial staff following the August coup.) The move was engineered by Khasbulatov, a frequent target of *Izvestiya*'s criticism, who accused the newspaper of waging war against the Supreme Soviet and seeking to drive a wedge between the President and parliament. On the same day, the Supreme Soviet debated a draft law on the media which would have established a parliamentary "supervisory council" to monitor State television and radio: the law was eventually adopted albeit in a diluted form.

In early September, Yeltsin told the Supreme Soviet that he had exercised his power of veto on 11 laws adopted by the Supreme Soviet before the summer recess (including the laws on defence, interior troops and hard currency regulation). However, when the autumn session opened on 22 September, an attempt by hard-line deputies to introduce a motion of no confidence in the government fizzled out, as did the call by a minority of democratic deputies for Khasbulatov's resignation. When Yeltsin addressed the Supreme Soviet on 6 October, he took a conciliatory line. He gave only ambivalent support to his government, which he criticized for its "too macro-economic" policy neglecting the needs of the population and industry, and for ignoring alternative proposals from groups such as the Civic Alliance. He criticized individual economic ministers by name but said the government itself should not resign. He appeared, however, to distance himself from Gaidar, who on the following day spoke robustly in defence of government policy and seemed somewhat at odds with Yeltsin's line.

Date of the Congress

On 16 October, in a speech to the Constitutional Commission, Yeltsin repeated an earlier call to postpone the Seventh Congress until March or April 1993, which he said would give time to complete work on the new constitution which could then be adopted at the Congress. In the same speech he was sharply critical of the Supreme Soviet for allowing meetings of the National Salvation Front to take place in the White House. The Supreme Soviet's vote on 21 October by 114 to 59 to reject Yeltsin's request for a postponement of the Congress and confirm that it would begin on 1 December (the date on which Yeltsin's special powers expired) was seen by the President's supporters as an "act of war". Hostility between the Opposition majority in parliament and the liberal wing of the presidential administration and the government had reached an unprecedented pitch.

The decision by the Supreme Soviet to reject Yeltsin's request to postpone the Congress, sharpened Yeltsin's tactical dilemma and the arguments among his advisers. A few days before parliament finally confirmed the date of the Seventh Congress Burbulis, Poltoranin, Kozyrev and Chubais held a briefing for foreign journalists at which they spoke in extravagantly alarmist terms of the danger of a parliamentary coup against the President. Poltoranin publicly described Khasbulatov as a "detonator of political stability" who had deliberately scheduled the Congress to coincide with planned subversive actions by pro-Communist forces. Khasbulatov responded by writing to the President to demand Poltoranin's dismissal.

During a speech to the collegium of the Foreign Ministry on 27 October, Yeltsin referred angrily to the Supreme Soviet decision to hold the Congress in December as "sheer confrontation". He said he was consulting on how to beat off the attack by the irreconcilable opposition and defend the reforms. He expressed support for Kozyrev saying that to sack him would be wrong morally and professionally. If the Congress attempted to force the resignation of the government "we must keep the Foreign Minister at least but the main thing is to keep Gaidar". The main theme of Yeltsin's address was the need for a more assertive foreign policy in relation to the CIS and the West (Yeltsin had been increasingly critical of the West for taking Russia for granted, e.g. over the political / economic costs of sanctions against Libya and Serbia). Immediately following this speech Yeltsin issued two decrees, evidently intended to mollify his democratic supporters as well as give vent to his own anger and frustration: one banned the National Salvation Front (on dubious legal grounds), the other disbanded the 5,000-strong parliamentary protection service popularly known as Khasbulatov's private army (which had recently taken control of the *Izvestiya* building following the Supreme Soviet vote to transfer the *Izvestiya* publishing house to the jurisdiction of parliament).

Yeltsin continued to vacillate between the options of seeking a *modus vivendi* with the parliament and settling accounts with it. He explained in his memoirs why the confrontation with the parliament was so long delayed: he had strong inhibitions, especially after

August 1991, against violating the law or constitution; the split with parliament had developed gradually, imperceptibly and at first he saw the possibility of co-operation; finally he admitted to an element of Russian "avos'" (something might turn up).[2] Elsewhere he wrote that Gaidar had been making progress in finding an understanding with the parliament and given a little more time might have gained acceptance.[3] But he also seriously considered replacing Gaidar by Skokov and a "technocratic government of directors"; and he discussed this with Skokov in the run-up to the Seventh Congress when he was "under massive pressure from parliamentary factions, parties, movements, economist and managers". By this time he was seriously alarmed by the economic situation: industrial output was down by 28 per cent on the previous year and food prices were rising by 4 per cent per week.

YELTSIN SEEKS BROADER SUPPORT: OCTOBER–NOVEMBER 1992

Civic Alliance

Yeltsin also considered the possibility of a coalition with the Civic Alliance, in the hope that this would help to protect the core of the government and its policies against the attacks of the opposition at the forthcoming Congress. Yeltsin was reported in the press to have had a number of meetings with the leaders of the Civic Alliance to discuss "correctives to the composition and policy of the government". Following a meeting on 3 November, the President said that their positions were close and he hoped that the Civic Alliance would influence the mood of the Seventh Congress and channel events into a constructive course. Volsky handed over the new Civic Alliance anti-crisis programme, but apparently over-reached himself by proposing also a list of Civic Alliance candidates for senior posts in the government and a list of ministers (including Kozyrev and Poltoranin) they wished to have removed. Yeltsin reacted angrily and at a press conference a few days later said that the Civic Alliance representatives had shown "immoderate appetites" in proposing so many changes to the government that it would virtually destroy the Yeltsin-Gaidar team. At a meeting of the Presidential Consultative Council a few days later he said it was essential to preserve at least the main part of the government headed by Gaidar – "The symbol and motor of reform". On 14 November, Yeltsin and Gaidar addressed the Civic Alliance Congress. Yeltsin expressed approval of some elements of the Civic Alliance programme but noted that other measures were "utterly unacceptable" and referred to barely disguised moves to return to the administrative command system.

War of Yeltsin's Ear

Yeltsin's apparent readiness to make concessions on policy and personnel increasingly alarmed the radical members of his entourage and of the government and the "War of Yeltsin's ear" intensified. Burbulis, Kozyrev, Poltoranin and others were urging him to go over the head of the Congress, dissolve it if necessary and call a referendum on the constitution and reform. The radicals argued that although such a step might be risky and unconstitutional it was the only realistic way to preserve the radical reform policy. Constant compromises were adding up to a "creeping coup" or a "silent putsch" by the opposition. The conservatives in Yeltsin's entourage, notably Petrov, the head of his administration, and Skokov, the Secretary of the Security Council, favoured the policy of compromise. They urged Yeltsin to broaden the base of the government with representatives of the Civic Alliance and drop some of the liberals on the Opposition's hit-list. Petrov in an interview in *Rossiiskaya Gazeta* of 11 November described himself as a "centrist" and a supporter of the Civic Alliance. He said he was in favour of gradual transition to the market and was implicitly critical of Burbulis.

Republics and Regions

In an attempt to shore up his position as the Congress approached, Yeltsin enlisted support for his constitutional powers and the government from republic and regional leaders. On 15 October he set up a Council of Heads of Republics (with Skokov as Secretary) which duly backed his request for a postponement of the Congress, but without effect. Subsequently Yeltsin established a parallel Council of Heads of Administration which duly put out a robust statement (21 November) expressing firm support for radical economic reform, calling for the extension of Yeltsin's additional powers and confirmation by the Congress of Gaidar as Prime Minister. The regional governors, mostly appointed by Yeltsin, were strong supporters of executive power and in many cases at loggerheads with their own regional legislatures. In the longer-term the tactic of deploying regional leaders as a counterweight to the parliament paid few dividends. It further stimulated the constitutional and political aspirations of the republics and regions, whose leaders in the event gave Yeltsin no effective support in his political battle at the Centre.

Notes

1   BBC SWB Part 1 of 7 November and 30 November 1992.
2   *Zapiski Prezidenta*, pp. 283–4.
3   *Zapiski Prezidenta*, p. 249.

8

Seventh Congress

PRELUDE: NOVEMBER 1992

The option of extra-constitutional action to remove the Congress was never far from Yeltsin's mind and as the temperature rose in the last few weeks before the Seventh Congress, it was openly discussed by his supporters and his opponents and hinted at by Yeltsin himself. On 13 November in the Supreme Soviet the extreme right-wing Deputy, Andronov who had links to the former KGB, claimed that he had information that the parliament would be dissolved on the 24th or 25th of November. On the following day Khasbulatov responded by declaring that a state of emergency would be unconstitutional unless approved by the Supreme Soviet; and it would be treated as a *coup d'état* and its organizers as state criminals. During a visit to Astrakhan, Yeltsin was asked about the possibility of "Presidential rule" and gave an ambiguous response. He did not want to violate the Constitution, which he described as outmoded, but his oath was to the Russian people.

Law on the Government

In the Supreme Soviet on 13 November, the law on the government had been adopted in a version directly at odds with what the President had requested: none of his proposed amendments to the draft had been accepted. The government would be subordinated to the parliament, the President could not appoint Deputy Prime Ministers or key ministers without discussion in parliament. The First Deputy Prime Minister Shumeiko stated that the draft was contrary to the constitution and he would advise the President not to sign it. Gaidar said the law would paralyse the work of the Cabinet if enacted.

At its session on 20 November the Supreme Soviet was in a relatively peaceable mood. A proposal by the right-wing Deputy Baburin to include impeachment of the President on the agenda of the Congress was rejected by 74 votes to 52 with 19 abstentions; and the Supreme Soviet adopted a statement on the Congress which declared inter alia that it was decisively minded to co-operate with the President and the government, and to support all proposals directed towards the further development of reform and ending the economic crisis.

But the opposition was stepping up the pressure. The Civic Alliance's Political Council said that it was considering demands for the resignation of the government if earlier "agreements" were not observed. It would demand in particular the removal of Kozyrev and Shokhin and the Foreign Trade Minister, Aven. On 21 November there was a meeting between the Civic Alliance and the hardline Russia Unity Bloc to discuss joint actions at the Congress which reportedly reached agreement on a vote of no confidence in the government unless it produced a new realistic programme and a list of Cabinet changes. Baburin was among the authors of a scurrilous article in *Sovetskaya Rossiya* of 21 November alleging that Burbulis, Poltoranin and by implication Yeltsin himself were acting as "agents of influence" of the USA.

Gaidar addressed the Supreme Soviet on 26 November on the government's anti-crisis measures in fairly bland and conciliatory terms. He described the programme as a merger of a number of aspects of rival economic programmes. The government could not accept resurrection of State distribution of resources; massive money emission; or a prices and wages freeze. But it was ready to agree to selective support for key industries; and greater emphasis on de-monopolization and support for entrepreneurs. Gaidar hoped that inflation could be curbed over the next four months and that it would be possible to create an "oasis" of growth in production. The deputies did not respond to calls for a no confidence vote and adopted a vaguely worded resolution calling on the government to work with parliamentary economic experts to amend the programme.

In a repeat of his tactic before the Sixth Congress, which had so demoralized his supporters, Yeltsin offered up the heads of some of his closest radical colleagues and advisers to mollify the opposition. The Deputy Prime Minister, Poltoranin, a particular enemy of Khasbulatov and near the top of the opposition hit list, resigned on 25 November; and Burbulis was removed as State Secretary and demoted to head of the President's group of advisers. The dismissal of Yegor Yakovlev as head of Ostankino television, was primarily a sop to the new Council of Heads of Administration which had criticized Moscow's television coverage of the ethnic dispute between North Ossetia and Ingushetia; but it was also welcome to the hard-line opposition.

SEVENTH CONGRESS: 1–14 DECEMBER 1992

About 900 deputies attended the Seventh Congress of the 1,041 eligible to do so (27 seats had fallen vacant); 694 votes constituted the two-thirds majority required for constitutional issues and 521 a simple majority. During the opening sessions a number of hostile resolutions put forward by the opposition received a majority but not a sufficient one. A proposal to put impeachment of the President on the agenda was defeated by 429 votes to 352 with 77 abstentions.

Yeltsin's Constitutional Deal

Yeltsin made a lacklustre opening speech, not conciliatory enough to appease the opposition or tough enough to frighten it. He spoke strongly in support of market reforms and privatization of land, but also stressed the "social orientation" of economic policy and selective support for industry. There was much emphasis on Russia's history, traditions and national interests. But the main theme was the conflict between the executive and the legislature. He proposed a constitutional deal. The Congress should adopt a resolution on a referendum for a new constitution and in the meantime take urgent measures to stabilize the political situation. He proposed that during a stabilization period of 12–18 months the law on the government should be set aside. The President would assume full responsibility for the economy and the Congress would confine its legislative activity to the constitution. In effect he was asking for the continuation of his special powers over appointments and economic policy in a different form. This was totally unrealistic and his speech and the constitutional proposals were poorly received.

The Speaker, Khasbulatov, in effect responded for the opposition. In a biting and effective speech, he painted a grim picture of a collapsing economy and made a scathing attack on the government's policy, describing it as a total failure. The government, he said, favoured a neo-classical liberal model of the market economy adopted in the USA. He proposed the socially oriented model adopted in western Europe, especially Scandinavia and also China and Korea. The Congress should choose. He referred to the "illusory" influx of Western capital and said that Russia must rely on its own resources. Khasbulatov indulged in a number of thinly veiled jibes at the President which drew laughter and applause, and he commented sarcastically on Yeltsin's constitutional deal. Stabilization was indeed needed but without departure from the constitution or the laws.

On the following day Gaidar made an effective and robust defence of his reform policies, yielding virtually nothing to the opposition. The tone of the subsequent debate was hostile to the government but there was a relatively calm atmosphere until a major row broke out at the end of the third day. Khasbulatov in the Chair appeared to manipulate a vote on the issue of whether crucial constitutional amendments designed to limit Yeltsin's powers of ministerial appointment, should be voted on openly or in secret. Democratic deputies approached the Chair to protest and when Khasbulatov called dramatically for protection there were fisticuffs as opposition deputies came energetically to his defence.

Constitutional Amendments

The Congress was now heading for confrontation with the President. Yeltsin made an unscheduled intervention in which he warned that constitutional amendments which would bring into force the law on the government adopted earlier by the Supreme Soviet were "unacceptable". They would create a serious imbalance between the executive and the legislature, and destabilize the political situation. However, the Congress reaffirmed its intention to vote by secret ballot on seven amendments. The President's press secretary said that the hostile attitude of the Congress was forcing the President towards an appeal to the people in a referendum. The Congress also began debating a draft resolution on economic reform which contained wholesale condemnation of the government's performance and policy. There was now open conflict between President and Congress on the two main issues dividing them: division of powers and economic policy.

The Congress refused to allow the President to nominate his Prime Minister until it had discussed the constitutional amendments which would effectively transfer control over Cabinet appointments from the President to the Supreme Soviet. It then proceeded to a secret vote on the amendments on the fifth day of the Congress. This first major clash ended in a narrow victory for Yeltsin. The most damaging amendments received a sizeable majority but just short of the two-thirds needed for adoption. The opposition took its revenge by rejecting all the President's amendments to its denunciatory resolution on the government's economic policy. With the Congress well underway there was no evidence of the compromises allegedly reached in advance on constitutional issues between Khasbulatov and Yeltsin and on economic policy between the government and the Civic Alliance. The "centrists" supposedly controlled by the Civic Alliance had failed to materialize and there was a solid opposition majority of close to two-thirds on most issues.

Yeltsin's Concession on Cabinet Appointments

Before the morning session on the seventh day of the Congress, Yeltsin discussed his proposed nomination of Gaidar with parliamentary fractions. He then addressed the Congress to make a significant concession to the opposition by proposing that the appointment of four key Cabinet Ministers (Security, Defence, Foreign and Internal Affairs) would require the agreement of the Supreme Soviet. Later he nominated Gaidar in a brief statement. The concession on Cabinet appointments was clearly intended to improve Gaidar's chances in the vote; indeed he had evidently reached some understanding on this with Khasbulatov. Gaidar had a meeting with parliamentary fractions to discuss his nomination. On the following day he made a spirited and effective speech in which he reaffirmed that the economic crisis could only be solved by deepening reform and not retreating from it. His speech was quite well received and the subsequent debate was relatively subdued and even-handed. However, the Congress continued to adopt constitutional amendments hostile to the President. It rejected his request for the right to call a referendum on his own initiative and the right to appoint the Chairman of the Central Bank of Russia. Despite a strong protest by First Deputy Prime Minister Shumeiko, who was acting as the President's representative, the Congress adopted a constitutional amendment to the effect that the President's powers would cease if he attempted to dissolve Congress.

On the eighth day of the Congress, Khasbulatov manipulated the order of business so that the Congress was able to pocket Yeltsin's concession on Cabinet appointments by adopting the relevant constitutional amendment before voting on Gaidar's nomination. Khasbulatov ignored calls for an open roll-call vote and gave deputies only the choice of two methods of secret voting. In the subsequent vote Gaidar was rejected by 486 votes to 467.

Yeltsin Confronts the Congress: 10 December

According to Yeltsin's memoirs, he went home that evening to his dacha "in a trance", locked himself in the *banya* from where he had to be forcibly extracted by his chief bodyguard, Korzhakov. He wrote that the parliamentary drubbing was a repeat of the psychological blow he had suffered in 1987 when he was humiliated at a plenum of the Moscow City Party Committee following his expulsion from the Politburo.[1] After late night consultations with a few advisers (he names Ilyushin and Shakhrai), he decided to challenge the Congress head on. When the Congress session opened the following day, 10 December, he made a short angry statement. Events at the Congress had forced him to appeal directly to the people. An attempt was being made to achieve what the August putsch had failed to achieve. He had made "unjustified concessions" but the agreements he had made had been violated. The Congress had rejected his proposals for a stabilization period; his proposed Prime Minister; his amendments to the constitution. Russian citizens had seen the insulting and disorderly behaviour of the Congress. It was impossible to work with such a Congress any further. He described Khasbulatov as the leader of an irreconcilable opposition which favoured cheap populism and demagogy, and hoped to restore the discredited Soviet system. The people would judge between President and Congress in a referendum to be held in January.

Yeltsin walked out inviting deputies who supported him to follow and convene in a neighbouring hall. His aim was to deprive the Congress of a quorum. But only about 150 deputies left; 700 or more remained and the Congress stayed in business. Khasbulatov made a show of offering his resignation, which was rejected. Crucially for the balance of psychological advantage, live television coverage of the Congress continued and the President was now off stage. Plainly floundering, he made an unconvincing appearance at the Lenin Komsomol Automobile factory, evidently to demonstrate working-class support. There were small opposing demonstrations on Red Square and a drive past of municipal lorries organized by the Mayor of Moscow, Luzhkov, which succeeded in stoking up the real or pretended fears of the deputies that a coup was in progress. They summoned the Ministers of Defence, Security and Internal Affairs, who all made cautious statements assuring the Congress of their loyalty to the Constitution and that no force was contemplated. Vice-President Rutskoi called for a compromise but his statement attacked the government and economic reform, and showed that he had clearly taken the side of the Congress. The Congress adopted a Constitutional amendment to block Yeltsin's proposed referendum by banning any plebiscite aimed at the dissolution of state bodies before the expiry of their term; it issued a Declaration accusing the President of destabilizing the political situation.

It was typical of Yeltsin to make a sudden dramatic move after a long period of indecision. It was conventional wisdom that when he did so he showed a sure political instinct. On this occasion it let him down badly. The challenge to the Congress went off at half-cock; the rejection of Gaidar by a narrow majority was not a strong enough pretext and many of his own supporters were dubious about the propriety of a referendum formulated in a way which put the executive and the legislature in direct confrontation. Yeltsin acknowledged in his memoirs that the walk-out was a bad decision. He had expected the Congress to split in two but he did not give his supporters time to think and react and "some of them stayed". According to Burbulis, Yeltsin was badly let down by the Chairman of the Constitutional Court, Zorkin, who had promised to intervene immediately after the President's statement and support his proposed referendum, but failed to do so.[2]

COMPROMISE AGREEMENT

The Congress was in confident and belligerent mood, and heard calls for the Procurator-General and the Constitutional Court to examine the constitutionality of Yeltsin's statement, as well as a proposal for a commission to investigate the mass media for alleged anti-parliamentary bias. However, following behind the scenes discussions to find a way out of the crisis, a joint statement by the President and the Congress was read out and approved, which declared that they were both resolved to solve disputes between the executive and the legislature only by constitutional methods. A meeting was held between Yeltsin, Khasbulatov and the Chairman of the Constitutional Court, Zorkin, which produced a nine-point compromise agreement. The main features were:

- a referendum in April on the basic principles of the new Constitution;
- some of the Constitutional amendments affecting the powers of the President to be suspended until the referendum (but not the key amendment on the appointment of four Cabinet Ministers);
- the Supreme Soviet not to introduce Constitutional amendments altering the existing balance of power between legislature, executive and judiciary before the Referendum;
- the President to put forward a number of candidates for Prime Minister and submit for Congress approval one of the three who received most votes in a preliminary contest.

As an unpublished part of the deal (according to Burbulis himself "Article One"), Yeltsin announced the dismissal of his chief adviser Burbulis, widely believed to have been instrumental in the decision to confront the Congress. Khasbulatov forced a snap vote which endorsed the agreement by a large majority. There were angry protests from some hard opposition deputies who complained that the Congress had been given no opportunity to debate the agreement. There were repeated attempts in subsequent sessions to force a new vote.

Election of Chernomyrdin

Yeltsin put forward a short list of five candidates for Prime Minister: Gaidar, Kadannikov (Director of the Volga car factory), Skokov (Secretary of the Security Council), Shumeiko (First Deputy Prime Minister) and Chernomyrdin (Deputy Prime Minister). In the preliminary vote Gaidar finished a poor third (400) behind Skokov (637) and Chernomyrdin (621). After consultations with the three candidates Yeltsin told the Congress he still favoured Gaidar but would not nominate him; Skokov was needed in his current post as Secretary of the Security Council; he therefore nominated Chernomyrdin who was duly confirmed by 721 votes to 172. In a brief acceptance speech, Chernomyrdin stated that he supported the deepening of reform provided the people were not impoverished in the process; he was in favour of the market but not the "bazaar". The overall tone seemed to confirm doubts about Chernomyrdin's reformist credentials. The Congress concluded on 14 December.

OUTCOME OF THE CONGRESS

Yeltsin's handling of the Congress had been dogged from the beginning by indecision and misjudgement. He had wavered between two courses – appealing to the people over the heads of an unpopular Congress with a dubious mandate, and appeasing his congressional enemies with tactical sacrifices. Either course pursued with energy and consistency might have worked. Yeltsin's failure to choose between them and the timing of his belated attempt at confrontation ensured his defeat.

Before the Congress even began Yeltsin had lost the first round by attempting and failing to persuade the Supreme Soviet to postpone it until the Spring. He had made thinly veiled threats to take unconstitutional action to deal with the Congress but backed away from them as the Congress approached and then demoted or sacked close colleagues in order to conciliate the opposition. His opening speech showed him still in two minds: a mixture of concessions and unrealistic demands which failed either to gratify or impress the opposition. At the Congress itself he was outmanoeuvred at every turn by Khasbulatov and failed to achieve either of his main objectives: the extension of his additional powers or the preservation of Gaidar. But his real defeat lay not in this or the terms of the compromise agreement with Khasbulatov but in the fact that he had challenged the Congress and had to back down. He had denounced Khasbulatov as the leader of the reactionary opposition and then had to come to terms with him having yielded the head of his chief adviser and Khasbulatov's personal enemy, Burbulis.

In the power struggle between the President and the parliament, Yeltsin had been fatally handicapped by the fact that the constitution was not only tilted in favour of the parliament but fully under the control of Congress. Once Yeltsin's support eroded to the point where the opposition had a two-thirds majority, they were able to change the rules of the game at will. The Seventh Congress was frequently an unedifying spectacle as communists and neo-nationalists vied to quote the Constitution and proclaim their devotion to the principles of parliamentary democracy. Yeltsin had faced an impossible dilemma with the constitutional cards stacked in favour of a basically undemocratic opposition. The Seventh Congress left him seriously weakened. He had what looked like a losing position in the power game against Khasbulatov and his authority and prestige had been severely dented to the point where an unconstitutional declaration of Presidential rule appeared to be no longer a serious option.

However, accusations by the radicals that Yeltsin had betrayed Gaidar and the reforms were unfair. He could have done a deal much earlier by sacrificing Gaidar but had defended him for as long as he could. The fiasco of 10 December left him in no position to provoke the Congress again by appointing Gaidar following his poor result in the preliminary ballot.

Balance of Forces in Parliament

Events at the Seventh Congress showed that there had been a strong drift away from reform and towards the Opposition. A subsequent analysis of voting patterns at the first seven Russian Congresses between March 1990 and December 1992 (by A. Sobyanin) showed that only three fractions, Radical Democrats, Democratic Russia, and Agreement for Progress (and its predecessors) had consistently supported reform; four fractions, Communists of Russia, Rossiya, Agrarians, and Fatherland had consistently opposed reform; while the other seven fractions had been inconsistent but had drifted steadily towards the Opposition. On a "reformism" scale of from +100 to −100, the Congress as a whole had shifted from +7 in March 1990 to −20 in December 1992. In terms of eligible deputies (not all were in attendance) at the Seventh Congress, 273 deputies had been strongly pro-reform; 88 moderately pro-reform; 125 moderately anti-reform; and 554 strongly anti-reform. This meant that strong opponents of reform had a simple majority and the reformists could barely muster a blocking third with the help of their moderately pro-reform colleagues. The opponents of reform were close to a permanent two-thirds majority. According to the same analysis the Supreme Soviet, after partial rotation of its membership at the Seventh Congress, was even more reactionary than the Congress with an overall "reform" rating of –23.

After the Congress

Following his set-back at the Congress, Yeltsin was anxious to regain the political initiative and reassert his authority. After press reports appeared suggesting that Civic Alliance leaders and Chernomyrdin were discussing government appointments behind his back, Yeltsin cut short his visit to China and returned to Moscow in order, as he put it, for "the boss to restore order". The composition of the new government announced on 23 December suggested that Yeltsin had succeeded in imposing a Cabinet largely of his own choice on the new Prime Minister. Aven was removed as Minister for Foreign Economic Relations but almost all the rest of the Gaidar team remained in place; two new Deputy Prime Ministers were appointed: Boris Fedorov, former Minister of Finance with strong reformist credentials and Yarov, a deputy chairman of the Supreme Soviet.

Yeltsin's decree of 25 December establishing a new Federal Information Centre headed by Poltoranin with the rank of First Deputy Prime Minister, also showed him in uncompromising mood. The choice of Poltoranin was a slap in the face to the Opposition, since he had been removed as Deputy Prime Minister on the eve of the Congress as a concession to Khasbulatov and the Civic Alliance. However, the FIC, to which State television and radio were to be subordinated, was widely compared to a Ministry of Propaganda and the move dismayed the President's liberal supporters as much as it angered his opponents. Yeltsin appeared to be staking everything on the April referendum and hoping that the FIC would ensure favourable coverage of the reforms and of his proposals for a presidential republic, while pre-empting further attempts by Khasbulatov and the Parliament to assert their own control over the media.

Notes

1   *Zapiski Prezidenta*, p. 292.
2   Private conversation, Moscow, May 1995.

Part IV

Constitutional Struggle Continues: January–September 1993

9

Battle for the Referendum

The focus of the political struggle in the early months of 1993 was the referendum on the basic principles of the new Constitution scheduled for 11 April. It was the key element of the Seventh Congress Compromise Agreement which, however, soon began to unravel. The constitutional crisis resumed with barely a pause.

The Supreme Soviet reconvened on 14 January with Khasbulatov in confident and aggressive mood. He instructed his deputy to agree with the government a date for submitting for the Supreme Soviet's approval candidates for the posts of Minister of Foreign Affairs, Defence, Security and the Interior. (Yeltsin, however, stuck to his position that the incumbent Ministers were not subject to parliamentary approval since they were appointed prior to the VII Congress Constitutional amendment.) Yeltsin was now showing signs of abandoning attempts to gain influence in the Supreme Soviet since he appointed two of its few moderates and liberals in leading positions to posts in the administration (which meant they had to resign their deputy's mandates): Filatov became Head of the Presidential Administration and Bragin, (Chairman of the key Mass Media Committee), Head of Ostankino TV. This had the incidental effect of helping Khasbulatov to tighten his grip on the parliamentary leadership.

Campaign against the Referendum

Khasbulatov began his campaign against the proposed referendum early in the New Year when, in a two-part article in *Rossiiskaya Gazeta* of 9th and 10th January, he raised the spectre of a low turnout leading to political instability. He argued that the Referendum had been agreed only as part of an attempt to save the Presidency and executive power from the consequences of its own impulsive behaviour. At the beginning of February, in a performance extraordinary even by Khasbulatov's standards, he made public comments contemptuously critical of President Yeltsin during an official meeting with the Swedish Prime Minister. He said the President had failed to cope with his tasks and the government should be free from his jurisdiction. The President had imposed a referendum and now did not know how to extricate himself. "We will have to rescue him again". The President's press spokesman described Khasbulatov's comments as "odious".

Yeltsin Retreats

Doubts about the referendum began to be expressed across the political spectrum, except for the radical democrats, on grounds that the territorial integrity of the Federation could be jeopardized if some republics and regions refused to hold it; and that a failed referendum would plunge the country into political chaos. Yeltsin himself was now getting cold feet about the risks involved. What seemed a final blow was dealt by the Council of Heads of Republics at a meeting attended by Yeltsin on 9 February, when the majority of the participants opposed the referendum which they said could lead to an uncontrollable power struggle. On the same occasion, the Chairman of the Constitutional Court, Zorkin, appealed to the President and the Supreme Soviet to postpone the referendum which could "threaten the constitutional system". (Although Zorkin himself had brokered the agreement of which it formed an integral part.) Yeltsin told the Constitutional Commission later the same day, that he would not insist on the referendum if the constitutional problem could be resolved through dialogue with the other branches of power; but he indicated that meanwhile preparations for it would continue. At the same time he proposed bringing forward parliamentary and presidential elections by one year (to 1994 and 1995 respectively).

Khasbulatov countered with a proposal for simultaneous pre-term parliamentary and presidential elections in Spring 1994 and said a question on simultaneous elections should be included in the referendum in order to increase interest and ensure an adequate turnout. Yeltsin now began to negotiate with Khasbulatov in an attempt to trade in the referendum for a new constitutional agree-ment. At a meeting on 16 February they agreed to set up a working group (co-chaired by Shumeiko for the government and Ryabov for the Supreme Soviet) to draw up such an agreement. On the same occasion Yeltsin proposed that an Extraordinary Congress should be convened in early March with the sole purpose of ratifying the agreement.

Yeltsin was weakening an already vulnerable position by showing readiness to give up the referendum, the only strong card he held. He was retreating from a venture in which he had invested a lot of political capital and his long suffering supporters in the democratic camp, who had rallied loyally to the referendum campaign, looked like being left in the lurch once more. Moreover Yeltsin's proposal of an Extraordinary Congress was a dangerous tactic, since he could not control its agenda and the Congress had ultimate constitutional power to set its own terms for a referendum or annul it without any quid pro quo. The opposition leadership and press meanwhile repeatedly denied that there was a "constitutional crisis" implying some need to adjust or bypass the constitution. They were content to play the game according to the existing rules since the constitutional cards were stacked in their favour. They were increasingly nervous about the possibility of some anti-constitutional solution such as Presidential rule and also of the possibility of early elections or a referendum which would bring into the equation the President's still considerable popular support. The hard opposition began to gun for Khasbulatov who was suspected of readiness to do an unconstitutional deal with the President in order to enhance his own influence and had publicly called for early parliamentary elections which the deputies were determined to avoid. There were calls in the Supreme Soviet for the removal of both the Speaker and the President. Khasbulatov was in fact bluffing in espousing early elections since he knew the Congress, which had the sole power to decide the issue, would never agree to them. Yeltsin could well have called his bluff and seized the high moral ground.

Draft Constitutional Agreement

Yeltsin now published his own draft constitutional agreement and presented it during a television address on 18 February. The key points were strict observation of the separation of powers and abolition of Article 104 of the Constitution which conferred supreme authority on Congress and a moratorium on other constitutional changes affecting the balance of power. It provided that if the President were to violate the agreement in the estimation of the constitutional court, he would resign; and if the Supreme Soviet did so it would be dissolved. Yeltsin's draft was essentially intended to strengthen the executive power and was patently unacceptable to parliament.

In the Supreme Soviet on 25 February, Khasbulatov said there was a powerful movement in favour of halting preparations for the referendum and convening a Congress; but he manoeuvred to avoid setting a date. The hard-line Russian Unity Bloc of deputies put down a motion calling for rejection of a referendum or any constitutional deal and for the convening of a Congress to annul the December agreement. The hard-line variant of their proposed agenda called for the resignation of both Yeltsin and Khasbulatov. Addressing the Civic Alliance forum at the end of February, Yeltsin spoke of the need for a choice between the absolute power of the Soviets or the division of powers. He was sharply critical of the Supreme Soviet which he said had started attacking the Seventh Congress Compromise Agreement as soon as it was concluded. The Supreme Soviet was seeking to concentrate executive power in its own hands and running a second government alongside the constitutional one. He called for a law on power to determine the division of power between the three branches.

Final Option

On 2 March Yeltsin addressed leaders of the democratic movement and warned that hard-liners could come to power through the Congress and reverse the reform policy. If the Congress were to reject both the April referendum and the President's draft of the constitutional agreement, he would use his right to appeal directly to the people. He said in conclusion that the constitution should be respected but if the hard-liners took extreme measure which might destroy Russia, he would have to find "other methods" of saving the country, democracy and reform. He hoped it would not come to that.

At its next Session in early March the Supreme Soviet in harshly critical mood voted to invite Yeltsin to explain his recent statements about the crisis and a possible "final option" for resolving it; and demanded publication of the minutes of Yeltsin's meeting with military commanders on 3 March which had reportedly endorsed firm action by the President. The session resolved to convene the Eighth Congress on 10 March with a two-point agenda: the April referendum; and "Observance of the constitution by supreme bodies of power and officials" (a formulation which raised the possibility of impeachment proceedings again the President). The Session debated President Yeltsin's draft constitutional agreement. Ryabov said the draft was unacceptable and appeared designed not to stabilize the situation but destroy constitutional structures. If adopted it would mean a death sentence on the Supreme Soviet. Shumeiko defended the draft but following a hostile debate, Khasbulatov declared that it was increasingly difficult to find a basis for co-operation in view of the aggressiveness of the executive. In advance of the Congress, the Supreme Soviet had in effect rejected both the referendum and Yeltsin's constitutional agreement on power-sharing.

On the same day the Cabinet met to discuss preparations for the Congress. Chernomyrdin said it was time to put an end to the intolerable situation when the Supreme Soviet was trying to supplant the government. The government was unanimous in its support for the President and ready to throw its entire weight behind him. There was also support for Yeltsin from the Siberian miners who had carried out a warning strike on 1 March and now added to their economic demands the political demand that the referendum should take place and that one of its questions should address lack of public confidence in the Congress.

In a television interview on 7 March, Yeltsin appeared still uncertain of his tactics. He said that if the referendum were annulled by the Congress, he would put forward his questions in a plebiscite without legal force. He had drawn up a new version of his constitutional agreement in the form of a law on power which he would submit to the Congress. But he again spoke of a "final option" implying some form of extra-constitutional solution such as Presidential rule. The Supreme Soviet leadership, reacting nervously to renewed speculation about the possibility of Presidential rule, had summoned the "power ministers" to a closed meeting of the Supreme Soviet presidium on 6 March to discuss "public order" during the Congress.

On the eve of the Congress, on 9 March, Yeltsin chaired a meeting of the Council of Heads of Republics, but the body which he had established to act as a counterweight to the parliament gave him only very limited support. The majority of republic leaders opposed a referendum while supporting the idea that Congress should· conclude a constitutional agreement. Its statement called for Congress to focus not on disagreements between legislature and executive but on adopting a law to implement the Federation Treaty. (The influence of the republic leaders in Congress was in fact very limited; they did not control the votes of deputies from their own territories.) Yeltsin had no greater success at a meeting on the same day of regional governors and presidential representatives. On the eve of the Congress, Yeltsin had been able to rally very little support in parliament and not much outside it for his various proposals to overcome the constitutional crisis. The opposition majority in Congress were in an uncompromising mood and Khasbulatov, as the power broker, in a strong position.

EIGHTH CONGRESS: 10–13 MARCH 1993

Khasbulatov and Ryabov

The Eighth Congress opened on 10 March in a fairly calm atmosphere. Khasbulatov's opening address was relatively restrained. He referred to continuing economic decline and complained about attempts to give a second wind to the discredited radical economic reforms. He noted that grave doubts had arisen over the wisdom of holding the referendum. The Congress would have to decide whether to approve it or find other ways of ending the political crisis. In an indirect attack on Yeltsin, who was present, he condemned "artificial and cynical actions to destabilize the situation" including attempts to draw the army and security services into the political process. In the debate on the agenda, the President's request to remove the second item on "observance of the constitution" (clearly directed against himself) was rejected. A motion to bring Yeltsin before the constitutional court for violations of the constitution achieved 418 votes, well short of a majority. The Deputy Chairman of the Supreme Soviet, Ryabov, delivered an uncompromising and aggressive report, subsequently described by the President's spokesman as confrontational. Ryabov, a signatory and the chief advocate of the Compromise Agreement of the Seventh Congress now said that it had been mistaken; it made too many concessions to the President and violated the constitution. He called for rejection of the referendum and said the President's proposed alternative, a plebiscite, would be unlawful. Ryabov defended the right of Congress to supreme authority enshrined in Article 104 of the Constitution. As for references in the Constitution to the separation of powers, this was reflected "at the second level" – the President, Supreme Soviet and Constitutional Court. He rejected any formal constitutional agreement but suggested the possibility of a working agreement including a moratorium on changes to the constitution affecting the balance of power; and early presidential and parliamentary elections. The tone of the debate was overwhelmingly hostile to the referendum and constitutional agreement. The Civic Alliance issued a statement calling for the four "power ministers" to be submitted to the legislature for confirmation.

Yeltsin and Chernomyrdin

On the second day, 11 March, Yeltsin addressed the delegates to express strong disappointment at the attitude of the Congress on the opening day and his alarm at the terms of the draft resolution which had been tabled rejecting the agreement reached at the Seventh Congress. He favoured strong presidential power as a guarantee of the integrity of the Federation and remained ready for dialogue and agreement in any legal form, e.g. a resolution or a law on power. If the compromise agreement were revoked, confrontation would result and a referendum would be the only solution to the conflict. Chernomyrdin spoke shortly after Yeltsin calling for the government not to be dragged into the political conflict and asking for government control over the Central Bank and other financial institutions. He also made a statement of support for strong presidential power as the real guarantee of reform, while admitting that the reform policy needed certain corrections.

The tone of the rest of the morning session was set by Khasbulatov who made an unscheduled, violent and at times near hysterical statement which was loudly applauded. The Congress wanted peace and accord; but any "agreement" had to be made within the framework of the constitution. Any other discussions or ephemeral ideas must not be taken seriously. Khasbulatov said he had been wrong to sign the compromise agreement at the Seventh Congress.

The mistake must be corrected and the resolution overturned. He said he had been disillusioned by the speeches that day of Chernomyrdin and Yeltsin: there had never been confrontation between the branches of power, only confrontation between certain institutions and the constitution.

Khasbulatov said the Congress was being put under pressure and must avoid falling into further traps. Becoming increasingly excited, almost incoherent, he complained bitterly about criticism of himself and the Supreme Soviet. It was not clear to the Congress whether Chernomyrdin was really Prime Minister or whether it was Shumeiko or Chubais. He called on the Congress to remove Chubais and complained that Yeltsin had promised many times to dismiss Kozyrev without doing so. Khasbulatov concluded with a further attack on Chernomyrdin and stated that the Supreme Soviet would not agree his budget and would take a decision to cut off salaries of government workers. Khasbulatov's performance was bizarre and embarrassing but it both reflected and further stoked the hostile mood of the Congress.

However, there were signs that some sort of compromise might be patched up at the end of the second day. A joint draft resolution on stabilization of the constitutional system was produced by Yeltsin and Khasbulatov at the head of an editorial commission and adopted by the Congress as a basis for discussion. But the tone of the subsequent debate was again hostile and when a hard-line deputy called for the President to be stripped of his powers, Yeltsin walked out.

Constitutional Amendments

During the debate on the draft resolution on the morning of the third day of the Congress (12 March), Yeltsin intervened to call for the removal from the Resolution of Article 2 which rescinded the Seventh Congress Compromise Agreement and Article 7 which brought into force several of the hostile constitutional amendments suspended according to the terms of that agreement (in particular the right of the Supreme Soviet to cancel decrees and resolutions of the President on the basis of a constitutional court opinion; and the Article removing the President's powers if he sought to dissolve the Congress). He warned that if the resolution were adopted, including those two Articles, he would have to consider taking "additional measures to preserve the balance of power in the country". The Congress rejected Yeltsin's proposed amendments to the draft resolution by 656 votes to 184 with 41 abstentions. Yeltsin and senior members of the administration and government left the hall. Subsequently there was a meeting behind closed doors of Yeltsin, Khasbulatov and Zorkin, which produced no reported result. During the third day the Congress voted to reject the referendum and to allocate the money earmarked for it to housing for the military – a transparent and provocative attempt to woo the army. The parliamentary leadership backed away from its own proposals for early parliamentary and presidential elections citing objections which had been raised that this would be contrary to the constitution which prescribed five-year terms in each case. The Congress confined itself to instructing the Supreme Soviet to examine the expediency of amending the constitution with a view to making it possible to hold early elections – in other words they put off the issue indefinitely. The Congress also voted to instruct the Supreme Soviet to examine ways of making the press and television answerable to Parliament.

By the end of the third day of the Congress there was a tense and nervous atmosphere reminiscent of the situation on 10 December following Yeltsin's challenge to the Seventh Congress. Opening the evening session, Khasbulatov proposed that since the "situation was not very favourable" the Congress should continue to sit on 13 March in order to "watch over the observation of the constitution by the executive". A right-wing deputy claimed that a column of lorries with armed men had been seen entering the Kremlin. The Congress voted in favour of live television coverage of its proceedings. There were widespread reports that Yeltsin was about to address the nation on television.

Congress "Appeal"

On its fourth and final day, on 13 March, the Congress issued an "Appeal" to the people which stated inter alia that attempts to resolve problems by investing special powers in the President had produced no positive results; and that the economic reform had turned against the majority of the people. In his closing speech Khasbulatov again attacked the failed economic reform. He noted that Western aid promised by two US Presidents to Gorbachev and

Shevardnadze in return for destroying the CMEA, the Warsaw Pact, and the USSR had never materialized. He stated that the main achievement of the Congress was the assertion of the overriding importance of observing the constitution (i.e. the repudiation of the compromise reached at the Seventh Congress).

Reactions to the Congress

A statement by the President's press spokesman on 15 March declared that by denying the people the right to express its will through a referendum, the Congress was violating the constitution and embarking on confrontation with the President. The Congress had attempted to concentrate power in the hands of the Soviets, and return the levers of administration to the communist *nomenklatura* and take away the democratic achievements of August 1991. The statement referred ominously to numerous appeals from the population to the President to uphold democracy and stop the communist restoration.

Conclusion

The Eighth Congress was another serious defeat which left the President further weakened and the reform programme in doubt. It was an easy win on points for the Congress which was not quite ready for a knockout punch (impeachment did not get on to the agenda). Yeltsin was in better form than in December but playing a very weak hand; his referendum and constitutional deal both rejected by the Congress determined to take a stand on the constitution already loaded in its favour and which it could now alter almost at will. The amendments frozen in the Seventh Congress compromise and now reinstated, allowed the Supreme Soviet to suspend any presidential decree or instruction pending a constitutional court verdict. The democratic press suggested that Yeltsin had suffered a crushing defeat and had been reduced to a figurehead. This was an exaggeration but the damage to his powers was serious and that to his authority worse. Yeltsin, with the support of the army and security organs in doubt, could rely only on his relative popularity. (His approval rating went up in Moscow during the Congress from 30 per cent to 36 per cent while Khasbulatov's remained at 12 per cent.)

YELTSIN'S DECREE ON "SPECIAL RULE": MARCH 1993

The week following the Eighth Congress was one of uncertainty and speculation about how Yeltsin would respond, with a national television statement expected daily. As usual he was considering options in the light of conflicting advice from his entourage. At a presidential council meeting on 17 March, some members were reported to have called for Presidential rule. Before setting off on a tour of CIS countries Khasbulatov gave a television interview, in the course of which he called on "all citizens" and the military and staff of the Security and Interior Ministries to "safeguard the constitution". On 18 March the Chairman of the Constitutional Court, Zorkin, cut short a visit to the United States to return to Moscow.

TV Statement on 20 March

On 20 March at 21.30 Moscow time, Yeltsin made his long awaited statement on national television. Looking strained but speaking firmly and decisively, he declared that all his attempts at compromise with the Congress had been rejected. He described the Eighth Congress as a "dress rehearsal for the *revanche* of the former party *nomenklatura*" and said that the Supreme Soviet leadership was planning an anti-constitutional coup. He must now use his power as popularly elected President in order to prevent the reversal of democratic and economic reforms and the restoration of a totalitarian regime. He had signed a decree that day instituting "special rule" until a referendum on 25 April on a vote of confidence in the President and Vice President, on the draft new constitution and a law on elections. The Congress and Supreme Soviet would not be dissolved or suspended and deputies would retain their mandates; but the Supreme Soviet would be confined to legislative functions. All civil rights would continue to be guaranteed.

A "special regime" as described by Yeltsin fell short of a state of emergency or Presidential rule. The legislature remained in place, no measures were taken against the opposition, there was no involvement of troops or police and the special regime was to last only until the popular vote the following month.

Despite Khasbulatov's absence from Moscow, Yeltsin's opponents were well prepared for his move. With rather naive optimism Yeltsin had hoped to split the opposition by linking Rutskoi to the vote of confidence. According to Yeltsin's memoirs, Rutskoi at first supported the move but, when shown the draft decree, had refused to endorse it and had evidently sent copies immediately to the parliamentary leadership and the constitutional court. The secretary of the Security Council, Skokov, also declined to initial the decree although according to Yeltsin he had in the past several times advocated the forcible dissolution of parliament.[1]

Opposition Reaction

The presidium of the Supreme Soviet was in session to discuss the statement before Yeltsin began speaking and an hour and a half after he had finished his statement, Rutskoi, Voronin (the Acting Speaker), Zorkin and the Procurator General Stepankov, appeared together on television to condemn his move. Rutskoi claimed he had tried to dissuade Yeltsin from his action and called for calm; Zorkin described it as a "coup from above". Voronin and Stepankov also warned that Yeltsin had acted unconstitutionally.

Khasbulatov cut short his tour of the CIS to return for a special session of the Supreme Soviet on 21 March. Immediately before the session the Supreme Soviet presidium issued an address to the nation declaring Yeltsin's actions authoritarian and unconstitutional. Khasbulatov ensured that this was the main theme of the Supreme Soviet debate and speaker after speaker condemned Yeltsin's move. The Prime Minister Chernomyrdin and government ministers spoke during the Session. Chernomyrdin said that the President had the right to appeal to the people but he avoided comment on the legality of Yeltsin's decree (the Government held an emergency Session on 21 March which adopted a resolution in support of Yeltsin and the action he had taken). The Security Minister, Barannikov, reiterated his Ministry's loyalty to the constitution and the law. The Defence Minister, Grachev, confirmed that the army would not become involved in politics and criticized hard-line attempts to play the army card. Skokov said that no orders had been given for emergency rule; he claimed he had tried to dissuade Yeltsin from signing the decree.

Reactions of regional and local leaders were mixed and fairly evenly balanced between support for and opposition to Yeltsin. Democratic and hard-line demonstrations took place in Moscow on 21 March but without clashes. Elsewhere in Russia the situation remained calm.

Constitutional Court Ruling

The Constitutional Court ruling, issued on 23 March in response to the application from the Supreme Soviet, was highly critical of the President's statement which, it said, breached a number of provisions of the constitution and the Federation Treaty. The Constitutional Court verdict was not unexpected but nonetheless a blow to Yeltsin since a ruling that he had violated the constitution provided the basis for a vote for impeachment by Congress (requiring a two-thirds majority). However, Zorkin's public credibility was now low. He had demonstrated his partiality by defending the legality of all the Eighth Congress decisions before they had even been considered by the Court. His appearance at the joint press conference with the parliamentary leadership and Rutskoi removed any doubt that he was playing a political rather than a judicial role in the crisis. Moreover his comments on that occasion were typically emotional and lacking in a sense of proportion. He spoke of a *coup d'état* when Yeltsin was proposing no more than limited Presidential rule for a five-week period before putting himself to a popular vote. Moreover the Constitutional Court had, contrary to its own procedural regulations, delivered a verdict not on the decree itself, which had yet to be published, but on Yeltsin's television statement.

Government's Position

The statement of support from the government, issued on 21 March, was reportedly signed by all the ministers, including those of Defence, Security and Internal Affairs. However, the statement was not wholly unequivocal. It defended the President's right to consult the people and asked Parliament to make this possible, but did not explicitly endorse the introduction of a special regime. At the Supreme Soviet the Prime Minister and the three "power" Ministers looked uncomfortable and spoke evasively without expressing direct support for the President or his statement. The fact that the Secretary of the Security Council, Skokov, disassociated himself from the President's action was another set-back for Yeltsin.

There were suggestions at the Supreme Soviet that Yeltsin's powers had already lapsed in accordance with Article 121/6 of the Constitution, since he had allegedly attempted to suspend parliament. The Supreme Soviet instructed the Procurator-General to consider criminal proceedings against officials involved in the preparation of the decree; it also issued an address to parliaments, governments and peoples of the world expressing surprise and regret at Western support for Yeltsin's anti-constitutional actions.

On 23 March, Yeltsin issued a decree instructing the Ministry of the Interior to protect television, radio and newspaper offices, and describing himself as a guarantor of the mass media. The preamble to the decree referred to a "real threat" to freedom of information, evidently a reference to calls at the Supreme Soviet for the parliament to take over control of the media. At the 21 March Supreme Soviet Session, Khasbulatov had declared that the media would "soon learn how to conduct themselves".

Tactical Retreat by Yeltsin

Faced with the rapid, determined and well co-ordinated counter-attack by his opponents and the defection of key figures, e.g. the Secretary of the Security Council, Skokov and the Procurator-General, Stepankov, who as his press secretary Kostikov put it had "failed the test of loyalty at the decisive moment", Yeltsin began a tactical retreat. His draft decree was considerably reworded and eventually issued in a much watered down form without any reference to a "special regime". The Supreme Soviet reconvened on 24 March to discuss calling an Extraordinary Congress to impeach the President. The Session went into recess while Yeltsin met the Chairman of the Constitutional Court, Zorkin together with Khasbulatov and the Prime Minister Chernomyrdin in an attempt to reach some form of compromise. The talks produced no result and the Supreme Soviet having reassembled resolved to call the Congress on 26 March to consider "urgent measures to preserve the stability of the constitutional system". On the following day the Supreme Soviet voted to ignore a discursive message from Yeltsin defending his proposed referendum and warning that as President he remained the guarantor of constitutionality; and it adopted a resolution to set up a parliamentary television and radio channel.

NINTH CONGRESS: 26–29 MARCH 1993

The Ninth Extraordinary Congress opened on 26 March. There were now 1,033 eligible deputies so that the two-thirds majority needed for impeachment or constitutional amendments was 689 votes. Khasbulatov made a brief opening statement in which he called for the government to be placed under firm parliamentary control and said that the President's administration was hampering the work of the government by creating "parallel structures". He said in conclusion that if the deputies decided that the root cause of the crisis was personal conflict, then he was ready to resign for the sake of accord.

Zorkin's Compromise Proposal

The Chairman of the Constitutional Court, Zorkin, defended the Court's hostile judgement against Yeltsin but called for the rejection of "extreme measures" including impeachment and attempts to dissolve parliament. Zorkin put forward a ten-point proposal for a compromise agreement, including a referendum on a new constitution, elections for the Presidency and for a new two-chamber parliament in the autumn of 1993; and a moratorium on further constitutional amendments until the elections were held. The last point of his proposal however, called for the dismissal and indictment of those who drafted the President's television appeal.

Speaking during the afternoon session, Yeltsin indicated approval for some of Zorkin's proposals, including the new constitution. He reiterated his call for a plebiscite on 25 April and suggested that it include a vote of confidence in the Congress as well as in himself. In the subsequent debate there was much hostility to Yeltsin but largely unco-ordinated and unfocused. The deputies failed to address any kind of compromise solution and Zorkin's proposals were largely ignored. It appeared that at the end of the first day of the Congress, the opposition was not sure what it could achieve short of impeachment. There were signs that the attack was being switched to the government with calls, led by Vice-President Rutskoi, for the removal of reformist ministers including Kozyrev, Chubais and Shumeiko, and for an end to the pro-Western foreign policy and, "so called" economic reform.

The debate on the second day of the Congress, 27 March, was fairly evenly balanced between speeches in support of the President and vituperative attacks on him by hard-line deputies who called for a secret vote to impeach him. A motion to put impeachment of the President on the agenda failed by 42 votes to achieve the necessary simple majority (it received 475 votes compared to 396 and 418 for similar motions at the Seventh and Eighth Congresses). The Prime Minister Chernomyrdin who spoke in the debate was generally, though not very explicitly, supportive of the President. He defended the government's recent actions and said he was in favour of broadening its composition but against a coalition which would lack political cohesion.

During the evening Session the Congress adopted as a basis for discussion, a resolution proposing a referendum on 25 April to include four questions:

- confidence in the President;
- support for his social and economic policies;
- early elections of President in 1993;
- early elections of deputies in 1993.

The President's representative, Shakhrai, objected to the second and third questions and to the proposed requirement that the confidence vote would require the support of 50 per cent of all those entitled to vote.

Draft Resolution

The Congress then considered a draft resolution on the constitutional crisis, accusing the President of violating the constitution in his television address of 20 March; suggesting that he and Khasbulatov should both resign; proposing a coalition government or government of national confidence; and calling for the dismissal of those in Yeltsin's entourage responsible for the television statement. Yeltsin intervened with a brief statement: he objected to the terms of the draft and proposed instead a resolution with only two points which he said would calm down the situation. The Congress would take note of the Constitutional Court's conclusion; the President, Chairman of the Supreme Soviet, Chairman of the Constitutional Court and Prime Minister would reach agreement within one week on co-operation between the different branches of power. When a hard-line deputy immediately afterwards again called for his impeachment or resignation Yeltsin walked out.

Compromise Rejected

On the third day the Congress took an unexpected and dramatic turn. A new compromise formula agreed overnight between Yeltsin, Khasbulatov and the government, involving Parliamentary and Presidential elections in November 1993 and cancellation of the proposed April referendum was presented to the congress. After a succession of speakers had angrily attacked the proposed deal, it was rejected as a basis for discussion by 687 votes to 130. There were repeated calls for the resignation or removal of both Yeltsin and Khasbulatov, and the Congress voted to place on the agenda the impeachment of the President and the removal of the Chairman of the Supreme Soviet. The opposition deputies were infuriated that Khasbulatov having piously declared at the conclusion of the Eighth Congress that its determination not to depart from strict observation of the constitution was its main achievement, had now again done an unconstitutional deal behind the backs of the deputies. Moreover he had offered early parliamentary elections which the deputies were above all determined to avoid. Yeltsin subsequently addressed a rally of some 50,000 supporters near the Kremlin. He told them he would not accept a Congress decision to remove him but would await the verdict of the people on 25 April.

While preparations for the secret ballot were being made, the Congress returned to their relatively calm debate on amendments to a draft resolution to "ensure freedom of speech on State radio and television" involving the setting up by Soviets at federal and local level of supervisory Councils on the media. The resolution was finally adopted despite protests that it violated both the constitution and the law on the media. A group of deputies petitioned the Constitutional Court to review the legality of the resolution.

Impeachment Vote Fails

The results of the voting on Yeltsin and Khasbulatov were announced late on the evening of 28 March. The vote to impeach Yeltsin fell 72 votes short with 617 in favour and 268 against. 339 deputies voted for the removal of Khasbulatov, 558 against. Khasbulatov thanked the deputies for what he described as a vote of confidence in himself. He added that it was "another matter" when a large number of deputies had almost impeached the President and Congress would need to consider the implications of what he described as "a serious national problem".

The principal result of the attempted constitutional deal was to galvanize a frustrated and moribund Congress into a renewed outburst of hostility which nearly ended in the President's impeachment. The deal also risked demoralizing yet again Yeltsin's loyal supporters who were at last beginning to mobilize effectively and at that moment were marching towards the Kremlin carrying banners in support of his referendum. Yeltsin had emerged diminished from each previous cycle of confrontation and compromise, and would have had little authority left if he had failed to stand his ground.

In the event the chaotic events of the third day of the Congress turned out fortuitously to Yeltsin's advantage. The failed attempt to impeach him rallied pro-Yeltsin support, which judging by opinion polls and the large turnout for the demonstration on 28 March was already gathering momentum; and the rejected deal had again discredited Khasbulatov in the eyes of the Congress. He did not receive the vote of confidence he blandly claimed since the vote against his removal was almost entirely due to a tactical switch by the hard-line Russia Unity Bloc of over 300 deputies. They wanted to be rid of Khasbulatov but anticipating that Yeltsin would survive did not want to oblige him by offering the head of his principal enemy as a bonus. The real extent of Khasbulatov's current popularity at the Congress was reflected in the majority of 614 to put his removal on the agenda.

A further effect of the failed attempt to impeach Yeltsin may have been to strengthen the link between the President and the government, a link which the Congress had been seeking to break. Chernomyrdin stood side by side with Yeltsin in front of the crowd of his supporters outside the Kremlin after the results of the vote were announced, as did the Minister for Security, Barannikov, and the Minister of the Interior, Yerin.

Conclusion of Congress

On the fourth and final day of the Congress, 29 March, the opposition majority gave vent to its anger and frustration at the failure of the impeachment vote. A number of deputies claimed that drug-crazed pro-Yeltsin demonstrators had attacked them (one of them made a dramatic appearance at the podium with a bandaged head). Khasbulatov, back in the chair, in buoyant mood called for the appointment of a "special prosecutor" as in the case of President Nixon, to investigate Yeltsin's responsibility for the incident. The Minister of Internal Affairs and the Mayor of Moscow who had been summoned to the Congress, later made firm and bland statements about the affair which then fizzled out.

The Congress adopted a sharply hostile resolution on urgent measures to preserve the constitutional system, which inter alia suspended a number of Yeltsin's decrees including the decree of 20 March; recommended a coalition government; abolished the Federal Information Centre; and abolished the institution of Presidential Representatives in the regions.

The Congress adopted a resolution on a referendum on 25 April comprising four questions:

Q1 Do you have confidence in the President?
Q2 Do you support the government's social and economic policy since 1992?
Q3 Do you want pre-term Presidential elections?
Q4 Do you want pre-term parliamentary elections?

The original references to elections in 1993 were therefore removed. The Resolution deemed all the questions to be constitutional issues requiring for a positive result a majority of 50 per cent of all those eligible to vote.

Winding up the Congress Khasbulatov suggested that the deputies might meet again before long since events were taking an extremely unpleasant and unpredictable turn. He said the Ninth Congress had met in order to deal with the consequences of an attempt at a *coup d'état* and had succeeded in defending the constitution in a critical situation. If the President's team's intentions had been realized it could have led to a return to totalitarianism or even civil war. Khasbulatov spoke of the need for a more professional and responsible government and criticized the Prime Minister, Chernomyrdin's inactivity during his first four months in office. Khasbulatov's remarks reflected the growing disillusion of opposition deputies with Chernomyrdin. Attempts to drive a wedge between him and Yeltsin had failed; and contrary to their expectations and the fears of the democrats, he had maintained the economic reform policy broadly on course. Yeltsin wrote in his memoirs that Chernomyrdin had "knocked the wind out of the sails of Rutskoi and Khasbulatov" and proved a bulwark for the President's policies.[2]

After serious defeats at the Seventh Congress in December 1992 and at the Eighth Congress earlier in March, Yeltsin had emerged from the Ninth Congress in a stronger position. The attempt to impeach him had failed; he retained the loyalty of his government; his main opponent Khasbulatov suffered a severe blow to his credibility; and he gained acceptance for an April referendum albeit one the Congress had rigged against him. Above all the Congress's attempt to remove him had galvanized the population of Moscow and other large cities into the biggest show of support for Yeltsin since August 1991. The Civic Alliance leader, Travkin, arguing during the debate at the Congress in favour of the compromise deal which the Congress rejected, said that the alternative would be a political fight and he warned the deputies that in a fight Yeltsin would be "in his element". The Democratic rally of 28 March was reminiscent of the massive Moscow demonstrations of 1990 and Yeltsin almost visibly drew strength from it.

APRIL REFERENDUM CAMPAIGN

After considering various options, Yeltsin decided not to add his own questions to the referendum (e.g. in a separate plebiscite). And he refrained from appealing to the Constitutional Court against the second question (on his social and economic policy); or the stipulation by Congress that a positive result for all the questions would require a majority of the whole electorate. (He did not wish to acknowledge the authority of the Constitutional Court or enhance its credibility.) But in the event the Constitutional Court decided on its own initiative on 21 April that a majority of those who voted, provided there was a 50 per cent turnout, would be sufficient for a positive result on the first two questions (confidence in the President and support for his economic and social policies); while a "constitutional" majority would be required for the two questions on pre-term elections.

Yeltsin decided to campaign for a "yes" vote on all four questions. This meant paradoxically supporting early Presidential elections but he argued that a four-times "yes" campaign would be more appealing and comprehensible, especially to elderly voters. (However, his supporters in most cases campaigned for "yes" "yes" "no" "yes"). During the Referendum campaign Yeltsin issued a number of patently populist decrees on economic issues, providing inter alia for an increase in the minimum wage, a ban on increases in petrol prices and rents in Moscow and an increase in student grants. He had a series of well-publicized meetings with veterans, students, editors etc. and made a visit to the Kuzbass mining region. The parliamentary leadership and the opposition at first did little to mount a referendum campaign. They probably counted mostly on popular apathy leading to a low turnout. They may also have felt confident that they could not lose the referendum given the way Congress had formulated the questions and set the terms for a valid result. Yeltsin might gain a majority in the confidence vote but not of the whole electorate; and in any case Question 2 on support for reform was expected to negate a positive vote for Yeltsin and amount to a vote of no confidence in his government and its policies. A majority in favour of the re-election of deputies was anticipated but it would have no legal consequences unless supported by 50 per cent of the whole electorate.

Rutskoi's Corruption Campaign

However, in the last two weeks of the campaign the opposition went onto the offensive. Rutskoi addressing the Supreme Soviet on 16 April, launched an onslaught on the reformists in and out of the government, alleging massive corruption in which Gaidar, Burbulis, Shumeiko, Grachev and Chubais were implicated. At the demand of the Supreme Soviet, Rutskoi's speech and answers to questions were transmitted live on the Russian television channel and then repeated that evening at peak viewing time. Rutskoi announced that he did not intend to resign and told journalists afterwards that only the people could determine his fate. He would be supported by deputies and those "who want to see their motherland a mighty and flourishing state rather than a raw materials appendage of the West". At the same session of Parliament the Deputy Speaker, Voronin, refused to comment on a report in *Izvestiya* that the presidium of the Supreme Soviet had commissioned, at public expense, millions of copies of an anti-Yeltsin leaflet purportedly issued by a mythical "reform for the people committee".[3]

In a television interview on the following day, 17 April, Khasbulatov said that Yeltsin was inclining towards dictatorship.

He was living in a make-believe world and did not understand how ordinary Russians lived. The referendum would be very useful in exposing his delusions. A rally of pro-communist groups in Moscow on 17 April attracted about 6,000 people who were addressed by two of those involved in the August putsch, Lukyanov and Shenin as well as Nina Andreeva and the leader of "Labour Russia" Anpilov. Khasbulatov had earlier continued his personal attacks on Kozyrev. He answered a question about ratification of START II in the Supreme Soviet on 13 April, by saying that the Treaty must be submitted by a Foreign Minister who enjoyed public respect and trust. Until Russia had such a Foreign Minister "it would be absurd to talk about START II".

Rutskoi demanded further air time for a live broadcast on government corruption but rejected the offer of a television debate to involve himself, Zorkin, Khasbulatov and Shumeiko, and accused the mass media of waging a propaganda campaign to make the population vote for "further plunder of the country". Rutskoi publicly declined to say whether he would vote yes to the confidence vote in the President and said he would offer his candidacy in the event of early presidential elections. Filatov, Head of the President's Administration, said that Rutskoi should have resigned before engaging in anti-Presidential activities. The break between Yeltsin and his Vice-President was now complete. In an interview on the 22 April, Yeltsin said that Rutskoi had broken his "officer's word of honour" not to confront him; he now regretted choosing him as Vice-President.

Yeltsin received the solid support of all the CIS leaders at the Minsk Summit on 17 April. The Ukrainian President, Kravchuk, stated publicly that the future of the CIS depended on the April referendum: it would not survive if Russia voted against reform. Yeltsin embarked on a campaign tour of provincial cities. In Vladimir he stated that the purpose of the referendum was to prevent Russia from returning to a "communist void". In the final days before the referendum Yeltsin was in the Urals. Speaking in Izhevsk he said, when asked what he would do if the referendum resulted in a vote of confidence, that he did not want to "divulge all secrets" but it would be necessary to take "a number of tough measures". This comment and other hints of strong action if he received popular backing were interpreted by his opponents as an allusion to the introduction of Presidential rule. The Supreme Soviet press service put out a story that he would do so on the night of 25–26 April.

Draft Constitution

On the eve of the poll, increasingly confident of a positive result, Yeltsin published his proposed draft constitution. It included strong powers for the President who would nominate the Prime Minister, Chairman of the Central Bank and the Constitutional Court Judges, and could dissolve parliament (which would consist of two Chambers – the Council of the Federation and the State Duma). In his final television appeal on 24 April Yeltsin outlined the basic provisions of the draft and said that votes cast in the referendum for the President would be regarded as in support of the new constitution.

REFERENDUM RESULTS AND REACTIONS: APRIL–MAY 1993

Results

Some 69 million citizens took part in the referendum on 25 April out of 107 million registered voters, i.e. a higher turnout than expected of 64.5 per cent. The results were as follows:

- 58.7 per cent of those who took part voted "yes" to the first question (Do you have confidence in President Yeltsin?)
- 53 per cent voted "yes" in the second question (Do you approve of the socio-economic policy carried out by the President and government since 1992?)
- 31.7 per cent of the electorate (49.5 per cent of those who took part) answered "yes" to the third question (Do you consider it necessary to hold pre-term elections for the President of the Russian Federation?)
- 43.1 per cent of the electorate (67.2 per cent of those who took part) voted "yes" to the fourth question (Do you consider it necessary to hold pre-term elections of people's deputies of the Russian Federation?)

The overall results were highly favourable to Yeltsin. He not only received a vote of confidence (with a higher share of the vote than he won in the Presidential elections in 1991) but a majority, albeit more narrow, for his reform policies. This was a pleasant surprise for his supporters and a severe blow to the opposition. The majority for early parliamentary elections was insufficient to make them mandatory; and the disparity in the numbers favouring early presidential and early parliamentary elections (49.5 per cent and 67.2 per cent respectively of those who took part) was less than might have been hoped (although he had himself called for a "yes" vote on Question 3). But the results as a whole gave the President every justification for claiming victory.

Regional Variations

There were significant regional variations in voting patterns. There was solid support for Yeltsin in large cities, especially Moscow, St Petersburg and Yekaterinburg, in Northern Russia and Siberia. Support was lower in rural areas and especially in the non-black earth zone of Central Russia; and it was patchy in the Republics, in only half of which he won the confidence vote. The Chechen Republic was the only region which failed to participate. In Tatarstan only 20 per cent took part in the referendum and the results were declared invalid.

Opposition Reaction

The opposition, in considerable dismay, interpreted the results as best it could. Khasbulatov, visibly shaken, told a press conference that the referendum had only succeeded in splitting society and Yeltsin's success was due to "Poltoranin–Goebbels propaganda". Rutskoi argued that a majority of the population had not supported either the President or his economic policies (32 million had voted for the president, while 71 to 72 million had voted against or stayed away). There could therefore be no talk of overall support and the reform programme had to be altered. Isakov, co-ordinator of the Russia Unity Bloc, described the majority support for the government's socio-economic policy as "inexplicable" but added that the results provided no basis for unconstitutional action.

May Day Riots

Hard-line opposition groups, including the National Salvation Front and the Russian Communist Party, vented their anger and frustration at the referendum results by provoking serious disturbances at a May Day demonstration in Moscow, which left 570 people injured including a number of militiamen, one of whom died. The parliamentary leadership seized on the incident to accuse the Moscow authorities of responsibility for the disorders and they set up a commission to investigate "the use of violence against peaceful demonstrators". An opposition rally the following week on Victory Day, 9 May, attracted some 20,000–25,000 people but passed off quietly.

The vote of confidence made Yeltsin secure for the time being from renewed attempts by the parliament to unseat him or further weaken his presidential powers, since it was bound to make some inroads on the hard-line Congress majority. But it did not change the constitutional structure, reduce the powers of the Congress, which was still able to block elections or a new constitution, or resolve the struggle between the executive and the legislature. Yeltsin now faced a battle to turn his psychological victory to real political advantage. As always, his entourage was divided on the tactics to adopt. Despite earlier hints and the urgings, private and public, of radical supporters, Yeltsin decided to avoid drastic action and instead to use the political momentum of the referendum victory in order to push for the rapid adoption of a new constitution.

Conclusion

In the light of subsequent events, Yeltsin would have done better to dissolve parliament and call new elections immediately after the referendum. Such action would have been unconstitutional, but in the circumstances politically acceptable to domestic opinion (and the West). The parliamentary leadership and opposition were demoralized by the referendum results and in no position to offer serious resistance. The army and security forces would almost certainly have supported a president who had just renewed his mandate. Yeltsin could have taken the initiative by convening the Congress to confront it with a demand for early elections and a new Constitution in the light of the Referendum results. The Congress would have refused but thereby put Yeltsin in a strong position to take extra-constitutional action. Instead, Yeltsin embarked on a complicated and lengthy manoeuvre to outflank the parliament by setting up a rival constitutional assembly as a vehicle for his own version of the new constitution. At first it achieved a measure of success; but inevitably it became bogged down in compromise and haggling and as the opposition recovered its nerve and regained confidence, Yeltsin's flanking manoeuvre ran out of steam.

Notes

1   *Zapiski Prezidenta*, pp. 305–6.
2   *Zapiski Prezidenta*, p. 326.
3   *Izvestiya*, 16 April 1993.

10

Battle for the New Constitution

Yeltsin's first official reaction to the referendum came in a television broadcast on the 6 May following the publication of the final official results. Yeltsin declared that the referendum had been "a major political defeat" for parliament and a defeat for Rutskoi "in whom he had lost confidence". He said he had relieved the Vice-President all the political commissions he had entrusted to him and had taken personal charge of the Anti-Crime and Corruption Committee. Yeltsin said that he would soon publish a draft law on elections to a new federal parliament and believed that the election should not be delayed beyond the autumn. He claimed that 68 per cent of the army had supported him in the referendum (this comment did not appear in the published text). The speech was a let-down for Yeltsin's radical supporters, who had seen no sign of the "decisive measures" and "package of decrees" promised during the referendum campaign in the event of victory. There was anxiety that he had lost momentum by failing to follow up more decisively. Boris Fedorov wrote in *Izvestiya* of 8 May, that the two weeks since the referendum had been effectively lost.

Cabinet Changes

Yeltsin did take advantage of the referendum to settle some accounts. He did not have the power to remove Rutskoi from office and the Vice-President refused to resign. But Rutskoi had been stripped of his responsibilities for Agriculture shortly before the referendum and for Crime and Corruption shortly afterwards. Yeltsin subsequently began receiving ambassadors' credentials which deprived Rutskoi of his sole remaining vice-presidential function; at the same time his staff and fleet of cars were severely cut. Yeltsin also dismissed the secretary of the Security Council, Skokov, who had failed to support him at the Seventh Congress and more conspicuously over the abortive 20 March decree on "special rule". But Yeltsin's cabinet reshuffle left his supporters and radical advisers confused and disappointed. The unexpected vote in support of his social and economic policies appeared to provide an opportunity to strengthen the reformist element in the government and perhaps bring back Gaidar. Instead, Yeltsin chose to mark time, or even retreat – almost as though he were implementing changes he had planned in the event of defeat on the second question. Although he removed the Deputy Prime Minister, Khizha, reputed to be the leading opponent of reform in the government, he also appointed two new First Deputy Prime Ministers with no reformist credentials, Lobov and Soskovets. Lobov was appointed First Deputy Prime Minister in charge of economic policy ten days before the referendum, apparently in an attempt to cultivate centrist opinion. Lobov was a personal friend and old associate of Yeltsin from his days in Sverdlovsk Party apparatus, which Lobov headed for two years after Yeltsin moved to Moscow (Yeltsin gave Lobov the task of forming a "government in exile" in Sverdlovsk in case of need during the August 1991 coup). Soskovets was appointed shortly after the referendum to be First Deputy Prime Minister in charge of industry.

Rival Draft Constitutions

Despite Yeltsin's brave words about pressing ahead with economic reform, he was relatively inactive on this front after the referendum although the position of Chubais, who had been under threat, was strengthened and the privatization programme regained momentum. Yeltsin focused his main political efforts on the battle for his new constitution. The tactic Yeltsin chose was to bypass and sideline the Congress by relying on the support and authority of heads of republics and regions to push through his own draft constitution. His chosen vehicle was a constitutional conference or assembly. On 29 April, Yeltsin presented the text of his draft constitution to the heads of republics and regions at a conference in the Kremlin and the full text was published in *Izvestiya* on the following day. He asked for amendments and suggestions so that a revised draft could be considered by the constitutional conference to which each subject of the Federation would send two representatives. He said he hoped that the conference would meet at the beginning of June to finalize the text. The appearance of Yeltsin's draft galvanized the parliament into unwonted enthusiasm for its own official draft constitution and the work of the Constitutional Commission of the Congress (of which Yeltsin was still formally the Chairman) was speeded up. The text was to be submitted to the Supreme Soviet by the end of June and the Congress was to be convened to adopt it on the 17 October. A race between two rival draft constitutions was now underway.

Republics and Regions

The problem with Yeltsin's tactics was that the constitutional conference had no legal status; and reliance on the authority of the regional leaders incurred the risk that some might not support it, thus jeopardizing the whole project; or that the regions and republics would extract a high price in terms of increased autonomy and economic favours. The other flaw which became increasingly apparent was that the republics and the regions had different and conflicting interests. Republics, with Tatarstan and Bashkiria in the lead, were demanding recognition as "sovereign states"; while *krais* and *oblasts* demanded equal economic and political status, and, to underline the point, some regions even started moves to convert themselves into republics.

On 20 May Yeltsin issued a decree convening his constitutional conference for 5 June to be attended by representatives of republics and regions, the federal parliament, political parties, trade unions, religious groups, industrialists, etc. A conference of 20 republic leaders convened by Yeltsin on 26 May gave generalized support for his constitutional conference but failed to endorse Yeltsin's draft constitution. The republic leaders' response to Yeltsin's bid to make adoption of his constitution a condition for measures to implement the Federation Treaty was simply to reverse the linkage which threatened seriously to obstruct Yeltsin's constitutional programme. The President's warning that failure to adopt his constitution quickly could give proponents of a unitarist state more time to mobilize, did not appear to impress. Yeltsin's only other lever, the demand of the regions for equal status with the republics, was too risky to deploy.

Splits in the Opposition

Yeltsin's manoeuvre had some initial success in splitting the opposition. Khasbulatov and Zorkin had denounced Yeltsin's plans to have the new constitution adopted unconstitutionally as "criminal"; and Khasbulatov declared that Yeltsin's "political games" would cause the disintegration of the Federation. However, at a session of the Supreme Soviet on 14 May which debated the issue, Ryabov, the deputy chairman, who had led the onslaught against Yeltsin at the Eighth Congress, unexpectedly argued for co-operation with Yeltsin's proposal. He commented that Khasbulatov had failed to understand the new balance of forces following the referendum and it would be "madness" to seek further confrontation with the President. The chairmen of the Council of Republics, Sokolov, and of the Council of Nationalities, Abdulatipov, took a similar line. Khasbulatov's authority suffered a further set-back when on 8 June eight members of the presidium of the Supreme Soviet, including Ryabov and Stepashin, chairman of the Defence Committee, and Ambartsumov, chairman of the Foreign Affairs Committee, signed a declaration criticizing Khasbulatov's style and methods, and asserting that the Supreme Soviet had lost the political initiative in the country since the referendum. They called for a constructive attitude towards the process of constitutional reform.

Khasbulatov denounced his critics as careerists but gave some ground. He put forward a number of conditions which would have to be met if the parliament were to participate in the constitutional conference: the Constitutional Commission must be involved; all proposed draft constitutions should be discussed; it should be agreed that the conference itself would be a purely advisory body; and the new constitution should be adopted only by the Congress of People's Deputies. He said that efforts to bypass parliament would be viewed by the Supreme Soviet and the subjects of the Federation as a "coup attempt". The Supreme Soviet adopted a resolution approving Khasbulatov's report and instructing him to attend the constitutional conference. Yeltsin declared unlawful a session of the parliamentary Constitutional Commission convened by Khasbulatov without consulting him and boycotted it as did about half the membership. He subsequently formed his own Constitutional Commission to include republic and regional representatives.

The Constitutional Court also split in the wake of the referendum. On 14 May, the deputy chairman, Vitruk, said he was ready to resign if Zorkin, whom he described as "politically prejudiced", stayed in office. He said the Court was in danger of becoming a political instrument. Zorkin refused to resign, acknowledging that there were differences but claiming that the Court was continuing to work in a "calm and constructive spirit".

Yeltsin's Draft

Yeltsin's draft constitution bore the scars of the political battles of the previous 18 months. It gave minimal powers to parliament in part because of the hostility he had encountered from it, and extensive powers to the republics because Yeltsin needed allies in his battle against Congress. It eliminated the posts of vice-president and chairman of parliament and emasculated the role of the Constitutional Court. It gave strong powers to the President but broadly comparable to those of the French president and hardly "dictatorial" as his opponents, echoed in some of the Western press, claimed.

Decree on Procedures

Yeltsin issued a presidential decree on 2 June setting out the procedure for the constitutional conference. Plenary sessions were to be chaired by Yeltsin himself; there would be five chambers or panels comprising representatives of federal organs; republics and regions; local governments; political parties, religious groups, etc.; industrialists, businessmen, etc. The chambers would be co-chaired by, among others, Chernomyrdin, Shumeiko, Shakhrai and Sobchak (Mayor of St Petersburg). The final draft was to be ready by 15 June. In the Supreme Soviet, the secretary of the Constitutional Commission, Rumyantsev, proposed a lengthier procedure protecting the prerogatives of the Commission and the parliament; but at this stage the Supreme Soviet had been effectively upstaged and had lost the initiative.

CONSTITUTIONAL CONFERENCE: JUNE–JULY 1993

The Constitutional Conference opened in the Kremlin on 5 June with an uncompromising introductory speech by Yeltsin. He attacked the Congress and Supreme Soviet as illegitimate remnants of the Soviet era and gave short shrift to the rival parliamentary draft constitution. He said it was impossible to reform Soviet-type power structures which lacked legitimacy and were therefore incompatible with democracy. The Supreme Soviet was not a parliament but an "organization with bosses and subordinates". The current political confrontation was between two independent political systems, not different branches of power. Yeltsin took a relatively firm line on the integrity and unity of the Russian Federation while continuing to offer inducements to republic and regional leaders in return for their support. He proposed a schedule for the adoption of his new constitution: text to be agreed by constitutional conference; initialled by the subjects of the Federation; approved as it stood by Congress; elections to a new parliament no later than October. If Congress were to reject the draft, there would be "other possibilities".

Khasbulatov Incident

Immediately following Yeltsin's speech, the parliamentary speaker, Khasbulatov, who was not scheduled to speak, forced his way to the podium. Yeltsin, in the chair, eventually allowed him to begin his speech but it was drowned out by continuous ironic applause from the President's supporters and Khasbulatov walked out followed by about 50 among the 700 people present. After further incidents in which the Procurator-General Stepankov was apparently man-handled and a Communist deputy Slobodkin (author of a third "Soviet" draft constitution) was forcibly removed, the chairman of the Constitutional Court and two of its judges also left the hall. Khasbulatov told reporters outside that the incident showed that Russia was moving towards dictatorship and said that Yeltsin's speech had been confrontational. Yeltsin said that Khasbulatov's behaviour was a "planned attempt to disrupt the Conference".

Khasbulatov was probably looking for a pretext to provoke a confrontation and stage a walk-out. However, Yeltsin made it easy for him by establishing a rigid agenda and procedure for the conference which gave the opposition little opportunity to state their views. It was understandable that Yeltsin could not resist giving the arch-manipulator a taste of his own medicine; but in not silencing his supporters and permitting Khasbulatov to speak, he antagonized some among the growing number of deputies who were ready to compromise. Ryabov, Deputy Chairman of the Supreme Soviet, criticized Yeltsin for being "unduly confrontational" during his opening address to the Conference. The hard-line opposition who had obtained permission for a demonstration of 100,000 people on Lubyanka Square to coincide with the opening of the conference on 5 June, could muster only 8,000 or 9,000.

At a session of the presidium of the Supreme Soviet on 7 June, Khasbulatov and other parliamentary leaders were criticized for their failure to involve themselves more actively in the process of constitutional reform; but the Presidium also expressed anger that Khasbulatov had been prevented from speaking at the Conference and objected to Yeltsin's assertion that the Soviets were not legitimate bodies of power. On 8 June, *Rossiiskaya Gazeta* published the speech Khasbulatov had intended to give. Khasbulatov stated that the Constitutional Conference had an important role to play in the adoption of a new constitution and parliament would co-operate to this end; but only if the law and constitution were observed. He alleged that Yeltsin was calling for "unlimited presidential power" which was unacceptable as was his proposal to eliminate the representative power in the guise of the Soviets. He insisted that the new constitution could only be adopted by the Congress.

Second Plenary Session

At the Second Plenary Session of the conference on 9 June, Yeltsin responding to resistance both from regional leaders and from parliament to his draft and his initial attempt to railroad it through the conference, adopted a more conciliatory approach. He said that the presidential and parliamentary drafts were not in competition and qualified his earlier assertion that the Soviets and democracy were incompatible. By conceding discussion of the parliamentary draft as well as his own, he managed to get members of the Constitutional Commission and most of the deputies who walked out of the opening session back on board. Khasbulatov, however, did not reappear at the conference, pleading illness at the Second Plenary and another engagement at the Third. He remained effectively sidelined. The five Conference Chambers got down to work on merging the two drafts in a relatively business-like spirit. Amendments were agreed reducing somewhat presidential powers, e.g. limitations were introduced to his power to dissolve parliament and references to the proposed Security Council were removed. But only limited progress was made on the four basic contentious issues:

- division of powers between President and parliament;
- division of power between the centre and republics and regions;
- relative status and rights of republics and regions;
- method for adopting the new constitution.

Republic Status

The question of an acceptable definition of the powers and status of republics was proving especially intractable. The concessions Yeltsin had made to obtain support from the republics were regarded as excessive, both by the leaders of the Russian regions and politicians of all persuasions at the centre. Yeltsin accordingly tried to claw back some of the ground he had given, notably a reference in the Declaration of Principles of the Constitution to the republics as "sovereign states" and to 50 per cent representation for the autonomies in the Upper Chamber of the parliament. When these were omitted from the new version of the Principles, a majority of republic leaders refused to vote for them and the leaders of Tatarstan and Karelia threatened to withdraw from the conference. When Yeltsin produced a compromise formulation referring to the republics as sovereign states within the Russian Federation, he antagonized leaders of the more numerous and populous *krais* and *oblasts*, some of whom (e.g. Vologda and Sverdlovsk) were now threatening to demand sovereign status and convert their regions into republics. Eventually Tatarstan walked out of the conference on the grounds that the final draft did not take account of its special status.

"Final" Plenary Session

The Constitutional Conference met for what was supposed to be its final Plenary Session on 26 June but failed to reach a conclusion. A single draft had now been drawn up and consensus had been reached or was close on the question of division of powers between

President and parliament; the main sticking point continued to be the structure of the Federation and relative standing of republics and regions. The final draft text gave republics superior political status in the form of special rights in citizenship, language, and their own constitutions; but guaranteed equality to all subjects of the Federation in the economic field.

At the final Plenary Session on 12 July, the Conference voted by a large majority to approve the latest text. Of the 585 present, 435 voted for the text and 62 against. However, a number of republic and regional leaders were not present and others voted against the draft. Yeltsin was the only speaker at the final Session. He said that it was wrong to argue that the constitutional question could not be resolved during the present difficult transitional period. Lack of a strong basic law had been a root cause of the conflict. A new constitution was essential for peaceful transition to a new statehood. And economic reform in particular, could not succeed without it. Yeltsin said the draft would now be submitted to each subject of the Federation for approval or further amendment. He declared that the Conference had successfully completed its first phase and acquired considerable prestige; it would now become a standing consultative body and its first task would be to work out a procedure for adopting a new constitution and to agree a draft electoral law.

The Constitutional Conference had achieved a measure of success. Yeltsin had seized and retained control of the constitutional reform process. The parliament had acquiesced in the proposed division of powers at the centre; and Zorkin had voted for the draft. The Supreme Soviet was sidelined and the continuation of the conference as a standing body was intended to keep it that way. But the process had been left incomplete. The intractability of the Federal question gave Yeltsin's opponents ample opportunities to derail it; and the invitation to regions and republics to take the text home and make further amendments was a recipe for unravelling it.

Loss of Momentum

Yeltsin's handling of the constitutional issue seemed to have lost urgency and direction. His failure to produce a draft Electoral Law meant that the original target of autumn elections was now out of reach. The loss of momentum threatened to allow Khasbulatov and the Parliament back into the game. They were waiting eagerly for the President's constitutional vehicle to stall and issuing solemn warnings that their fears that Yeltsin's initiative would lead to the break-up of the Federation were proving justified. When Yeltsin wound up the Plenary Session of the Constitutional Conference on 12 July, he said the next session would be held in August when the conference would take decisions on how to adopt the constitution and discuss a law on elections. But he set no agenda or deadline for finalizing the text of the constitution.

On 24 July, responding to alarm in democratic circles at a growing sense of drift and inaction, Yeltsin issued a decree on procedures for adopting the new constitution, which, however, contained nothing new of substance. During a visit to Orel in August, he claimed that the constitutional process was gaining momentum as it was actively discussed in regions and republics. He said he had a recipe for reconciling the differences between the republics and regions and he would try to resolve the problem at a meeting in Petrozavodsk in mid-August. He expected the final session of the Constitutional Conference to take place in September when the draft would be initialled. The Moscow press reacted with scepticism. It was in fact now clear that Yeltsin's constitutional process was becalmed in the republics and regions. A survey of 46 regions in *Segodnya* of 10 August showed that where the draft was being discussed at all it was being considered alongside the original parliamentary draft Constitution. The paper concluded that a large number of representatives of the subjects of the Federation would arrive at the next session of the Constitutional Conference either with no agreed position at all or with substantial amendments.

By now virtually no hope remained that the constitutional draft would obtain the clear support of two-thirds of the subjects of the Federation including a majority of republics which was regarded as essential to give it legitimacy. One of the principal gains of the Constitutional Conference, a single agreed basic text, had been allowed to slip away and the parliamentary text was back in contention. Without the support either of the parliament or of the republics and regions, there was no legitimate way in prospect for Yeltsin's Constitution to be adopted in anything like its existing form.

SUPREME SOVIET'S SUMMER OFFENSIVE: JULY–AUGUST 1993

As Yeltsin's constitutional process ran into the sand, the Supreme Soviet hard-liners began to recover their nerve and return to a more aggressive stance. At a session on 24 June, Khasbulatov started a purge of Parliamentary Committees whose chairmen had adopted a moderate or positive attitude to the Constitutional Conference. The Legislation Committee was split in two with the key Constitutional Legislation Committee henceforth headed by the Communist hard-liner, Isakov. Ryabov accused Khasbulatov of imposing "a personal dictatorship" on the Supreme Soviet. Khasbulatov was again tightening his grip on the Supreme Soviet apparatus, a task made easier by Yeltsin's tendency to nominate its few democrats and moderates in leading positions to posts in the administration. The Supreme Soviet also resumed the campaign against alleged government corruption on the basis of a report by the Deputy Procurator General (head of a six-man commission set up to investigate Vice-President Rutskoi's allegations made back in April). The deputies adopted a resolution expressing no confidence in First Deputy Prime Ministers Shumeiko and Poltoranin and demanding their dismissal. Khasbulatov claimed that the facts revealed in the report were enough to justify the resignation of the entire government. The Presidential spokesman and the liberal press dismissed the accusations as a last-minute opportunistic attempt to throw a spanner into the works of the Constitutional Conference.

With Yeltsin's draft in the doldrums, the new head of the Constitutional Legislation Committee was sufficiently emboldened to advocate the course which had always been favoured by the majority of hard-line deputies – the continued amendment of the existing old constitution. He argued that proposed amendments to the law on government would dispense with the need to adopt a new constitution whether the presidential or parliamentary version. The law, as amended, would transfer most of the President's powers either to the Supreme Soviet or to the government, leaving him a figurehead. The law would also provide that the incapacity of the President to carry out his duties should be established by the Constitutional Court on the basis of the recommendations of a State Medical Commission appointed by the Supreme Soviet.

Rouble Exchange Row

As its summer session drew to a close, the Supreme Soviet lashed out with further aggressive decisions. It rejected the government's budget, approving instead a substantial increase in the budget deficit and it voted to annul a presidential decree accelerating mass privatization, referring it to the Constitutional Court. The opposition deputies were quick to exploit the apparent disarray in the government following the botched implementation of the rouble exchange (the withdrawal of all pre-1993 Soviet and Russian banknotes by 26 July announced by the chairman of the Central Bank on 24 July without consulting Boris Fedorov, the Minister of Finance, who was in the USA) and the unexplained dismissal of the Minister for Security, Barannikov on 27 July (for corruption, as revealed subsequently in Yeltsin's memoirs)[1] and the Deputy Minister of the Interior, Dunaev. The departure of Barannikov who had demonstrated apparent loyalty to Yeltsin during the attempt by the Ninth Congress to impeach him, caused mixed reactions among the President's supporters. The Supreme Soviet was due to debate Barannikov's removal on 31 July but in the event failed to do so, apparently because of fears that the President would retaliate by releasing documents implicating Rutskoi and others in corruption. Yeltsin issued a Decree modifying the terms of the rouble exchange but did not rescind the measure which in liberal circles was regarded as a political provocation against the President.

Khasbulatov, winding up the Sixth Session of the Supreme Soviet, said that the Parliament was going into recess at a very complex moment and "abrupt turns in the political situation" could not be ruled out. Parliament must be ready to reconvene quickly without warning in response to any possible complications. In one of the last acts of the Session the Supreme Soviet called for the dismissal of the Minister of Interior, Yerin and the Mayor of Moscow, Luzhkov who had been sharply criticized in the Parliamentary Commission's report on the May Day riots. The extra-parliamentary opposition also geared itself up. The National Salvation Front held its Second Congress on 24–25 July and issued a statement that it planned to launch an all-out offensive since if it failed to replace the "criminal regime" it would itself be crushed. It called for all power to be transferred to the Soviets, the formation of a government of national salvation vested with emergency powers and the elimination of the presidency.

The opposition press renewed its insinuations about Yeltsin's health and drinking. A report published simultaneously in *Pravda* and *Rossiiskaya Gazeta* on 31 July claimed that a meeting of the Political Council of Democratic Russia had discussed a sharp deterioration in the health of the President and the possibility of his resignation or forced retirement. *Pravda* threw in a story of a plot to assassinate Vice-President Rutskoi and Khasbulatov, alleging that Barannikov's removal was intended to facilitate the attempt. At the Extraordinary Session of the Supreme Soviet on 31 July, the hard-line deputy, Chelnokov claimed that the Mayor of Moscow had gone to the headquarters of the Dzerzhinsky Division to draw up a list of opposition figures for internment following an imminent coup.

Yeltsin cut short his holiday and returned to Moscow on 25 July evidently in response to panic and confusion over the rouble exchange and amid appeals from his supporters to assert his authority in face of the increasingly aggressive behaviour of the Supreme Soviet. *Izvestiya* of 24 July carried a banner headline "When Democracy is under threat Russia must hear the Voice of its President". A front-page editorial said that events seemed to be developing in accordance with a scenario written not in the Kremlin but in the White House (seat of the Supreme Soviet). If Yeltsin continued to allow matters to drift in a direction desired by his opponents, he took the risk that like a previous president, he would return to "a different country". An appeal issued the previous day by Democratic Russia claimed that the Parliament's attack on the reforms had split the government and created a situation tantamount to a "constitutional coup". It was "inadmissible" that the President should continue his holiday during such developments.

CRISIS ATMOSPHERE: AUGUST 1993

By the beginning of August there was an increasingly feverish political atmosphere in Moscow. The democratic camp was in one of its periodic bouts of panic; Yeltsin's post-April referendum political offensive seemed to have petered out and let Khasbulatov regain the initiative; the opposition and parliamentary leadership were in increasingly aggressive mood while frustrated at their inability to inflict serious damage. The situation was heading back into acrimonious stalemate with suspicions on both sides that the other might resort to desperate measures. A *Nezavisimaya Gazeta* article portrayed the presidential camp as demoralized by fears of conspiracies and splits in the government. Yeltsin was saying nothing on the key issues and losing authority. The paper referred to a sense that no one was in control, August '93 was starting to look like August '91 and the "shadow of forcible solutions loomed".[2]

Proposal for Federation Council

A meeting in Petrozavodsk, 13–14 August, attended by Yeltsin, the Council of Heads of republics, and representatives of 8 inter-regional associations (Siberian Accord and others), discussed implementation of the Federation Treaty and the adoption of a new constitution. Yeltsin declared that the process of redefining Federal and Regional powers must take place in the context of a single and united state. Russia would remain an integral state, either through civilized constitutional changes "or through the use of crude force and arbitrary dictatorship". Thoughts of separation were a mistake. Yeltsin proposed the formation of a new body, the Federation Council, to co-ordinate the views of republics and regions with two representatives from each subject of the Federation. The Constitutional Conference would meet again in September when it was "quite possible" that a law on a transitional period would be adopted allowing for new elections to resolve the problem of "dual power" before the latter brought the country to a standstill.

Yeltsin Predicts a Hot September

Yeltsin told a press conference before leaving for Petrozavodsk that September would be a "super-combative" month and decisive for the future of the constitution, elections and the fate of authority in Russia. He predicted several weeks of intense political conflict to resolve his struggle with the parliament. August should be used for a "preparatory artillery barrage". Yeltsin said that elections must take place in the autumn; if deputies did not take the decision the President would take it for them. Radical supporters welcomed Yeltsin's statement but expressed fears that it would remain mere bluster as had similar threats in the past. In retrospect, however, Yeltsin had perhaps started to signal his punch. In a statement on 12 August Khasbulatov, in response to what he called the threatening statements of the President and his entourage, defended the Supreme Soviet's decisions on the budget and privatization and warned that "provocations" were planned for the August coup anniversary.

On 18 August the President's Anti-Corruption Commission, headed by the recently appointed Acting Minister of Justice, Kalmykov, claimed at a televised news conference that it had evidence of corruption against Vice-President Rutskoi including details of a million dollar account in a Swiss bank. There was also reference to the involvement of Procurator General Stepankov in an alleged plot to murder the chief Government lawyer Makarov. Little solid evidence was provided for the allegations but they had their presumably intended political effect of neutralizing the accusations of corruption against Shumeiko and Poltoranin.

Suspension of Rutskoi and Shumeiko

The nervous and uncertain atmosphere was further fuelled by the offer of resignation by Marshal Shaposhnikov a little more than a month after his appointment as Secretary of the Security Council. Shaposhnikov gave a number of reasons for his resignation, including the failure of the Supreme Soviet to ratify his appointment and the insults he had publicly received from some deputies as well as the lack of any clearly defined role for the Security Council and the fact that any mention of it had been dropped from the new draft constitution. On 1 September, Yeltsin issued a decree simultaneously relieving Vice-President Rutskoi and First Deputy Prime Minister Shumeiko of their responsibilities pending the outcome of investigations of corruption against them. The move, which was on dubious constitutional ground in the case of Rutskoi, amounted to the sacrifice of a piece in order neutralize the Vice-President if not remove him from the board. The Supreme Soviet on 3 September responded predictably by suspending the Presidential Decree in the part relating to Rutskoi. The President retaliated by having the Vice-President barred from his Kremlin offices.

Notes

1   *Zapiski Prezidenta*, pp. 335–7.
2   *Nezavisimaya Gazeta*, 3 August 1993.

Part V

Climax of the Constitutional Crisis: Elections and Referendum: September– December 1993

11

The September/October Crisis 1993

Yeltsin states in his memoirs[1] that he took the decision to dissolve parliament in early September without telling even his closest aides. He instructed his Chief of Staff, Ilyushin, to prepare a decree with a small team of advisers including the then Legal Adviser, Baturin, who played his part "correctly and professionally". On Sunday, 12 September, Yeltsin informed his "closest comrades", the Minister of Defence, Grachev, the Minister for the Interior, Yerin, the Acting Security Minister, Golushko, and the Foreign Minister, Kozyrev. (The Prime Minister, Chernomyrdin, was on a visit to the United States.) Yeltsin says he had no doubts about the loyalty or support of any of these except Golushko whom he did not know well. (Golushko was only officially appointed Acting Minister of Security on 20 September.) All expressed support for the proposed decree, Kozyrev commenting that his only reservation was that it was long overdue. The proposed date was 19 September with the intention that the Dzerzhinsky Division should take control of the White House which on a Sunday would be empty. (According to Yeltsin "mountains of weapons" had already been stockpiled there.) This would prevent the Supreme Soviet from convening and from using the building as the headquarters for co-ordinating opposition. On the same day Yeltsin spoke to Korzhakov, his chief bodyguard, and Barsukov, head of the Security Directorate. (It is almost certain, however, that Yeltsin's close confidant, Korzhakov, was involved from the beginning.)

On the following day he met Chernomyrdin on his return from the USA who signed the draft decree without hesitation and "with a flourish". On 14 September he floated the dissolution of parliament as a theoretical possibility at a meeting of the Presidential

Council but received less support than he expected. On 15 September the Security Council, including those members not already informed, endorsed the plan. On the following day Yeltsin visited the Dzerzhinsky Division of Interior Troops. (Two weeks earlier he had visited the Kantemir and Taman Divisions.) On 18 September Gaidar was appointed First Deputy Prime Minister in place of Lobov who became Secretary of the Security Council.

On Friday 17 September, Yeltsin held a final consultation with the "power ministers" and according to Yeltsin's own account the plans nearly ground to a halt. One after another they argued for postponement until the end of the following week on the grounds that the CIS summit scheduled for 24 September would be disrupted with consequent loss of face for the President; and because Khasbulatov and Rutskoi had got wind of the decree, it would be no longer possible to seize an empty White House since it would be occupied by supporters of the Parliament. Yeltsin agreed to postpone but only by two days and asked Yerin, Grachev, Golushko and Barsukov to work out alternative plans for occupying the White House without bloodshed. But Yeltsin adds that what he had most feared was going to happen: the White House would become a centre of resistance. By now there were serious doubts in the presidential entourage; there was a row on 19 September between Barsukov and Grachev, the former arguing that the military plans were inadequate; and Yeltsin's Head of Administration, Filatov, who learned of the plan only on 17 September, desperately tried to persuade Yeltsin not to go ahead.

The opposition were aware in general of Yeltsin's intentions and made no secret of the fact. In a speech on 17 September Rutskoi warned that Yeltsin was proposing to introduce Presidential rule, abolish the Supreme Soviet and replace it with the Federation Council. He called on citizens to defend the constitution and on the army not to become involved. On the following day Khasbulatov, addressing an All-Russian Conference of People's Deputies at the Parliamentary Centre, claimed that the President had been sounding out reactions in the West to the dissolution of the Supreme Soviet and the imposition of a state of emergency. He made a number of insulting comments about Yeltsin, including an imputation of drunkenness. The opposition was well prepared. By 19 September, the White House was crowded with deputies and their supporters including hard-line opposition groups, some with contingents of armed men.

DECREE NO. 1400: DISSOLUTION OF PARLIAMENT:
21–29 SEPTEMBER

Yeltsin made his speech to the nation on television, pre-recorded earlier the same day, at 2000 local time on 21 September. At the same time Decree No. 1400 "on the stage by stage constitutional reform" was issued. Yeltsin said that attempts for over a year to reach compromise with the deputies had failed. The Supreme Soviet majority was flouting the will of the people, expressed in the April referendum, and seeking to weaken and eventually remove the President. Power in the Supreme Soviet had been seized by a group which had turned it into the headquarters of the irreconcilable opposition. But "the security of Russia and its people was of higher value than formal compliance with the contradictory norms created by a legislative power which had utterly discredited itself". The existing constitution provided no way out of the crisis. The only way to resolve the paralysis of state power was to hold new elections to a new parliament, the Federal Assembly, based on the draft constitution approved by the Constitutional Conference. Elections would take place on 11–12 December; thereafter he favoured early presidential elections. In the meantime the Congress and Supreme Soviet were suspended and powers of deputies ceased. The presidential decree additionally recommended that the Constitutional Court should not convene until the Federal Assembly met. Local executive and representative organs would retain their powers. On 23 September, Yeltsin issued a further presidential decree announcing presidential elections for 12 June 1994.

Opposition Reaction

The Supreme Soviet, with a large number of deputies already in place, reacted swiftly and predictably by formally dismissing President Yeltsin and swearing in Vice-President Rutskoi as President at a late-night session on 21–22 September. It acted on the basis of the constitutional amendment, adopted by the Seventh Congress, providing that the President's powers ceased if he attempted to dissolve parliament. The deputies then voted to dismiss the Ministers of Defence, Security and the Interior and appointed in their place Generals Achalov, Barannikov and Dunaev respectively. Achalov instructed army units to proceed with weapons to the White House but there was no response. It was a tactical blunder to "dismiss" the power ministers since it removed any possibility that they might waver in their loyalty to Yeltsin. Of the new appointees one, Achalov, had been heavily involved in the August putsch, the other two had recently been dismissed for corruption by Yeltsin. A crowd of about 2,000 supporters gathered round the White House and built barricades which were manned by armed paramilitary groups.

Khasbulatov attempted to convene a Congress. The number of deputies was insufficient for a quorum so the rules were changed and the resulting rump congress voted to hold early elections of parliament and President. The Constitutional Court, despite the recommendation in Yeltsin's decree and attempts to bar it from the Constitutional Court building, met and voted by 9 votes to 4 that there were grounds for impeachment, but that only Congress could dismiss the President.

Support for Yeltsin

There were statements of support for the President's action from the Prime Minister who denied that there was a *coup d'état* and from the Minister of Defence, Grachev, who made it clear that there would be no use of armed force to implement the decree. There were also expressions of support from G7 countries, whose ambassadors had been briefed by Kozyrev an hour before the announcement; and from Ukraine, Belarus, Moldova and the Baltic States. On 24 September all CIS leaders arrived in Moscow for the scheduled Summit. The Russian government remained solid apart from the Minister for Foreign Economic Relations, Glaz'ev, who resigned. (He had offered his resignation a few weeks earlier following corruption allegations.) The Central Bank, after a slight delay, indicated support for the President.

The first violence occurred on 23 September when an armed group lead by Terekhov of the Officers' Union attacked the CIS headquarters building. Two people were killed, a militia Captain and a woman onlooker. On the following day as a result of this incident a serious blockade of the White House by militia was instituted. People were allowed to leave but not to enter; hot water and electricity were cut off (telephones had been cut off from the first day but some remained in operation). Deputies were offered inducements, including employment and retention of their flats, to leave the building. As the siege continued the parliamentarians increasingly came to be dominated by hard-liners who in turn fell increasingly under the influence of extremist political groups and armed paramilitaries who had rallied to the opposition. The arms build-up had continued; according to Filatov in a public statement on 28 September, groups of armed men had come from Abkhazia, Transdniestria and former OMON forces in Riga and Vilnius.

Ultimatum

On 29 September, extending an earlier ultimatum, the Russian and Moscow governments demanded evacuation of the White House and the handover of arms by 4 October. Failure to comply would have "grave consequences". All who left by the deadline would have immunity. On the night of 28 to 29 September there were prolonged clashes between police blockading the White House and about 5,000 demonstrators attempting to break through the cordon, led by Anpilov the leader of "Labour Russia". By now only about 200 deputies remained in the parliament building.

STALEMATE: 29 SEPTEMBER–1 OCTOBER

Yeltsin appeared to have won the first round. The besieged parliamentary leaders had appealed without success for support from army units and for nation-wide strikes. They found themselves, as Yeltsin put it, "in a vacuum". The rump congress, with no effective levers to pull, had petered out. Senior Supreme Soviet figures, including Ryabov, Stepashin and Ambartsumov were among many deputies to leave the White House. But a possible lifeline for the parliament emerged from the regions and republics where reactions to Yeltsin's action had been cautious. Regional leaders on the whole saw little advantage in a victory for the President and the re-assertion of strong undivided central authority. A stand-off provided the opportunity to increase their influence by assuming a mediatory role. A regional meeting in St Petersburg on 26 September to discuss the crisis gathered representatives from fewer than half the regions. But a subsequent assembly in Moscow in the guise of a "Council of Components of the Federation" attracted representatives from 62 of the 88 subjects of the Federation. It met under the auspices of the Chairman of the Constitutional Court, Zorkin, and endorsed the "zero option" he had earlier proposed, i.e. a return to the status quo before 21 September with suspension of the decrees and decisions of both sides including Yeltsin's Decree No. 1400. The Assembly also called for simultaneous parliamentary and presidential elections and a bigger role for the regions in drawing up legislation.

Negotiations

The presidential camp was becoming concerned at attempts by regional leaders to exploit the crisis. The President's press spokesman Kostikov, in a statement on 28 September, referred to attempts to siphon power from the centre to the regions and rejected calls for the Council of the Federation to "take control of the situation" since the President and government he said were in full control. The regional initiative had raised the spectre that the body Yeltsin had created as a counterweight to parliament might now seek to supplant his authority. (It is significant that Yeltsin makes virtually no reference to the regional dimension of the crisis in his own account of these events.) Fears that he might lose the political initiative if the stalemate continued was evidently one reason why Yeltsin responded positively to the offer of mediation by the Orthodox Church on 29 September. (Contacts between the government and the chairmen of the two Chambers of the Supreme Soviet had been taking place throughout the week.) Talks began in the Danilov monastery under the chairmanship of the Patriarch with Filatov, Soskovets and Luzhkov on the presidential team and Sokolov and Abdulatipov representing the parliament. They reached provisional agreement on initial steps for the storage of White House weapons under joint control in return for the restoration of light, heating and some telephones to the White House; to be followed in a second stage by the removal of armed formations from the White House and armed militia blockading it. But the talks broke down when the agreement was denounced by hard-line leaders now effectively in control of the parliamentary building. They later resumed and were continuing aimlessly when overtaken by the violence on 3 October.

DENOUEMENT: 2–4 OCTOBER

Attack on Ostankino

One of the hard-liners, Ilya Konstantinov, leader of the National

Salvation Front, left the White House on 29 September evidently
to organize the subsequent demonstrations. On 2 October between
2,000 and 4,000 demonstrators built barricades on the Moscow ring
road which they subsequently set on fire. Many militiamen were
injured and the MVD forces were patently unable to cope. Encouraged by their success the demonstrators gathered in increased
numbers on the following day and broke through the cordon round
the White House. Rutskoi, addressing the crowd from the balcony,
urged them to form detachments and attack the Mayor's office and
the Ostankino television station; Khasbulatov added that the Kremlin too should be seized. Armed demonstrators stormed the Mairie
close to the White House and occupied it. Using commandeered
trucks they moved to the Ostankino television station, which was
subjected to prolonged siege. Part of the building was occupied and
at about 2000 all television channels except the Russian channel,
operating with reserve facilities, went off the air. The Tass building
was also besieged by a mob but not taken over. A state of emergency
was declared and Yeltsin arrived in the Kremlin from his dacha
by helicopter to avoid demonstrators. After a six-hour siege the
partially occupied Ostankino building was retaken by Government
forces.

Seizure of the White House

Gaidar and other democratic figures and politicians appeared on
television later in the evening to appeal to the public to defend
democracy. Between 10,000 and 20,000 people gathered during the
night outside the Mossovet building. In his own account Yeltsin
denies that there was panic and confusion in the Kremlin (and by
implication suggestions that he had been drunk and incapable). He
acknowledges that the fate of the country "hung by a thread". On
3 October the militia had virtually disappeared from the capital
and army units had not arrived although apparently ordered into
Moscow hours earlier. Armed bands of parliamentary supporters
were encountering very little resistance. In the early hours of 4
October Yeltsin went to the Ministry of Defence building to join a
meeting in which the Prime Minister and the Minister and Deputy
Ministers of Defence were already taking part. The discussions were
inconclusive until Yeltsin's chief bodyguard Korzhakov put forward
a plan for the shelling by tanks and then storming of the White

House. This was endorsed by the Generals present but Grachev insisted on a direct instruction from the President for the use of force. (In a later television interview [26 November] about the crisis, Yeltsin complained that Grachev had been unwilling to take decisions on his own authority.) The operation to take the White House was carried out on the following day. According to Yeltsin's own graphic account,[2] the Alpha special forces group assigned to storm the building refused orders to do so, including orders from Yeltsin himself. They eventually took part in the operation only because one of their number was killed outside the White House. In the attack on the White House on 4 October and in the violence of the previous day about 144 people, none of them deputies, were killed. Rutskoi, Khasbulatov and other ring-leaders were arrested and taken to Lefortovo Prison.

The disappearance of the MVD forces from the capital on 3 October and the delay in the appearance of the military gave rise to a conspiracy theory that the authorities had deliberately allowed opposition extremists a free run in order to have a pretext for violence against the White House. The ultimatum was due to expire on 4 October and Yeltsin would have faced a difficult decision on whether to use force (which meant persuading the Army to take action) or appear weak by again postponing the deadline. The weakness of the theory, apart from the lack of any evidence, is that no one in the Russian leadership could have calculated on such a chaotic situation developing in accordance with a pre-planned scenario and the risks involved were far too great. The attack on Ostankino very nearly succeeded – had it done so the psychological / political boost to the Opposition could well have turned the scales.

AFTERMATH: OCTOBER

Anpilov and Konstantinov, who played leading roles in fomenting the disturbances, were at large for some days before being arrested and joining the other ring-leaders in Lefortovo. Together with Rutskoi, Khasbulatov, Achalov, Barannikov, Dunaev and Makashov, they were charged under Article 79 of the Criminal Code with incitement to mass disorders (carrying a penalty of from 2 to 15 years imprisonment). Hard-line deputies who played no direct part in the violence, e.g. Baburin and Isakov, were briefly detained before being released without charge or sanctions. The Procurator-General, Stepankov was dismissed (replaced by Aleksei Kazannik). Zorkin resigned as chairman of the Constitutional Court (but not as a judge). The Constitutional Court was suspended by presidential decree until the Federal Assembly met. The Minister of Interior, Yerin was made a Hero of the Russian Federation; Grachev and Golushko received lesser awards.

State of Emergency Measures

In connection with the state of emergency which was extended until 18 October, a number of extremist parties and organizations were suspended including the National Salvation Front, the Russian Communist Workers Party, the Russian National Assembly and the Moscow branches of the Russian Communist Party and the Popular Party "Free Russia" (Rutskoi's Party). A dozen publications were banned including *Pravda, Sovetskaya Rossiya,* and *Den'* (a quasi-fascist broadsheet). The first two were eventually allowed to resume publication and *Den'* did so illegally under a new name. Censorship which had led to ostentatious blank spaces in protesting liberal and centrist newspapers was lifted after 48 hours on 6 October. The emergency measures aroused some concern in Russian liberal circles and in the West, especially when the Moscow authorities took the opportunity to evict thousands of Caucasians (popularly believed to be heavily involved in black market and criminal activities) from the capital.

Yeltsin issued a decree on 9 October on reform of the regional Soviets (a majority of which had sided with the parliament during the crisis). The Soviets were instructed to dissolve themselves in favour of regional Dumas with from 15 to 50 full-time members; republic Soviets / parliaments were recommended to do likewise. In a symbolic gesture of some resonance the guard of honour was removed from the Lenin Mausoleum. A day of mourning was declared on 7 October.

Yeltsin addressed the nation on television on 6 October. In a balanced and sober speech he said Russia had suffered a very great tragedy; there should be no talk of victory or defeat. He was sharply critical of the Supreme Soviet and Congress, which had become the "chief patrons" of organizations inciting and preparing violence, the Constitutional Court, the regional Soviets and the so-called Council of the Components of the Federation which had set itself up as an enemy of the Executive Branch. He spoke of the need for further reform of the army and security Services.

August '91 and October '93

In his memoirs, Yeltsin discusses the bitter irony of the close parallels between the defence of the White House in August 1991 and September / October 1993.[3] He writes that the memory or "complex" of August 1991 was strong on both sides. The White House defenders were convinced they could repeat the successful scenario of two years earlier. The leadership in the Kremlin was afraid of finding themselves in the role of the Putschists and of acting indecisively and clumsily. But according to Yeltsin there were crucial differences: in August the streets were packed with troops and armour; in October there were no troops in Moscow until 4 a.m. on the 4 October. Unarmed passive resistance in August had prevailed; armed revolt in October led to defeat. The army had refused orders to storm the White House in August 1991; they carried out their orders in October 1993.

Balance Sheet

The balance sheet in the aftermath of the October insurrection was complex and contradictory. From one perspective this was the end of the Soviet era. The Soviet structures which survived August 1991 and the collapse of the USSR had been or were apparently about to be demolished, removing the prime cause of the protracted and debilitating constitutional crisis and opening up the way for progress on economic and political reform. The reassertion of undivided central authority offered better prospects for containing the growing ambitions of republics and regions and safeguarding the integrity of the Federation. But Yeltsin's authority and prestige, and to some extent those of reformists both in and out of government, were permanently scarred by the events of September / October. The television pictures of the shelling of the White House and its blackened façade made an unpleasant and lasting impression in Russia and in the West. Unfortunately for Yeltsin there was no or negligible coverage of Rutskoi's incitement to violence from the balcony of the White House, of the violent assault on Ostankino, or of the paramilitaries with swastika arm bands and hammer and sickle flags defending the White House. And despite Yeltsin's apparent victory, there were still serious unanswered questions about the performance and attitude of the army and security services and the prevarication and opportunism of republic and regional leaders.

Notes

1 *Zapiski Prezidenta*, pp. 347–59, give Yeltsin's detailed account of preparations for the dissolution of parliament.
2 *Zapiski Prezidenta*, pp. 11–13.
3 *Zapiski Prezidenta*, pp. 128–31.

12

Duma Elections and Constitutional Referendum

NEW CONSTITUTION

Yeltsin issued an order on 11 October to reorganize the Constitutional Conference into two Chambers: a State Chamber comprising representatives of federal, republican and regional organs and a Public Chamber comprising representatives from parties, religious groups, industry and local government. The Constitutional Conference was instructed to finalize a draft by 3 November to allow time for its publication on 10 November one month before a referendum to approve the constitution which would be held simultaneously with the parliamentary elections on 12 December. In the event the key decisions were taken in a restricted working group chaired by the head of Yeltsin's administration, Filatov. (The Constitutional Conference never reconvened in Plenary Session to approve the final draft.) Yeltsin decreed that a simple majority vote in favour would be sufficient for the adoption of the Constitution provided there was a 50 per cent turn-out of the whole electorate.

The main thrust of the amendments adopted was to claw back concessions made in June / July to ambitious regional and republic leaders who had been taking advantage of the deadlock at the centre, and to the rival parliamentary draft constitution. The principal changes involved deleting references to the "sovereignty" of the republics and affirming the equality of all subjects of the Federation in relation to the federal authorities. The republics were now described as States but not sovereign; they no longer had their own citizenship. The Federation Treaty was removed from the body of the constitution and it was stated that the Constitution would prevail in the event of any contradiction between it and the

Federation Treaty. As a concession to regional leaders, the "Upper Chamber" of the new parliament, the Federation Council, which was to be elected on 12 December for the first Federal Assembly, would thereafter comprise nominated representatives of the republics and regions.

The main criticism of the revised draft centred on the powers of the President (although these were little changed in comparison with the Constitutional Conference draft of 12 July). The President had the power to dissolve parliament (to be followed immediately by new elections); parliament could impeach the President but the procedure was made much more difficult. In the section on transitional arrangements the draft constitution specified that Yeltsin would serve out his full term; it also abolished the upper age limit of 65 for the President (Yeltsin would be 65 in 1996). Even in the democratic camp it was argued that the draft had given too much power to the President which Yeltsin might use responsibly but a successor might not. One newspaper summed up the new constitution in the words: "In one bound he was free". In an interview in *Izvestiya*, Yeltsin acknowledged that the presidential powers in the draft were "indeed considerable . . . but what can you expect in a country accustomed to Tsars and leaders with extraordinarily weak executive discipline and steeped in legal nihilism?"

The hard opposition and to a large extent the centrists, made opposition to the constitution a central issue in their parliamentary election campaigns. The communists and agrarians called for a "no" vote or a boycott. The Civic Alliance and Travkin's Party, the DPR, had withdrawn in October from the Constitutional Conference in protest at the procedure for revising the draft and took the line that the new parliament should have been entrusted with approving the new constitution. The democratic camp was far from solidly in favour. Shakhrai expressed reservations and Yavlinsky came out strongly against approval of the constitution. In the light of such attitudes and some worrying opinion poll forecasts there was serious concern in the presidential camp as the referendum approached. Senior members of the government were galvanized into campaigning more vigorously for a "yes" vote issuing dire warnings of the dangerous political vacuum that failure of the referendum could create. Yeltsin declared that politicians should not use air time allocated to them for the parliamentary election campaign for attacks on the constitution.

PREPARATIONS FOR ELECTIONS

Presidential Elections

In a television speech on 15 October, Yeltsin reaffirmed that the parliamentary elections would take place in December in accordance with Decree No. 1400 and presidential elections in June 1994 unless the new parliament decided otherwise. However, there were already signs that his preference was to avoid presidential elections and serve out his term until June 1996. Filatov at a press conference on 20 October said that the undertaking for presidential elections in 1994 was made as a compromise and under pressure from the Soviets. At a meeting with news media on 6 November, Yeltsin now declared that he wished to serve out his full term. He would find and groom a successor and would not stand in 1996: "Everyone knows how many blows I have endured . . . it is too much for one man" (i.e. another election campaign). Yeltsin's decision to go back on the promise of elections (in his decree of 23 September) was supported by the Prime Minister, by Gaidar and Kozyrev but predictably came under sharp attack from the opposition as reneging on a public commitment. It was also criticized in the liberal media notably *Izvestiya*, and revived apprehensions that Yeltsin was showing authoritarian tendencies in the wake of his October victory. In reaction to such criticism Yeltsin changed tack yet again, stating in an interview in *Izvestiya* on 16 November that he had not rescinded his decree of 23 September, which however had been issued in a bid for compromise that was rejected by the Supreme Soviet. This gave him the right to go back on his word but the new parliament would have the final say.

Parliamentary Elections: Background

Although the question on re-election of deputies did not receive a sufficient majority in favour, there was a general assumption after the April referendum that early parliamentary elections were now on the agenda. Parties and movements began to manoeuvre and regroup in that light. A democratic electoral coalition, Russia's Choice, was founded on 10 June. It comprised Democratic Russia plus a number of small parties and movements; its organizational committee included A. N. Yakovlev, Chubais, Gaidar, Shumeiko and Burbulis. However, the prominent democrats, Shakhrai and

Yavlinsky stood aside from Russia's Choice and began to organize their own political parties. In the centre the Civic Alliance was showing few signs of life. Travkin's DPR withdrew from it during the summer on the grounds of Rutskoi's extremism. There was also a split in the hard opposition. At the second Congress of the National Salvation Front (July 24–25) Baburin's Russian National Union (ROS) withdrew because of the extremist language about a "national liberation struggle"; Lysenko's National Republican Party also pulled out for other reasons.

Central Electoral Commission

Preparations among the parties intensified when Yeltsin on 12 August stated that there would be early elections in the autumn with or without parliamentary agreement. Three days after his decree dissolving parliament Yeltsin issued a further decree (24 September) setting up a Central Electoral Commission to prepare for State Duma elections headed by Ryabov, former Deputy Chairman of the Supreme Soviet who had defected to the President's camp after the April referendum. The CEC's responsibilities were subsequently expanded to include elections to the Federation Council and the referendum. On 14 October the Ministry of Justice published a list of 91 registered political parties and movements eligible to compete in the elections; it excluded 10 or so parties suspended or banned after the events of 3–4 October including Zyuganov's RCP and Rutskoi's Popular Party "Free Russia".

Election Rules

The regulations in the Electoral Statute, published on 8 October, prescribed that the lower house of the Federal Assembly, the State Duma, would comprise 450 deputies half elected on the basis of party lists; half on the basis of a simple majority in single-member constituencies. The Upper House or Federation Council would comprise two representatives from each subject of the Federation, regardless of population, elected in 2 member constituencies. The criterion for registration of parties / electoral blocs was 100,000 signatures (but not more than 15 per cent from any one city or region). The threshold for representation of parties in parliament was 5 per cent. The criterion for registration of candidates in constituency elections was the signatures of one per cent of the electorate (but in no case more than 25,000) or inclusion on a party electoral list. Candidates and lists had to be registered by 4 November. It was assumed that the 50 per cent proportional representation in the Duma elections would favour the democrats whose votes tended to be concentrated in big cities and were therefore liable to be "wasted" in constituency elections.

A presidential decree of 19 October banned six parties / movements from the elections: the National Salvation Front and five organizations affiliated to it. The ban did not include the two large parties, the Russian Communist Party or the Popular Party "Free Russia". The decree disqualified from participation in the elections those facing criminal charges in connection with the insurrection – Rutskoi, Khasbulatov et al. (but not the August 1991 putschists, several of whom stood as candidates).

Electoral Blocs

Thirty-five parties / blocs presented lists to the Central Electoral Commission, of which 21 submitted the required 100,000 signatures, or claimed to have done so by the deadline of 6 November. The CEC disqualified eight lists, leaving 13 to contest the elections:

Pro-reform – 4
Russia's Choice (Gaidar);
Russian Unity and Accord (Shakhrai);
Russian Democratic Reform Movement (Sobchak / Popov);
Yabloko (Yavlinsky, Boldyrev, Lukin).

"Centrist" blocs – 7
Democratic Party of Russia (Travkin);
Civic Alliance (Volsky);
Women of Russia (Lakhova);
Russia's Future – New Names;
Ecological Movement "Cedar";
"Dignity and Mercy";
Agrarian Party (mostly communist including several hard-liners).

Hard-line Opposition Parties – 2
The Communist Party of Russia (Zyuganov);
Liberal Democratic Party (Zhirinovsky).

Among the parties whose lists were disqualified was the right-wing nationalist Russian National Union (ROS) led by Baburin who claimed that 22,000 of his signatures had been stolen in a raid on his headquarters. But democrat contenders were also disqualified and the remaining parties covered a wide political spectrum. 1,397 candidates were registered for the 225 State Duma constituencies; 483 for the 89 two member Federation Council constituencies. No candidates were nominated from Chechnya (which boycotted the elections).

The electoral blocs had mostly been put together in an ad hoc and back-to-front manner. Well-known names gathered under vague banners before discussing policies. There were some odd bedfellows and a good deal of rowing and in-fighting and jockeying for position on the national lists. Candidates were not permitted to switch lists once registered.

ELECTION CAMPAIGN: NOVEMBER–DECEMBER 1993

The formal three-week election campaign began on 21 November. When he announced the elections in September, Yeltsin had guaranteed all registered candidates and parties equal access to television and radio air time. This was formalized in a decree of 29 October setting out the rules. Parties could buy airtime up to 22 November. Thereafter each party list or candidate was to have one hour's free airtime at peak viewing hours during the campaign proper; the hour could be divided into 20- or 30-minute slots and the time when they were shown was decided by lot. The main television channels took the obligation of fair coverage so seriously that they were reluctant to risk any political commentaries or discussion programmes during the campaign.

Yeltsin adopted a neutral position. He did not speak as had been expected at the Russia's Choice Congress and he refused to say "for the time being" which party he would vote for. On 26 November he met leaders of the 13 blocs / parties and confirmed that he would stay "above the battle" and would not endorse any party. He complained of attacks on the constitution by politicians during their free election broadcasts and told them "not to touch the constitution" but stick to expounding their own programmes or else live transmissions might be stopped. This was followed by a letter from Shumeiko to the Central Electoral Commission demanding disqualification of the RCP and DPR for abusing their party political broadcasts to criticize the constitution. (Yeltsin's spokesman disavowed this ploy.) On 9 December Yeltsin made a nation-wide television speech in support of a "yes" vote in the referendum and said that the threat of civil war would hang over Russia until a new constitution was adopted. The speech indicated sympathy with "democratic and reformist blocs" but there was no endorsement of Russia's Choice.

Opponents of the Constitution held a rally in Moscow on 3 December at which the speakers included Zorkin and Rumyantsev, former Secretary of the Parliamentary Constitutional Commission, who denounced the draft as dictatorial. The Referendum was widely seen as a verdict on the events of September / October and a vote of confidence on Yeltsin.

Television Campaign

There was resentment in the Russia's Choice camp at the tactics of the rival democratic parties which concentrated their fire not on the communists or the LDP but on Gaidar and Russia's Choice, distancing themselves from "shock therapy" economics and the October violence while promising stability and reforms without tears. Yavlinsky's television clip began with shots of the shelling of the White House and also featured a picture of Gaidar alongside Stalin and Zyuganov as politicians Russians had seen enough of. The series of party political broadcasts by the contesting electoral blocs ended on 8 December. The campaign was relatively uneventful and without major scandals. Russia's Choice's campaign was lack-lustre and hampered by internal divisions and personal jealousies; its main television clip cacophonous and confusing. The neo-fascist Zhirinovsky conducted a skilful and lively television campaign. He was not taken seriously by the other parties and his demagogy went unchallenged. (An anti-Zhirinovsky documentary was belatedly televised on 10 December, but was probably counter-productive.)

The last opinion polls to be published (the electoral rules forbade publication after 2 December), showed Russia's Choice still leading but with its support slipping; the Yavlinsky bloc in second place and the Russian Communist party third. Until the beginning of the television campaign no poll showed Zhirinovsky above 5 per cent. Later unpublished polls showed a sudden surge in support for the

LDP in the final days of the campaign; the final predictions were that Zhirinovsky would finish a close second to Russia's Choice.

Duma Results

In the event the LDP came a clear first of the eight blocs which surmounted the 5 per cent barrier in the party lists contest for the State Duma. The LDP obtained 22.8 per cent of the vote which translated into 59 seats in the Duma. Russia's Choice came second with 15.4 per cent (40 seats) followed by the Russian Communist Party 12.3 per cent (32 seats); Women of Russia 8.1 per cent (21); Agrarian Party 7.9 per cent (21); Yabloko 7.8 per cent (20); Russian Unity and Accord party (PRES) 6.8 per cent (18) and Democratic Party of Russia 5.5 per cent (14). Of the five blocs which fell below the 5 per cent barrier, the Russian Democratic Reform Movement obtained just over 4 per cent which meant nearly 2½ million "wasted" democratic votes; the remainder including the Civic Alliance took under 2 per cent.

The results of the constituency elections significantly changed the picture. The LDP elected only five declared candidates compared with 30 for Russia's Choice. On preliminary estimates this left Russia's Choice as the largest party in the Duma with 70 deputies followed by the LDP with 65; the Communist Party 48; the Agrarian Party 33; Women of Russia 23; Yabloko 23; PRES 19 and the DPR 14. However, 119 deputies elected in the constituency had no declared affiliation and the real state of the parties was still not clear. Elections were not held in six constituencies; five in Tatarstan and one in Chechnya.

Federation Council

Elections to the Federation Council did not take place in Chechnya, Tatarstan and Chelyabinsk, and in two of the other two member constituencies only one candidate was returned leaving the Federation Council eight short of its full complement of 178. The successful candidates were predominantly local notables with relatively few national figures or party representatives. Party affiliation was of less significance than regional concerns in the Federation Council. The high preponderance of regional government leaders and presidential representatives made it seem likely that the "Upper Chamber" would be a more moderate and conservative body than the Duma. Figures published subsequently[1] confirmed that the membership of the Federation Council was dominated by the regional elite. Of the 170 members: 108 were senior figures from the Regional/Republic administrations and Soviets (including 59 Presidents, Prime Ministers and Governors; 23 were directors of regional industrial or agricultural complexes. There were 12 Communists and 8 from Russia's Choice; the LDP was not represented. Forty-four members of the Upper Chamber were former Supreme Soviet deputies.

Referendum

The official results of the Referendum on the Constitution were declared by the Central Electoral Commission on 20 December. 54.8 per cent of the electorate (58 million people) took part in the vote, of whom 58.4 per cent (nearly 33 million) were in favour of the Constitution. The Commission accordingly declared that the poll was valid and the new Constitution adopted. Both the Referendum and the election results were subsequently questioned by the respected (and pro-democrat) analyst Sobyanin, whose report claimed that the turn-out for the Referendum had been below 50 per cent, making the poll invalid; and that there had been widespread electoral fraud in favour of the Communists and Zhirinovsky. There was very little attempt by either the opposition or the democrats to make capital out of these findings (which were at odds with those of international observers) and they have been largely ignored.

POST MORTEM: DECEMBER 1993

The narrow victory in the referendum for the new constitution was inevitably highlighted by the presidential camp as the most important political outcome of the poll and another vote of confidence in the President and his policies. But the success for Zhirinovsky, and the weak performance of Russia's Choice in the parliamentary elections, sent shock waves through Russia and the West.

Zhirinovsky

Zhirinovsky's political career began in 1989/90 when he was involved in attempting to start up various political parties including

a so-called "bloc of centrist forces". He was also involved with
several Jewish groups. There is good evidence that he did this
under the auspices of the KGB, who hoped to siphon support
away from the burgeoning democratic movement. His political
party was eventually born in April 1990 (just after the Communist
Party abandoned its leading role) with the attractive and woefully
inappropriate name "Liberal Democratic". Its founding Congress
received unprecedented coverage on the front page of *Pravda*.

In the RSFSR presidential elections in 1991 Zhirinovsky,
campaigning on preservation of the USSR and cheap vodka, won 7.8
per cent (nearly 6 million) of the vote behind Yeltsin and Ryzhkov.
In August 1991 he jumped on the putsch bandwagon, immediately
supporting the state of emergency and attacking Yeltsin. Thereafter
he faded to the margins of the political scene. In June / July 1993
Zhirinovsky was adopting a more statesman-like posture, playing
a more or less constructive role at the Constitutional Conference
and winning unexpected rounds of applause for his humorous and
generally positive contributions. He earned Yeltsin's approval to the
extent that the President, to the disgust of many delegates, invited
him to address the final plenary session. Having learned his lesson
in August 1991 Zhirinovsky took no part in the parliamentary
revolt in October 1993. His reward was to escape the ban which
fell on other extremist parties and qualify for the parliamentary
elections by gathering the required 100,000 signatures (which he
did with remarkable speed) for registration in the contest for half
the seats in the State Duma. His election campaign was based on
aggressive nationalism and blatant economic populism featuring
extravagant and contradictory promises to virtually all sections of
the population.

Inquest

The inquest in the democratic camp led to much recrimination.
Shakhrai and in particular Yavlinsky were accused of allowing
personal ambition to stand in the way of a united democratic
front. *Izvestiya* (16 December) said that Yavlinsky's "inordinate
ambition" had become legendary and added that his claim on
the eve of the poll that the threat from Zhirinovsky had been
deliberately contrived was a case either of political ignorance or
"sheer careerist demagogy". The same issue of *Izvestiya* attacked

Popov, leader of the Russian Movement for Democratic Reform, who in a televised round-table debate a few days before the elections had chosen to ignore racist remarks by Zhirinovsky and devote all his comments to a demand for an investigation into the finances of Russia's Choice.

Yeltsin's Statement

Yeltsin issued a short "political declaration" on 13 December which celebrated the fact of free multi-party elections and the adoption of the constitution. It concluded with an implicit allusion to Zhirinovsky promising to guarantee the irreversibility of reforms and erect a solid constitutional barrier to any attempts to undo this democratic choice. There were several scapegoats: the President's political adviser Stankevich was dismissed; as the man charged with advising the President on political parties and movements, he had clearly failed to anticipate the rise of Zhirinovsky (in which, however, he was not entirely alone). Among other heads to fall was that of the head of Ostankino TV, Bragin, evidently held responsible for the television environment in which Zhirinovsky had flourished so spectacularly. Zhirinovsky's ostentatious embrace of Bragin at the televised post-election extravaganza in the Kremlin (which turned into a wake) was evidently the kiss of death.

Russian political analysts attributed the electoral set-back to divisions among the democrats which resulted in Russia's Choice coming under attack from all sides during the campaign; Yeltsin's passivity and refusal to endorse Russia's Choice; and a (in retrospect) predictable backlash against the reform policies from those who had lost out. Ominous comparisons with Hitler and Weimar Germany were made.

However, the evidence of opinion polls (reasonably accurate, at least in regard to trends) suggests that Zhirinovsky's success was very largely due to the television campaign which coincided exactly with the sudden surge in his support from 2 per cent to 23 per cent. There was no other charismatic personality in the field. People responded to his direct and personal style of address; and they identified with his exploitation of populist themes (e.g. while Gaidar continued to lecture the viewers on the principles of market economics, Zhirinovsky was shown haranguing swarthy market traders about their exorbitant prices).

Russian voters in the first Russian multi-party elections were confronted simultaneously with at least four ballot slips: for the Party list and constituency elections to the Duma; for the Federation Council elections; for the Referendum; and, in some cases, for local elections as well. The unprecedented choice between 13 parties caused confusion. And there was a tendency to vote for familiar names. If there was a genuine protest vote against the reforms, it is difficult to explain the success in the constituency elections of a number of prominent reformist ministers standing for Russia's Choice – Kozyrev, Boris Fedorov, Pamfilova, Shumeiko – all of whom were returned with healthy majorities.

Impact on the Government

The elections left the government divided and in some disarray. Senior members of the government joined competing electoral blocs – Russia's Choice, PRES, Agrarians, Yabloko – and campaigned against each other while the Prime Minister, Chernomyrdin, stood aloof from the campaign (though reputedly having links to Russia's Future – New Names, effectively the junior branch of Civic Alliance). Chernomyrdin evidently resented the widespread assumption that in the event of the anticipated victory for Russia's Choice, he would be replaced as Prime Minister by Gaidar; while Gaidar resented the fact that during the elections he had to carry the can for the government's economic policy and performance over which he had had only very limited influence, while Chernomyrdin sat out the campaign and emerged politically unscathed.

First indications were that the government would not be extensively reorganized. (Yeltsin was under no constitutional obligation to present a new government to the Duma.) At a press conference on 22 December (when he gave several hostages to fortune), Yeltsin denied that the elections had been a defeat for democracy or reform. A coalition cabinet would not be formed though the government would be seriously restructured. Gaidar would stay. Economic policy must take account of two contradictory objectives: social protection of the needy and control of inflation. Yeltsin also remarked that one-third of the voters in the army had supported Zhirinovsky which was worrying and appropriate measures would be taken. Yeltsin said that the results of the elections had finally convinced him that it was time to create a presidential party. At an end of year press conference, Gaidar said that the leaders of his Russia's Choice parliamentary faction had met Chernomyrdin and had been told there was no question of any fundamental changes in economic policy. It was generally assumed that the reformists in the government had after all survived the electoral set-back.

Note

1   *Nezavisimaya Gazeta*, 7 April 1994.

Part VI

Russia under the New Constitution: 1994–1996

13

Political Amnesty and Civic Accord: January–April 1994

The political fall out from the parliamentary elections had led to divisions in the government on economic policy. For Gaidar and Fedorov the electoral set-back pointed to the need to accelerate reform in order to get results and produce more winners in society, thus reducing the social base for Zhirinovsky's neo-fascism. The Prime Minister, Chernomyrdin, drew the more cautious and obvious lesson of the need to slow the pace and reduce the pain of the economic reforms. Chernomyrdin was ready to keep Gaidar and Fedorov in the government but on his terms. The Prime Minister's position had been strengthened by the perception that Russia's Choice had lost the elections; his stature had grown at the expense not only of Gaidar but of the President.

Cabinet Crisis

Gaidar resigned on 16 January stating that he had decided not to accept the offer of the post of First Deputy Prime Minister because more and more decisions had been taken in the government without his advice or in opposition to it (he cited in particular plans for monetary union with Belarus); he could not stay in the government and at the same time oppose it. At bottom Gaidar was unwilling to continue to bear the main responsibility for the country's economic problems while enjoying ever diminishing influence on government policy. Yeltsin accepted Gaidar's resignation on the following day while stressing the irreversibility of the reformist course. The other leading reformist in the government, Boris Fedorov, posed tough personnel and policy conditions for remaining in the Cabinet. He dropped his original demand for the removal of the Chairman of the Central Bank, Gerashchenko, but insisted that he would not accept to serve as Finance Minister without the status of Deputy Prime Minister if this meant subordination to other Deputy Prime Ministers determined to increase spending (notably Zaveryukha who oversaw Agriculture). He also demanded that precise limits be set to government borrowing. There were lengthy and messy negotiations involving Yeltsin, Fedorov and Chernomyrdin in which Yeltsin fought hard to preserve Fedorov. But the Prime Minister would not accept Fedorov's terms and Yeltsin had to back down. Chernomyrdin was in a strong position. The elections had undermined the position of the reformists and when it came to the crunch Yeltsin had either too many democratic scruples or too little determination to confront the Prime Minister and the parliament. The supposedly authoritarian new Constitution did not give him much room for manoeuvre. He could not appoint a new Prime Minister without the approval of the Duma and the dismissal and appointment of the Chairman of the Central Bank was the prerogative of the Duma.

The outcome of the Cabinet reshuffle was a government which looked much less reformist, with Russia's Choice retaining only a toehold: Chubais, whom Yeltsin personally appointed Deputy Prime Minister in a separate decree, Foreign Minister Kozyrev, Deputy Prime Minister Yarov and the Ministers for Science, Culture and Environment. Reformist representation in the government had been steadily whittled away by the attrition of conservative pressure, since Gaidar picked his own team at the end of 1991 and was now at its lowest ebb.

Prime Minister vs. President

Chernomyrdin told a press conference when the new Cabinet was announced, that the new government would not be blown off the reform course but policies would be modified. The emphasis would shift from the fight against hyperinflation to the fight against hyperslump; and the government would turn away from predominantly monetarist measures. "Market romanticism" was over but would not be replaced by "production fetishism". Gaidar and Fedorov predicted a rapid increase in inflation, the

"Ukrainization" of the economy with disastrous consequences ("social explosion" according to Fedorov). Fedorov made an emotional appeal to Yeltsin, in which he declared that the old Supreme Soviet's dreams had become a reality and the country had suffered an "economic coup". Yeltsin's effective defeat in the Cabinet crisis after a protracted struggle left him looking isolated and weakened. His relations with the reformist leaders were further soured. Both sides felt let down – Gaidar because Yeltsin had not supported Russia's Choice in the elections and Yeltsin because Gaidar and Fedorov's uncompromising attitude had put him in an impossible position. A new element of tension and rivalry had appeared in relations between the President and the Prime Minister who had emerged in a strong political position from the government crisis. The friction became public when Yeltsin's chief aide, Ilyushin, accused the government press spokesman of "unseemly haste" in announcing senior Cabinet appointments before the President had made his final decision.

FEDERAL ASSEMBLY: OPENING AND ELECTION OF OFFICIALS

Yeltsin

Even before the opening of parliament there was some friction with the President over his refusal to restore the White House to the new parliament and his assignment to each Chamber of separate, ill-equipped and inconvenient buildings. The impression was created that Yeltsin wanted to play down the significance of the new parliament and even hamper its effectiveness. Despite the historic nature of the occasion, when the first democratically elected parliament in Russia's history opened on 11 January, Yeltsin did not address a ceremonial joint session or attend the Duma. He spoke briefly at the opening session of the Federation Council (as laid down in the constitution), while Chernomyrdin read out a message from him to the Duma (in mid-1996 Yeltsin had still not set foot in the Duma).

In his speech to the Federation Council, Yeltsin's main themes were the need to continue the strategic course of reform; maintain the integrity of the Federation; promote free and peaceful integration in the CIS; and ensure constructive co-operation between President and parliament. Chernomyrdin told the Duma that 100 bills had been prepared for its consideration; he said the government's priorities would be support for production and social policy with no ill-considered "shock" decisions.

Duma: Election of Speaker

After a somewhat chaotic opening day of its first session on 11 January, mainly due to the disruptive behaviour of Zhirinovsky and incompetent chairmanship by a member of his fraction (presiding as the oldest deputy), the Duma made its first significant decision by electing the Speaker. Rybkin, a moderate communist and member of the Agrarian faction was elected with a bare majority of 223 votes in a run off against a hard-line nationalist, Yu Vlasov. The strongest placed democrat, Lukin, (ambassador in Washington) received only about 160 votes in the preliminary straw poll. Rybkin had a typical party official's career rising to be Party Secretary in Volgograd in 1987, i.e. when *perestroika* was already underway. He had taken a generally hard-line position as a deputy in the Supreme Soviet and was strongly opposed to Yeltsin during the September/October crisis, though prudent enough to leave the White House before the shooting started. Mityukov of Russia's Choice was elected First Deputy Chairman with Vengerovsky (LDP), Fedulova (Women of Russia) and V. Kovalev (Communist) as deputies.

Committee Chairmen

In the elections of Duma Committee Chairmen (agreed as a package deal between the fraction leaders), the reformists fared reasonably well with members of democratic fractions heading the Finance, Foreign Affairs and Defence Committees. The bad news for Yeltsin was the election of two extreme hard-line opponents of the President to head the key Committees for Security (Ilyukhin) and Legislation (Isakov). Ilyukhin was a former Soviet Procurator- General who tried to indict Gorbachev for treason and in 1993 published a series of inflammatory articles in *Pravda* attacking Yeltsin and his entourage. Isakov was the last Chairman of the Supreme Soviet Constitutional Legislation Committee, and in that capacity took a very aggressive line in seeking to strip away Yeltsin's presidential powers. Both were last ditch White House defenders in October

1993. Although Zhirinovsky's LDP was allocated more committees than any other fraction (five), none of them were very influential. They included an absurd Geo-Political Committee invented as a sop to Zhirinovsky who was frustrated in his ambition to gain control of the Foreign Affairs Committee.

Federation Council

On 13 January after two days of tense voting, Vladimir Shumeiko, First Deputy Prime Minister and one of the leaders of the Russia's Choice bloc, was elected Chairman of the Federation Council. His main opponent was Petr Romanov, director of a large military enterprise in Krasnoyarsk and member of the Russian National Assembly (an extreme Red/Brown organization led by ex KGB General Sterligov). Romanov appeared to enjoy the support of the Communists and was only two votes behind Shumeiko in the second round. Shumeiko's success in the final vote evidently owed much to arm-twisting overnight, principally by Chernomyrdin. His election was a notable gain for the presidential camp but the Federation Council, expected to be moderate and supportive and a counterbalance to the Duma, had been shown by the close vote to contain a strong hard-line element. Shumeiko's deputies were Abdulatipov (Chairman of the Council of Nationalities of the former Supreme Soviet) and Viktorov (Prime Minister of the Chuvash Republic).

THE DUMA AND THE NEW POLITICAL BALANCE

Despite the chaotic opening day, the Duma made a positive start, avoiding the anticipated prolonged procedural wrangling and getting itself efficiently organized within about 10 days. This was largely due to the institution of the Duma Council comprising the heads of the nine fractions plus Rybkin with a casting vote, which took decisions on the agenda and organization by consensus. Rybkin as Speaker, in striking contrast to Khasbulatov in the former Supreme Soviet, turned out to be moderate and reasonable; and although Zhirinovsky's antics continued and monopolized media attention, he made relatively little impact on the serious business of the Duma.

Balance of Forces in the Duma

On the other hand, as the balance of forces in the Duma became clear, it was apparent that the democrats were outnumbered by communists and nationalists. Early significant votes showed that the hard opposition comprised roughly 180 deputies: of which Communists, 45, LDP 64, Agrarians 55, Russia's Path (a nationalist group headed by Baburin and Lukyanov), 14. The democrats mustered about 160: Russia's Choice 74, PRES 30, Yabloko 27, Union of 12 December (a new reformist fraction later joined by Boris Fedorov) 25. The centrists numbered about 100: New Regional Policy (mostly independent constituency deputies) 66, Women of Russia 23, Travkin's DPR 15. But the centrists leaned heavily towards the opposition and the voting pattern suggested that up to 259 deputies were generally against reform and the government and 185 generally in favour. But the hard-liners were about 20 to 30 votes short of a hostile working majority. At this stage Zhirinovsky tended not to vote with the Communists and Agrarians on "anti-Yeltsin" or constitutional issues. The only seriously confrontational Resolution adopted during the first month of the Duma was the decision on 9 February, sponsored by Baburin, to set up a parliamentary investigation into the events of 3–4 October (which had the support of Zhirinovsky).

Yeltsin and the Duma

Yeltsin was developing a good relationship with Rybkin with whom he had several long meetings. Hard-line deputies had already begun to criticize Rybkin as a renegade and appeaser and were threatening to restrict the powers of the Duma Council. Yeltsin's initial attitude to the Duma was ambivalent. He was uncertain whether to seek a co-operative relationship or to sideline it. Its powers to influence and obstruct the executive were limited compared to those of the former Supreme Soviet. The new Cabinet had been formed without reference to the Duma, which apart from giving assent to the appointment of a new Prime Minister had little power over appointments and no say in the membership of the government. (The one significant exception being its powers to dismiss and appoint the chairman of the Central Bank.) The Duma could pass a vote of no confidence in the government which the President could ignore unless it was repeated within three months. In that event he was obliged either to dismiss the government or dissolve the Duma. (But he could not dissolve the Duma on those grounds during the first year of its existence.) The Federal Assembly could impeach the President but only on grounds of treason or another serious crime and the procedure under the new Constitution was much more difficult than under the old: it required a two-thirds majority in the Duma, a three-quarters majority in the Federation Council plus the support of the Constitutional Court and the Supreme Court. The President's veto on legislation could be overridden by a two-thirds majority in both Chambers. The balance in the Duma suggested that the government would lack a majority for any radical reformist measures, while the opposition would be able to obstruct government legislation but would be short of a sufficient two-thirds majority to force through its own legislation or initiate hostile constitutional amendments. The potential nationalist majority in the Duma raised the prospect of difficulty in ratifying treaties and the adoption of hostile resolutions on foreign policy and CIS issues.

President/Government/Parliament

The elections and the new Constitution had produced a different and more complex relationship between the President, the government and the parliament. In a sense the main winner of the December elections was not Zhirinovsky, whose party list gained most votes, but Chernomyrdin who took no part in them. Having won the argument over the formation of the Cabinet, Chernomyrdin now looked a strong Prime Minister and an independent political figure. The Duma appeared ready to give the benefit of the doubt initially to his government, shorn of the principal reformists and apparently distanced somewhat from the President. Yeltsin's authority seemed diminished, but he retained some important levers. The Foreign, Defence and Interior Ministries and the Security and Information Services were subordinated directly to the President. The government was thus largely focused on economic policy (in accordance with a tradition from Soviet times). However, the President could also influence economic policy, e.g. through presidential decrees and *ex cathedra* pronouncements on policy which the Prime Minister could not easily ignore, and by exercising his constitutional right to chair sessions of the government.

The presidential spokesman had early on distanced Yeltsin from the new government stating that the President would monitor the Government's performance closely: "using his constitutional powers and guided by the people's democratic expectations he was determined to protect the reform". In early February the Prime Minister's radical chief Economic Adviser, Illarionov, resigned in the wake of signs that the Government were moving away from financial stabilization and preparing to give large subsidies to agriculture. In March for the first time the monthly list of one hundred leading politicians published by the newspaper *Nezavisimaya Gazeta*,[1] rated in order of current importance by a group of experts, put Yeltsin in second place behind Chernomyrdin at the top. This embarrassed the Prime Minister and prompted a fulsome declaration of loyalty to the President at the expanded session of the government on 4 March. Rejecting press speculation about his presidential ambitions Chernomyrdin said that any such talk was unethical while Yeltsin "our one national leader elected by the whole people" was in office. He added that any attempt to drive a wedge between the President and the Prime Minister was a waste of time. Chernomyrdin was beginning to confound his critics by maintaining a tight-credit policy and acquiring a more reformist profile, e.g. he visited Nizhny Novgorod and gave his backing to the local land privatization scheme. There was a serious effort to achieve stabilization and monthly inflation fell from 18 per cent in January to 7 per cent in March.

The democratic movement had been left once more in some disarray by the elections and their aftermath. Russia's Choice with its participation in the government much reduced was in quasi opposition in the Duma, generally supportive on foreign policy issues, critical on some economic questions. There was little evidence of the democrats regrouping effectively. Yavlinsky was taking the line that his main mistake during the election campaign had been not to attack Yeltsin and Gaidar more fiercely.

POLITICAL AMNESTY CRISIS: FEBRUARY 1994

Duma Resolution of 23 February

After six weeks of the new parliament, with Yeltsin about to deliver his state of the nation address to the Federal Assembly, there seemed to be a real possibility that a reasonable working relationship between the President and the Parliament would develop. But on 23 February, on the eve of Yeltsin's address to the parliament, the Duma voted in favour of a wide-ranging resolution which included an amnesty for those involved in the August 1991 putsch and the violent events of 1 May and 3–4 October 1993. The vote was 252 in favour, with 67 against and 28 abstentions. Several earlier attempts had been made by hard-line opposition fractions, especially the LDP and the Communists to push through an amnesty for one or both sets of putschists, but the motions had fallen well short of a majority. The vote succeeded on this occasion because it was wrapped up in a complicated "compromise" package, which also included a motion proposed by the President but rejected earlier by the hard-liners for an amnesty in honour of the new constitution for persons convicted of minor criminal offences; an amnesty for economic "crimes" committed in the Soviet era; a decision to abolish the recently established Commission to investigate the events of October 1993; and a so-called Memorandum of Accord.

These added elements were evidently sufficient to obtain support for the portmanteau resolution from the Women of Russia and New Regional Group fractions and the neutrality of Yavlinsky's fraction. However, the crucial role was played by Shakhrai, leader of the Russian Unity and Accord fraction (PRES) who sponsored the package and openly supported the political amnesty. He was accused of treachery by Russia's Choice deputies, the only fraction to oppose the package unambiguously. Russia's Choice spokesman argued that the amnesty was confrontational and intended to prepare the ground for an attack on the President and his eventual impeachment.

Release from Lefortovo

Leaders of Russia's Choice and members of the presidential team reacted to the vote with anger and alarm, describing it as "a declaration of civil war". Gaidar said the release of the putschists would destabilize the political situation and could lead to violence on the streets. The President's press spokesman called the vote a challenge to Russian democracy. There was speculation that Yeltsin might react by postponing his address to parliament. In the event, he spoke as planned: he did not refer to the amnesty specifically but included a sharp critical allusion to it. It was widely assumed that the Duma's Resolution would not be implemented but, on 26 February following its publication in the official government newspaper, *Rossiiskaya Gazeta*, the leaders of the parliamentary insurrection were released from Lefortovo Prison in Moscow. They included the former Vice-President Rutskoi, the former Speaker, Khasbulatov, the former "Ministers" for Internal Affairs and Defence, Dunaev and Achalov (the Security Minister, Barannikov had been released into hospital earlier on health grounds), the National Salvation Front leaders, Konstantinov and General Makashov and the hard-left agitator Anpilov. They were greeted by a small raucous crowd of supporters waving red flags (and by Zhirinovsky claiming credit for their release) and were borne away in limousines.

Yeltsin made a belated and unsuccessful attempt to prevent their release by urging the Procurator-General, Kazannik, to suspend implementation of the amnesty. Kazannik sent a letter to the Duma questioning the legal basis of the amnesty but then, without waiting for a reply, authorized the release before calling a press conference to announce his resignation. He said that the parliament and strict observation of the letter of the law had forced him to take an action he regarded as immoral. Yeltsin accepted his resignation with unprecedented alacrity and appointed the head of the Presidential Control Administration, Ilyushenko, acting Procurator-General, pending confirmation of his appointment by the Federation Council. It appeared that the release was deliberately accelerated by a Deputy Procurator, Kravtsev, in order to pre-empt any further presidential move to prevent it.

Political Effects

The released rebels presented no immediate threat, but the episode had poisoned the political atmosphere, demoralized the democratic camp and rejoiced the President's hard-line opponents. Once again the divisions among the democrats and the disarray in the Presidential Administration had been exposed. His numerous advisers offered an array of conflicting opinions and advice but between them failed to devise an effective response. The hard-liners in the Duma had exploited a Constitution supposedly tailored to protect the President and limit parliamentary powers in order to deal a heavy political blow to Yeltsin, whose position had already been weakened by the failure to preserve the reformists in the government during the previous month's Cabinet crisis. Some moderate deputies and commentators argued, however, that the release of the Lefortovo inmates had its positive aspects in that it would have been impossible to prosecute them successfully and the longer they stayed in jail the more they would have appeared as martyrs and victims; and that the emergence of the rebels would divide the hard-line opposition and undermine Zhirinovsky, despite the fact that he had campaigned for their release.

Yeltsin was reported to be about to deliver a television address to the nation on 28 February and there was speculation that he planned a tough response. In the event, following meetings with the Speakers of the two Chambers on 1 March, he issued a press statement in which he deplored the amnesty and the haste with which the rebels had been released, but warned against over-reacting. He saw no danger for civic accord and was in full control of the situation. He did not plan tough measures in view of the stated intention of the Duma to act for national conciliation. On 28 February, Yeltsin issued a decree dismissing the Head of the Federal Counter-Intelligence Service, Golushko, evidently because officials of the security services which still controlled Lefortovo had acted to facilitate the release of the coup leaders. On 1 March the military collegium of the Supreme Court announced that it had decided to halt the trial of the August 1991 putsch leaders on the basis of the amnesty declared by the State Duma.

The Duma opposition was ambivalent in its attitude to the former Supreme Soviet leaders whose release it had engineered. Opposition deputies were happy to strike a blow against the President but had no desire to be upstaged by former opposition forces outside the new parliament. However, the amnesty episode gave a boost to the hard-liners who stepped up their attacks on the President. At the first Duma session following the release of Rutskoi et al., Isakov, Chairman of the Legislation Committee (who had masterminded the amnesty resolution) made a personal attack on Yeltsin referring to the "evident disintegration of the President's personality". He went on, true to past Supreme Soviet form, to attack the institution of the presidency, proposing that the next president should be elected not by popular vote but by the Federal Assembly and regional representatives, which he said was more in accord with Russian traditions. This proposal received little support and Rybkin, seeking to mend fences with the President, criticized Isakov's remarks as those of "a former Supreme Soviet deputy" not the Chairman of the Legislation Committee. (Isakov had not discussed his proposal with members of the Committee.)

YELTSIN AND CIVIC ACCORD: FEBRUARY–APRIL 1994

State of the Nation Address

Yeltsin's address to the two chambers of parliament on 24 February gave clear indications of the shift of emphasis in policies as a result of the elections and the perceived threat from Zhirinovsky. The leitmotif was the strengthening of Russian statehood and defence of Russia's national interests. He also addressed a number of the concerns which Zhirinovsky had exploited, promising tough action on crime and corruption and protection of Russian minorities in the CIS. On the economy, he took a middle road, emphasizing continued reform, private ownership of land etc., but also spoke of giving policy a more "social orientation". He said a balance had to be struck between the speed of reform and its social costs and spoke of an "optimal" participation of the State in the economic process. On foreign policy he said there should be an end to unilateral concessions and warned sharply against NATO expansion without Russia, which was "not a guest in Europe but an equal participant in the greater European community". On the CIS he noted a trend towards co-operation and integration and commented that the "euphoria of independence" was passing.

Civic Accord Proposal

Yeltsin, having contemplated but rejected a tough response to the political amnesty, elected instead to seize the high moral ground. He put forward a conciliatory proposal for an Agreement on Civic Accord, which was intended to "neutralize the negative consequences of the amnesty". The President, government, parliament and all political and social forces and religious groups would undertake: to play by the new rules and not rake up the past; pursue political aims by non-violent means; agree in effect to a two-year truce during which they promised not to destabilize the political process. The President's aim was to underpin the new political order and the new Constitution, divide the opposition and isolate the extremists who, it was presumed, would refuse to sign. Yeltsin first floated the idea at the expanded session of the government on 4 March, explaining that given the choice between a new spiral of confrontation or expanding the basis for co-operation he had naturally opted for the latter. The weakness of this initiative was that a new deal between the President, parliament and other political forces tended to devalue the Constitution whose authority he wished to reinforce; and it was difficult to reconcile a proposal for harmony and consensus across the political spectrum with the President's commitment to continue strong reformist policies.

The proposal was partly a riposte to the Memorandum of Accord which formed part of the Duma's amnesty package. The Duma's memorandum provided for round tables involving the executive and legislature in discussions of political and economic measures to resolve the national crisis. Its real purpose was to give the Duma leverage over the political and economic agenda. Yeltsin formally launched his Civic Accord process at a meeting in the Kremlin on 11 March with a fairly representative group of political figures. In turn, the hard-line opposition responded by launching on 17 March a new manifesto "Accord for Russia", likewise open to signatures of "all people of good will", which was supported in the first instance by the former Supreme Soviet Red / Brown leadership now rallying round Rutskoi. Among other signatories were Zorkin, Zyuganov, Baburin, Lapshin (Agrarian fraction) and Glaz'ev (DPR). (Zhirinovsky was conspicuously excluded.) A fierce political struggle for preeminence in reconciliation and harmony was now underway.

Opposition

The amnestied rebels appeared untroubled by any spirit of reconciliation. Apart from Khasbulatov, who said he would return to academic life for the time being, they were quickly back in political business and making aggressive noises. Rutskoi announced that he would stand in future presidential elections and in an article in *Pravda* called for Yeltsin's removal. When the former US President Nixon had an amicable meeting with Rutskoi during a visit to Moscow, Yeltsin reacted angrily and refused to receive Nixon. Rutskoi rejected any agreement with the "regime of bloodstained swindlers and villains" and announced in a television interview (24 April) that he was ready to lead a united opposition of all political forces opposed to the Civic Accord. Duma opposition leaders also took an uncompromising line. Zyuganov at the Russian Communist Party Conference in Zvenigorod called for a complete change of economic and social policy as a precondition for civic peace and declared that "Western bourgeois civilization" and Russian civilization were incompatible. The Agrarian leader, Lapshin, announced he would not sign the Agreement since this would amount to acceptance of the new Constitution.

Terms of the Accord

The text of Yeltsin's Civic Accord, published on 7 April, contained the following principal political undertakings:

- recognition of the existing Constitution; and a moratorium on "destabilizing" constitutional amendments;
- renunciation of violence in pursuit of political ends;
- no agitation for pre-term elections;
- no attempts by subjects of the Federation to change their status (this commitment was later deleted);
- a Conciliation Commission would monitor any violation of these obligations and co-ordinate round table meetings to find common approaches on principal areas of policy;
- to conciliate the opposition an additional obligation upon the government to reduce inflation and guarantee financial stability in 1994 was added to the text.

Kremlin Ceremony of 28 April

Yeltsin presided at the grand ceremonial signing of the Civic Accord in the Kremlin on 28 April, flanked by the Prime Minister, Patriarch Aleksii, and the speakers of the two chambers. The turnout, which included many religious leaders and the governors or presidents of all the 89 subjects, except Chechnya, and leaders of seven out of the nine Duma fractions, looked colourful and impressive. But not all present signed the document, and many who did repre-sented insignificant organizations and movements anxious to raise their public profile. In his introductory speech, Yeltsin recalled the series of conflicts and atrocities which had followed from the 1917 Revolution and suggested that a page was now being turned by the agreement committing signatories to pursue political goals by non-violent constitutional methods. In the event, only Zhirinovsky of the opposition leaders signed. (He kept the press guessing about his intentions until the last moment in order to keep in the limelight.) Zyuganov was present but did not put pen to paper; several regional governors also abstained. Yavlinsky refused to participate, as did the Agrarian fraction. The concessions which had been introduced into the text in the end antagonized the democrats without bringing any significant opposition figures on board. The major objective of the exercise – to divide the opposition and isolate the extremists – was only very partially achieved.

Opposition Demonstrations

Yeltsin claimed, with some justice, that the civic accord agreement had taken the wind out of the sails of the hard line opposition. Although they took the opportunity as usual of the May Day holidays (May Day and Victory Day on 9 May) for a show of strength they could muster no more than 10,000 on either occasion. On 9 May Rutskoi was the principal speaker at a rally on Lubyanka Square when he called for the overthrow of the "police regime" before next year's 50th anniversary of Victory, followed by the restoration of the Soviet Union. The Russian flag was publicly burned during the demonstration which led to a procuracy investigation into that incident and reports of incitement to violence. The Red/Brown leadership, augmented by the release from Lefortovo, were showing no evidence of unity and there were public differences on this occasion and subsequently over who should be the opposition candidate for presidential elections.

Note

1   *Nezavisimaya Gazeta*, 3 March 1994.

14

Relative Calm before Chechnya Storm: May–December 1994

YELTSIN REGAINS THE INITIATIVE: MAY–JUNE 1994

Political Reverses and Rumours

In the early months of 1994 Yeltsin had suffered several political reverses (notably the departure from the government of Gaidar and Fedorov and the political amnesty), his authority seemed in decline and he was the target of constant rumour-mongering about his health. He suffered two bouts of flu in the early part of the year (the first in February had delayed his State of the Nation address to parliament). And when he left Moscow for a two-week holiday in mid-March after a further bout of flu there was widespread speculation about his health and political future, and the possibility of early presidential elections. He was clearly feeling the effects of the flu and of the back injury he had incurred in Spain in 1990 but there was no serious evidence of the various chronic or terminal conditions ascribed to him by rumour. However, the opposition made a great play of his illness and absences; Yavlinsky, echoing a newspaper headline, dubbed him "Mr Not There". A sensational story appeared in the press alleging that moves had been made to have him declared unfit for office, masterminded by Skokov (former Secretary of the Security Council) and involving several senior figures in the administration including Chernomyrdin. (This appears to have been a deliberate hoax but was symptomatic of the current political atmosphere.)

Yeltsin Come-Back

However, Yeltsin's albeit qualified success with the civic accord process enabled him to regain the initiative and to some extent restore his political fortunes. In an interview with the German magazine *Der Spiegel* at the end of April, he said that he would not express a view on whether he would stand in 1996. He had agreed with his team not to discuss the issue for the next two years. The decision would depend on whether reforms were irreversible by then; if they were he would be able to go with a quiet conscience. Speculation about Yeltsin's health had subsided as he took a higher public profile with successful visits to Spain and Germany and a series of domestic public appearances, including the launch of his memoirs *View from the Kremlin* (*Zapiski Prezidenta*) and the Victory Day ceremony on 9 May.

New Boost for Economic Reform

Yeltsin now began pressing the government to keep up to the mark in implementing the economic reform programme, modifying the earlier impression that he had distanced himself from the management of the economy. At a six-hour meeting with Chernomyrdin on 17 May he took the Prime Minister to task for slow implementation of economic reforms and the state of the economy. At a subsequent meeting together with the Prime Minister attended by directors of large enterprises, Yeltsin took the line that the civic accord agreement had achieved the necessary base of political stability for a new push ahead with economic reform measures. Later in the month he issued a package of decrees, including measures on reduced taxation and abolition of export quotas which *Izvestiya* summed up as "a powerful lurch by the Chernomyrdin government in the direction of the market".

At his press conference to mark Independence Day on 12 June, Yeltsin struck a note of renewed confidence. He announced a second package of economic reform decrees and described the past year as politically a breakthrough. Glossing over the October events he celebrated their results:

- the end of the Soviets and the beginning of real separation of powers;
- fruitful co-operation with the new parliament and a better

political climate following the civic accord agreement;
- erosion of support for the irreconcilable opposition and acceptance of civilized means of political struggle.

In a further move to reassert leadership (and undercut Zhirinovsky), Yeltsin issued a decree giving police wide powers to deal
with the "mafia". It was criticized by liberal politicians and press on
legal and human rights grounds and the Duma passed a resolution
on 22 June calling for it to be suspended. Yeltsin modified some of
its provisions but did not rescind it.

Shumeiko's Trial Balloon

By the end of June, Yeltsin felt able to tell a group of Western
businessmen that in recent months Russia had been politically more
calm than at any time since the reforms began. He believed that the
stability would continue though he expected some turmoil before
the presidential elections in 1996. It was now generally assumed
that Yeltsin would not only remain in power until the summer of
1996 but would run for a second term; and his recent active political
schedule was seen as the beginning of his election campaign. The
Chairman of the Federation Council, Shumeiko, had proposed a
referendum on extending the parliament's mandate by two years
with the simultaneous extension of Yeltsin's term. This produced
a non-committal reaction in Yeltsin's entourage and a generally
hostile reaction from all sides in parliament.

END OF THE FIRST SESSION OF THE NEW PARLIAMENT: JULY 1994

Duma

After the political amnesty crisis the Duma reverted to its previous
uneasy equilibrium; hard-line motions falling about fifty short of a
majority. An attempt on 23 March to table a no-confidence motion
in the government had failed. The Duma met on 11 May after a
short recess in new premises (the former Gosplan building opposite
Red Square) and in a more constructive frame of mind. Following
a non-confrontational budget debate, Chernomyrdin said that the
government was building constructive relations with the Duma;

while Rybkin said in an interview that after four months "mutual understanding and interaction" had been achieved between the Duma, the President, the government and the Federation Council. Rybkin, who had strongly supported the civic accord agreement, seemed committed to making the new political order work and was proving its linchpin. As a result he became increasingly unpopular with the opposition fractions. Zhirinovsky and Baburin had both called for his removal and he was receiving only grudging support from the Communists and his own fraction the Agrarians. A vote of confidence in the Speaker might now have produced the reverse of the pattern of the vote to elect him, with democratic fractions likely to support him.

At the end of its first six-month long session, one-quarter of its constitutional term, the Duma was given fairly good marks by most politicians and commentators, especially in the light of widespread expectations following the elections that it might prove worse than the former Supreme Soviet. In his concluding remarks on 22 July Rybkin gave plan fulfilment figures in traditional style: 223 laws had been considered of which 46 had been adopted. Despite predictions that the new parliament would destabilize the political situation, it had succeeded in "establishing business-like co-operation with all the power structures". Rybkin singled out as the main achievements of the Session the adoption of the budget (in record time for recent years), the law on the Constitutional Court and (in its second reading) the first part of the Civil Code (a fundamental piece of reformist legislation which had been described as an economic constitution). The Duma also adopted a law on electoral rights of citizens and made substantial progress with the revised criminal code and land code. Contrary to expectations it succeeded in adopting a number of constitutional laws, requiring the two-thirds majority at first thought to be unattainable.

The main criticism of the Duma was that it had been too ineffectual to achieve much either for good or ill. It had limited powers under the constitution to start with and the absence of a working majority either for the government or the opposition, meant that its decisions tended to be either laborious compromises or spur of the moment reactions. The balance of forces in the Duma remained fairly stable throughout the session; the hard opposition (Communists, Agrarians, LDP, Russia's Path) 192 and the democrats (Russia's Choice, Yabloko, 12 December and PRES) 154. There had been no significant drift across the floor in either direction despite a series of noisy defections (especially from the LDP). However, the opposition advantage in numbers had tended to be increased by their better attendance and higher work rate on the floor of the Duma where communists and "liberal democrats" took turns at the microphone with little response from the democrats. However, there had been no serious attempt to pass a vote of no confidence in the government or force a confrontation with the President since the political amnesty decree, although an LDP proposal shortly before the end of the session to debate a no confidence motion received 174 votes. The main opposition fractions seemed to have their eyes now on future elections and were prepared to play the parliamentary game in the belief that they could win under the existing rules. But the communists continued to make no secret of their readiness to leave the parliamentary path as soon as they caught sight of a "revolutionary situation" and the Reds / Browns generally, in and out of parliament, were still counting on a "social explosion", though now perhaps with declining conviction.

Federation Council

In April the Federation Council rejected Yeltsin's proposal to dismiss the Procurator-General Kazannik, who had resigned during the political amnesty crisis but later changed his mind and decided that he wanted to stay in office; the upper chamber subsequently refused Yeltsin's new candidate for the office, Ilyushenko and rejected three of Yeltsin's six nominees for vacancies on the Constitutional Court, including Mityukov, his preferred candidate for Chairman of the Court. The Federation Council also rejected the Civil Code, already passed by the Duma, because of its provisions on private property in land. The Federation Council authorized Shumeiko to sign the Civic Accord agreement and did not seek confrontation with Yeltsin. But its stance over the Procurator-General and other issues including agricultural reform, showed that it was becoming increasingly obstructive, contrary to earlier expectations that it would provide reliable support for the President.

POLITICAL PARTIES AND MOVEMENTS: SUMMER 1994

Zhirinovsky

The release of the ringleaders of the October insurrection led to some regrouping of the opposition but in the short term at least had a relatively limited impact on the political situation. Hard-line leaders of the Duma made some gestures of co-operation towards the amnestied rebels but on the whole preferred to keep their distance. Zhirinovsky was the principal loser from the political amnesty he had been instrumental in engineering. He now had to compete for publicity with the former opposition leaders who ungratefully ignored him. The Liberal Democratic Party had failed to build on its electoral success and was invisible in the March local elections. (They were marked by considerable voter apathy and parties at both ends of the spectrum fared badly.) Zhirinovsky's antics in the Duma and during his travels abroad (notably in Strasbourg) and the trickle of revelations about his past (including documentary evidence that his father was Jewish and his real name Edelshtein) did nothing to enhance his presidential prospects. Zhirinovsky also had trouble keeping discipline in his fraction; his repeated attempts to push through the "imperative mandate" (which would give him the right to expel deputies from his fraction who broke ranks) were defeated. However, later in the year Zhirinovsky began a systematic attempt to build up LDP branch organizations in the regions.

"Accord in the Name of Russia"

The inaugural conference took place at the end of May of Accord In The Name of Russia, the latest attempt to create a united opposition front. The Accord movement was an attempt to cross the Civic Alliance with the National Salvation Front and it gathered on one platform, Rutskoi, Zyuganov, Baburin, Prokhanov, Tsipko (Gorbachev fund) Petr Romanov (Federation Council), Lipitsky (Popular Party Free Russia). Zorkin was to have attended but was warned off such overt political activity by his fellow judges of the Constitutional Court. Rutskoi was aggressive and uncompromising; the new parliament was powerless and useless; there was no centrism in Russian politics and only two parties – the Party of National Betrayal and the National Opposition of Left and Right. The opposition's aim was to achieve power, by elections "if necessary", and restore order within the frontiers of the USSR. Zyuganov gave no hint that he accepted the new constitution and referred to the anti-democratic, illegal and even criminal regime; he called for the denunciation of the Belovezhsky agreement, the restoration of the Union and the abolition of the Presidency. There was little sign of unity among those on the platform. Rutskoi clearly regarded Russian Accord as a vehicle for his presidential ambitions but Baburin (who soon withdrew from the movement) and Zyuganov (opposing the institution of the Presidency itself), made it clear they would not endorse him. Rutskoi had simultaneously launched a new "social patriotic" movement, Derzhava (power) with distinctly neo-fascist overtones. His increasing identification with a hard-line national patriotic platform was alienating the Popular Party Free Russia of which he remained nominally leader. (The party changed its name in May to the Russian Social Democratic People's Party (RSDPP) and re-elected Rutskoi chairman.)

Gaidar's Party

At an inaugural Congress on 12–13 June a new liberal conservative party, "Russia's Democratic Choice", based on the Russia's Choice electoral bloc, was formed and elected Gaidar leader virtually unopposed. The party appeared to have limited horizons. Chubais was the only nationally known democrat to join Gaidar in the leadership; and its policy statements were designed to appeal primarily to the educated electorate especially intellectuals and entrepreneurs. However, five years after the first significant nationwide democratic association, the Inter Regional Group was formed during the first USSR Congress of People's Deputies, a serious mainstream democratic political party had at last been created. It developed a fairly solid network of regional branches and appeared to be soundly financed. Filatov and Kostikov from the Presidential Administration were present at the Congress, representing a benevolent but detached interest on the part of the President, who still showed no sign of setting up his own party or linking himself directly to the democratic movement. The Democratic Russia Movement which had diverged further from Russia's Choice since the electoral campaign did not support the new party.

Political Campaigning

During the long summer parliamentary recess, a number of leaders took the opportunity to campaign in the provinces and start organizing for eventual elections. Yeltsin set off for a working cruise down the Volga and Don on 11 August with stop-offs for meetings with local leaders in Nizhny Novgorod, Kazan and Rostov. He was followed down the river by Zhirinovsky in another boat who reaped maximum publicity for himself and caused considerable annoyance and embarrassment to local authorities en route.

Rutskoi was now campaigning energetically in the regions in an effort to build up his new right-wing political movement, Derzhava having given up pretending to be a centrist or a social democrat. As a consequence his former party, now the Russian Social Democratic People's Party, split and the Chairman, Lipitsky, dissociated himself from Rutskoi at a press conference on 5 August. Lipitsky proposed convening a congress to unite all social democratic forces and expressed scepticism about Rutskoi's national patriotic movement.

Varennikov

The acquittal of the 1991 putsch leader General Varennikov by the military collegium of the Supreme Court was loudly welcomed by the hard-line opposition press. (Varennikov had refused to accept the terms of the February Duma amnesty and insisted that the trial should continue.) However, the August coup was still divisive for the opposition. Rutskoi, Baburin, Khasbulatov and others, though they no longer advertised the fact, were leading opponents of the putsch. Both liberal commentators and members of the presidential entourage reacted with cynical indifference to the verdict (which was outrageous both from a legal and political standpoint) on the grounds that it damaged Gorbachev politically rather than Yeltsin. The third anniversary of the attempted coup was marked by public apathy.

DEBATE ON TIMING OF ELECTIONS: SEPTEMBER–OCTOBER 1994

When the political season reopened in September, Yeltsin for once had not lost the initiative during his absence on holiday. He seemed to control the political agenda and there appeared to be no immediate threat to the atmosphere of relative stability which had prevailed since Spring. The opposition leaders continued to predict economic disorder leading to political upheaval, but more from habit than conviction. The head of the Counter Intelligence Service, Stepashin, gave his professional opinion in an interview for *Interfax* that despite continuing socio-economic difficulties, expectations of Autumn political cataclysms were absolutely groundless.

The focus of political debate was the timing of elections. Shumeiko's trial balloon (a two-year postponement of presidential and parliamentary elections), though shot at from all sides, was still in the air. Rybkin, after at first giving qualified support to this idea, shifted ground and spoke of proposals reaching the Duma from all directions for simultaneous parliamentary and presidential elections in June 1996. The head of the Presidential Administration, Filatov, endorsed this idea.

The hard opposition rejected any delay in elections as unconstitutional, while Zyuganov continued to campaign for early presidential elections. The democrats had made no progress towards agreeing an alternative candidate and there was some pressure developing for Yeltsin to stand again. Gaidar stated that Yeltsin was the only candidate capable of uniting the democrats; Sobchak said that the democrats should unite around the "worthy figure" of Yeltsin, adding that if he were to refuse to stand for a second term this would cause serious damage to the democratic movement. The leaders of Democratic Russia indicated qualified approval for Yeltsin's candidacy while proposing that the President should conclude an agreement on policy in return for Democratic Russia's support. However, Yavlinsky continued to promote himself as the democratic alternative and Shakhrai, also harbouring presidential ambitions, was non-committal.

Row in Yeltsin's Entourage

The Autumn calm was disturbed by two minor incidents which revived the perennial question of Yeltsin's drinking habits and led to a serious row in his entourage. His over-exuberant demeanour while attending troop withdrawal ceremonies in Berlin at the end of August, provoked sharp criticism in which unusually the main liberal newspaper, *Izvestiya*, took the lead.[1] He appeared to have laid the ghost of this episode with an effective performance on his subsequent visits to the UK and USA but at a stopover in Shannon on 30 September on the way back, he failed to emerge from his aircraft for a scheduled meeting with the Irish Prime Minister. Four of the President's key aides, including Kostikov and his Foreign Affairs Adviser, Ryurikov, had been omitted from the US visit, reportedly in disgrace for signing a letter criticizing Yeltsin's behaviour in Berlin. But Kostikov lent substance to rumours of a power struggle in the President's entourage by speaking in a press statement of a battle to preserve the "President democrat" against those promoting opportunistic policies. The issue was power for the sake of democracy and reform or power at any price. In his statement Kostikov took the occasion to remind democrats who criticized Yeltsin that despite his faults he was "the shield and battering ram" of democracy, who could see them through to the year 2000 (i.e. the end of his second term). Press speculation suggested that some of the President's aides were pressing him to postpone elections at the price of a deal with the opposition, including the replacement of Chernomyrdin by Skokov and the formation of a coalition government to include communists and agrarians. This strategy would involve less risk for the President but above all a more secure future for his aides during an extended presidential term (and subsequently should his opponents eventually come to power).

Yeltsin sought to put such speculation to rest at a major press conference on 4 October to mark the first anniversary of the October insurrection. He stated that the timing of parliamentary elections was a matter for the parliament (not strictly true, according to the Constitution); but as for the presidential election he was opposed to any postponement. Asked about reports of anxiety about his commitment to reform and the democratic cause, Yeltsin declared that he would remain true to the democratic choice he had made in 1991. In the run up to the presidential election he intended to rally all the democratic parties and movements. There would be no change in the strategic course of reform "at least until the election of a new President in mid-1996". He added that he and Chernomyrdin had in fact agreed recently that reform would even be strengthened and "toughened" a little wherever they could be confident that the social consequences would not be unacceptable. Yeltsin had also earlier dismissed, in incautiously categorical terms, suggestions that Chernomyrdin might be replaced. During his visit to the United States he declared that Chernomyrdin would stay Prime Minister as long as he remained President.

NO-CONFIDENCE MOTION AND GOVERNMENT RESHUFFLE: OCTOBER 1994

Insurrection Anniversary

The hard-line opposition staged marches and rallies in central Moscow on 21 September and from 2 to 4 October to mark the anniversary of Yeltsin's decree on the dissolution of parliament and the subsequent violence of 3 to 4 October. The turnout was only a few thousand and it looked especially modest in the light of the hard-line leaders' predictions of a nation-wide campaign of mass unrest. There were widespread reports that the opposition was organizing to force through a no-confidence motion early in the new Duma session with Glaz'ev, head of the Duma's Economic Policy Committee (former Minister for Foreign Economic Relations turned hard opposition leader) the prime mover. Yeltsin adopted a conciliatory approach to the Federal Assembly, holding a high profile meeting with the Prime Minister and the Speakers of both Houses to discuss the legislative programme and practical steps to speed up the passage of important bills; and subsequently a further meeting with Rybkin and his deputies soon after the session began. At a press conference on the eve of the new Session he hinted that there might be one or two ministerial changes and Filatov did not rule out a communist joining the government.

"Black Tuesday", 11 October

In the early weeks of the Session, which opened on 5 October, the Duma flexed its muscles by, for the first time, overriding a presidential veto. The bill at issue, on procedure for adopting the 1995 budget, gave the Duma greater powers to control the Finance Ministry and included a provision that the government should resign if the Duma rejected the budget for a second time (after government amendments following an initial rejection). Yeltsin eventually signed the bill with a rider that the no-confidence clause was unconstitutional. The inveterate communist hard-liner Ilyukhin (head of the Security Committee) caused a scandal by denouncing Yeltsin's behaviour in Berlin and Shannon as a "national disgrace" and describing him as "an alcoholic incapable of running the country". Rybkin brushed aside the speech with the comment that "subversives come and go but our President continues his work".

The threat to the government appeared to have receded but the collapse of the rouble by 25 per cent on 11 October ("Black Tuesday") and the subsequent recriminations, seriously undermined confidence in the government's economic policies and competence. Yeltsin reacted sharply by dismissing the acting Finance Minister, Dubinin, and calling for the removal of the chairman of the Central Bank, Gerashchenko and he instructed the Security Council to investigate the causes of the crisis and identify those responsible. Chernomyrdin, who resumed his holiday when the crisis subsided, was the target of renewed rumours about his impending resignation, fuelled by his failure to return to Moscow in time for the arrival of HM The Queen on her State Visit. However, Yeltsin reaffirmed his "complete confidence" in the Prime Minister. (The rouble had by now stabilized at 3,000 roubles to the dollar, slightly below its level before the collapse.)

Failure of No-Confidence Motion

However, the financial crisis, compounded to some extent by the murder of a young investigative reporter, Kholodov, who had accused the Commander of the Western Group of Forces in Germany and the Defence Minister of corruption, stoked a hostile mood in the Duma. When Chernomyrdin presented his budget and medium-term economic programme on 27 October, the debate concluded with a no-confidence motion: 194 deputies voted against the government, 54 in favour and 55 abstained. The government thus survived fairly comfortably by 32 votes. In an attempt to influence the vote Yeltsin had announced the appointment of a member of the Agrarian fraction, Nazarchuk, as Minister for Agriculture. As a result a third of the Agrarians did not support the no-confidence motion; but two thirds of Russia's Choice deputies refused to vote for the government in protest at the appointment. The communists and liberal democrats voted solidly against the government; none of the democratic factions gave it solid support, Yavlinsky's fraction boycotting the vote. Travkin's Democratic Party of Russia fraction was split, Glaz'ev sponsoring the no-confidence motion while Travkin (appointed a Minister in May) supported the government.

The outcome of the vote left the relationship between the Duma and the government in considerable disrepair. Nearly 200 deputies had voted against the government, 200 had abstained or taken no part in the vote. The prevailing mood was one of dissatisfaction and alienation with the government and frustration with the Duma's own powerlessness. Yavlinsky during his intervention in the debate had spoken of "elements of a constitutional crisis" and said it was pointless to attack the government when the problem was the President and the constitution. Shakhrai (a deputy Prime Minister) also spoke of a constitutional crisis and called on the President to consult the parliament and government and form a new government with majority support in the Duma. He added that his fraction might propose the convening of a constitutional assembly in order to change the constitution. However, Gaidar praised Chernomyrdin's report on the economy as exactly right; it would have been priceless if delivered two years earlier but "better late than never".

Government Reshuffle

In the wake of the failed no-confidence motion there was a protracted and confusing government reshuffle in which the balance seemed to swing away from and back to the reformists on several occasions. The new Finance Minister, Panskov, had served for three years as USSR First Deputy Finance Minister; and three new Deputy Prime Ministers appeared to have few reformist credentials: Bolshakov, responsible for CIS affairs; Davydov, Foreign Economic Relations (in place of Shokhin who resigned over Panskov's appointment); and Polevanov, Governor of the Amur region who replaced Chubais as Deputy Prime Minister in charge of privatization. On the other hand, Chubais was promoted First Deputy Prime Minister in overall charge of economic policy; the liberal economist, Yasin, became Minister for the Economy; and the head of the Government Administration, Kvasov, a long time bugbear of the reformists (also a close associate of Chernomyrdin) was sacked. Yeltsin had earlier nominated Paramonova chairman of the CBR in place of Gerashchenko.

PRELUDE TO CHECHNYA CRISIS:
NOVEMBER–DECEMBER 1994

Background

Chechnya's declaration of independence on 1 November 1991 was followed by an abortive state of emergency declared by the Russian leadership and a failed mini-intervention. After that the republic was largely left to fester for the next two years, the Russian leadership imposing economic sanctions and political isolation and making occasional half-hearted attempts to negotiate. The events of October 1993 and the adoption of the new constitution, which seemed to put an end to separatist threats elsewhere in the Federation, put Chechnya back on the agenda in 1994. Yeltsin laid down the new policy in his State of the Nation address to parliament in February: democratic elections should be held in Chechnya followed by negotiations with legitimate new authorities on the division of powers, on the lines of the agreement with Tatarstan. This approach was endorsed by the Duma in March. In May, Chernomyrdin set up a government delegation led by Shakhrai to hold meetings with representatives of state authorities and political movements in Chechnya and work out a draft treaty. But no progress was achieved.

Several factors underlay the tougher and more activist line towards Chechnya: a desire to outflank Zhirinovsky's nationalist agenda; growing concern and frustration at the extent of the criminal activities organized and financed from Grozny, dramatically highlighted by a series of terrorist hijacking and hostage-taking incidents in the Russian North Caucasus (the latest of which occurred at the end of July); growing economic and political chaos in Chechnya with rival opposition groups controlling pockets of territory and mounting sporadic assaults on the capital and assassination attempts on Dudaev. (The situation was further complicated by the arrival in Chechnya of the former Speaker Khasbulatov to organize his own opposition force.)

Covert Action

When it became clear that a negotiated settlement with Dudaev was impossible (assuming it was ever seriously contemplated), Moscow attempted a strategy of removing him by proxy, building up with political, financial and military support the main opposition group in control of the republic's northern Nadterechny district. A Russian government statement on 29 July denounced the Dudaev regime as the major destabilizing factor in the North Caucasus and declared that the situation in Chechnya was out of control. This aggressive line was intended to galvanize the internal opposition and the Opposition Provisional Council duly declared themselves the Chechen government on 2 August. With covert Russian military help, opposition forces mounted several inconclusive offensives against Grozny before launching, on 26 November a serious assault spearheaded by 30 armoured vehicles (allegedly purchased in the CIS). The attack was a fiasco; 58 Russian "mercenaries" were taken prisoner and later revealed to be Russian servicemen recruited for the operation by the Federal Counter Intelligence Service.

Intervention: 11 December

Yeltsin responded to the débâcle by issuing a statement containing an ultimatum that he would declare a state of emergency in Chechnya unless all the parties laid down their weapons within 48 hours. The ultimatum was withdrawn as the deadline arrived when an "authentic" text of the statement was released on 1 December with no reference to it. But shortly afterwards Russia deployed army and Interior Ministry forces in strength around the borders of the republic and Russian aircraft began bombing raids on Grozny. On 11 December Russian forces entered Chechnya. Russia's military intervention in Chechnya on the eve of the anniversary of the adoption of the new constitution threatened to alienate, perhaps terminally, Yeltsin's remaining reformist allies and to push him further towards dependence on a narrowing circle of advisers advocating a tougher, nationalist line in domestic and foreign policy.

Note

1   *Izvestiya* of 3 September; front-page article by A. Plutnik.

15

Parliamentary and Presidential Elections, 1995–1996

POLITICAL SITUATION: 1995

The political situation remained volatile in 1995, a year dominated by uncertainties about Yeltsin's health, about whether he would seek to postpone the Duma elections scheduled for December 1995 and/or the presidential elections due in June 1996, and whether he would stand if the presidential elections were to go ahead. The President had returned to work in the Kremlin at the end of December 1994, following an operation on his nose earlier in the month but the recurrent doubts about his physical fitness resurfaced in February when he stumbled in public at the CIS Summit in Alma Ata. (Yeltsin has often found it difficult to remain upright on these particular occasions.) However, he was in good form for the annual State of the Nation address to both houses of parliament on 16 February, when he strongly reaffirmed in familiar terms his commitment to democracy and reform, and, rather more significantly, to the electoral timetable. He also attempted to reassure Democrats who had voiced fears that the intervention in Chechnya could be a prelude to the establishment of an authoritarian regime in Russia proper.

Disarray in Yeltsin's Camp

While Yeltsin's electoral intentions remained unclear, his authority was to some extent weakening; and the presidential camp appeared to be in some disarray as the struggle for influence in the Kremlin led to in-fighting and settling of accounts among members of his entourage and former political allies. The murder at the beginning of March of a prominent television personality, List'ev, provoked intense media and public indignation, which Yeltsin sought to deflect by calling for the dismissal of the Moscow procurator and police chief. His demand was resisted by the Mayor of Moscow, Luzhkov, hitherto a loyal supporter of the President but increasingly viewed as a potential political rival. Luzhkov threatened to resign and publicly attacked key figures in Yeltsin's entourage – Korzhakov, Chief Security Head of the Presidential Security Service, and Barsukov, Head of the Chief Security Directorate. In the event, Luzhkov stayed put and the affair subsided.

Yeltsin's intention had evidently been to cut Luzhkov down to size, not remove him. The real instigator of the row was probably Korzhakov, whose men in December 1994 had carried out an armed raid on the Moscow headquarters of the MOST financial group which has close links to Luzhkov. The head of the President's Administration, Filatov, publicly expressed concern at the excessive influence wielded by Korzhakov (Yeltsin's former bodyguard and his closest confidant), the first time such views had been voiced by a member of Yeltsin's team.

Yeltsin and the Parliament

In its second year, the outgoing Duma continued to be inconsistent and unpredictable, combining sporadic aggressive moves and hostile political resolutions with a more responsible approach, especially where economic issues were involved. In general, the tactics of the opposition in the Duma were focused more on securing electoral advantage in December than seeking serious confrontation with the administration in the meantime. The "Upper House", the Federation Council, ended a protracted deadlock in February by finally electing the remaining six members of the Constitutional Court, which was thereby enabled to function. The election of Tumanov as chairman and Morshchakova as his deputy gave the Court a fairly liberal orientation and (in contrast to its predecessor) it adopted a moderate and non-interventionist posture.

Chernomyrdin's government survived a no-confidence motion in July, principally because the opposition parties, having made their political gesture, did not want to precipitate a dissolution leading to early elections. Later in the same month, a motion to set up a commission to begin impeachment proceedings against the President achieved only 164 votes against the requisite majority of 226. The move was a blatant electoral ploy mounted by the Communists and it was doomed when Zhirinovsky withdrew the support of his 50 deputies, ostensibly because of Yeltsin's illness. The aftermath of the Budennovsk crisis in June (see below) gave Yeltsin the opportunity to defuse some of the opposition's head of steam by sacking the heads of the FSB (Stepashin), MVD (Yerin, a close crony of Yeltsin's) and the Nationalities Minister Yegorov (who later made a soft landing as Head of the President's Administration). But Yeltsin once again ignored the Duma's calls to give parliament a say in the appointment of the "power Ministers". As the end of its term drew near, the Duma reverted to its responsible mode, appointing the relatively reformist Sergei Dubinin as Chairman of the Central Bank (having earlier twice rejected Yeltsin's nomination of the Acting Chairman Paramonova), and adopting the 1996 budget (the 1995 budget had been passed by both houses only in March).

CHECHNYA: 1995

A Russian three-pronged armoured assault on Grozny at the turn of the year was a bloody fiasco. It failed to dislodge the Dudaev forces and resulted in heavy loss of life and armour. Grozny was not finally captured until the beginning of March, following prolonged and ferocious artillery and air bombardment and at the cost of heavy civilian and military casualties on both sides. By the end of March, Russian forces had taken all the key towns in the lowlands controlled by Dudaev after his withdrawal from Grozny. But fierce partisan fighting continued and the Russians continued to suffer heavy losses. With the main population centres occupied, Yeltsin was ready to negotiate, but not with Dudaev and only on the basis of recognition of Russian sovereignty and surrender of weapons by the Chechen fighters. For his part, Dudaev insisted on withdrawal of Russian forces before negotiation. On 26 April, Yeltsin declared a moratorium on military action in Chechnya in the hope of securing peace during the 50th anniversary VE celebrations in Moscow on 9 May, which were attended by major Western leaders. But Dudaev responded by launching an attack which coincided with Yeltsin's summit meeting with President Clinton on 10 May. Soon afterwards, Russian forces resumed their offensive.

Following a successful three-week campaign by Russian forces in southern Chechnya in June, Dudaev's forces retaliated by attacking the Russian town of Budennovsk, north of Chechnya. Hundreds of civilians were taken hostage and dozens killed in the fighting. Prime Minister Chernomyrdin negotiated a safe retreat for the Chechen rebels in return for the release of the hostages. It was to some extent a political success for the Prime Minister but the well-televised episode was a humiliation for the Russian military and political leadership as a whole.

The Budennovsk incident was followed by negotiations and a cease-fire agreement on 30 July, which provided for withdrawal of Federal troops and the disarming of Chechen fighters. The agreement was not implemented but fighting was at a relatively low level until Chechen forces launched an attack on the town of Gudermes shortly before the December parliamentary elections, only to be driven out a week later after heavy fighting. As a result of the elections in Chechnya, organized by the Russians and generally regarded as fraudulent, Doku Zavgaev, the former Chechnya CPSU leader, was elected Head of the Republic and confirmed as leader of the pro-Moscow administration.

Yeltsin's Health

The Chechen war was a major factor in the progressive erosion of Yeltsin's political standing. Another factor was the perennial issue of the state of his health. Yeltsin was hospitalized on 11 July for twelve days with heart problems. On 26 October, following his return from a visit to France and the USA, he suffered a further heart attack, remaining in hospital for a month and spending another month convalescing before returning to work in the Kremlin only at the end of December (as he had done a year before). It was by now widely assumed that Yeltsin could not be a credible presidential candidate in 1996, if he survived that long.

The Chechen war and Yeltsin's physical decline created an inauspicious climate for the government and the democratic parties in the run up to the Duma elections scheduled for 17 December. There had been significant improvement in the economic situation in 1995: inflation was down to 4–5 per cent monthly in the second half of the year, compared to over 17 per cent in January; the rouble was stabilised and the fall in production reduced to 4 per cent compared to 1994. But these encouraging statistics failed to generate a feel-good factor among the population and the Communist and Nationalist opposition was increasingly confident.

DUMA ELECTIONS: DECEMBER 1995

The Yeltsin administration's electoral strategy was unveiled at the end of April, when it was announced that Prime Minister Chernomyrdin would lead an electoral bloc called Russia, Our Home, (Nash Dom Rossiya – NDR), while the Duma Speaker, Rybkin, would lead a centre-left "loyal opposition" bloc. The NDR was generally supported by regional leaders, who, it was evidently believed, would be able to deliver the local vote in traditional style. Rybkin was expected to draw support from moderate Communists and a number of small social democratic parties. The two blocs would thus occupy most of the centre ground and marginalize the Reds/Browns and the democrats. At the same time, Yeltsin tried to push through an amendment to the electoral law to increase the number of seats to be filled through constituency elections to 300, leaving 150 to be filled via party lists on the PR system, a 2:1 ratio as against the 50:50 division which had operated in the 1993 Duma elections. (It was believed in the presidential camp that the party list system had favoured Zhirinovsky in the 1993 elections, when he won very few constituency seats, and would benefit the Communists in 1995). In the event, the Duma majority repeatedly rejected the proposed change. The Federation Council (which was in favour of the 2:1 ratio) eventually adopted a compromise electoral law in which the 50:50 division was retained but the proportion of regional candidates on party lists increased.

As the election campaign got underway, it became clear that Yeltsin's two-bloc ploy had not worked. The NDR stood for stability and continuity, but the status quo had no appeal for a largely discontented population. The image of the "party in power" damaged the NDR and Chernomyrdin as it had damaged Russia's Choice and Gaidar in 1993 and, like Russia's Choice, the NDR found itself under attack from all sides. Many regional leaders back-pedalled from their earlier overt support; in the campaign itself, a number of NDR candidates even ran as independents to improve their chances. As for Rybkin, although he eventually cobbled together a bloc of some 50 small parties and organizations, the Rybkin bloc as a political force never left the ground. Among the parties/blocs officially registered for the party list contest, the front-runner by some distance was the CPRF (Zyuganov) with the LDPR (Zhirinovsky), the NDR, the Agrarians and several democratic parties (which once again and inevitably had failed to reach agreement among themselves) among the other contenders. Apart from the NDR, the only significant new blocs formed since the 1993 elections were: the Congress of Russian Communities (KRO), headed by Yury Skokov and Alexander Lebed, the charismatic and insubordinate General who resigned from the army in May in order to pursue a political career; Forward, Russia!, led by Boris Fedorov; and Derzhava, led by former Vice-President Rutskoi. In all, 43 parties/blocs were registered, most of which, including, for example, the Beer Lovers and the Cossacks, had no serious hope of surmounting the 5 per cent barrier for representation in the Duma.[1]

Duma Election Results

In the poll on 17 December, the turnout was significantly higher than in 1993 at 64.3 per cent. Only four blocs passed the 5 per cent threshold: the CPRF with 22.3 per cent (15.1 million votes), the LDPR 11.18 per cent (7.5 million), NDR 10.13 per cent (6.7 million) and Yabloko 6.89 per cent (4.7 million). Among the parties which failed to reach the 5 per cent were Women of Russia with 4.6 per cent, Labour Russia – Communists for the USSR (Anpilov) 4.53 per cent, the Congress of Russian Communities 4.3 per cent, Russia's Democratic Choice (Gaidar) 3.9 per cent, and the Agrarians 3.78 per cent. On the basis of their percentage of the votes in the party list contest, the Communists received 99 seats in the Duma, the LDPR 50, NDR 45 and Yabloko 31. Taking account of the results of the constituency elections, the Communist faction in the Duma numbered 149, the NDR had 55, the LDP 51, Yabloko 46, the Agrarians 35 and Power to the People (Vlast Narodu) a Red/Brown party headed by Nikolai Ryzhkov, the former Soviet Prime Minister, and Sergei Baburin, 35. The Communists, together with their allies, were now within easy reach of a simple majority of 226 in the Duma, although not a "constitutional" majority of two-thirds, ie 300 votes. The Reds and Browns, should they vote together, could muster about 270 votes.

The result was a serious set-back for Yeltsin, the government, the democratic parties and the cause of reform. The total vote for the Red/Brown parties had gone up from 43 per cent in 1993 to 52 per cent in 1995, which did not augur well for the presidential elections due six months later. One consolation was that Zhirinovsky's vote had been halved, but his loss was almost exactly matched by the Communists' gain. (Indeed, together with Anpilov's Stalinist party, the Communists achieved some 27 per cent of the vote.)

Aftermath of the Duma Elections, January 1996

Yeltsin reacted in characteristic fashion to the Communist success in the parliamentary elections. In the face of the unfavourable electoral wind, he dropped ballast in the shape of some of the more liberal and reformist among his close colleagues. He was not obliged by the constitution to nominate a new prime minister following the elections and he did not do so. (He had said when voting on 17 December that he would retain Chernomyrdin as Prime Minister and not retreat from reform whatever the results.) But he made a series of changes in his administration in January 1996 which seemed designed to alter its complexion in line with the conservative mood of the electorate and which deepened the gloom of liberal and democratic circles. Foreign Minister Kozyrev, who had been under constant attack for four years from Communists and nationalists for his pro-Western orientation, departed at last to be replaced by Primakov, the Head of the Foreign Intelligence Service. The Head of the President's Administration, Filatov, was replaced by Nikolai Yegorov, the hard-line former Minister for Nationalities (in which capacity he had presided over the débâcle in Chechnya in 1994–95); and, most significantly of all, the last of the leading economic reformers in his Cabinet, the Deputy Prime Minister Chubais was dismissed in favour of Kadannikov, an industrialist with no strong reformist credentials. (Kadannikov had been among the candidates for Prime Minister nominated by Yeltsin in December 1992.)

The dismay of the democrats was compounded by another humiliating and bloody hostage-taking incident at Pervomaiskoe on the border of Daghestan and Chechnya, in which 150 people were killed during an ill-judged assault by Russians troops. This episode prompted what was billed as the "final and irrevocable" break between Gaidar and the President, and he and a group of other prominent democrats resigned from the Presidential Advisory Council; Sergei Kovalev resigned as Chairman of the President's Human Rights Commission. However, it was also characteristic of Yeltsin that his ominous reshuffle proved to be more in the nature of a tactical retreat aimed at improving his prospects for re-election than a serious change of direction.

PRESIDENTIAL ELECTIONS: JUNE–JULY 1996

On 15 February (shortly after his 65 birthday), during a visit to his hometown of Yekaterinburg, Yeltsin announced that he would stand in the presidential elections. At the beginning of the campaign, his prospects seemed poor. He had alienated his only solid, if small, democratic constituency and he was trailing in the opinion polls well behind Zyuganov and Yavlinsky. One poll, published by the All Russian Centre for Public Opinion (VTSIOM), suggested that in a second round run-off Zyuganov would receive 33 per cent of the votes compared to 19 per cent for Yeltsin. Yeltsin, however, began to position himself for the elections, adopting populist economic policies, including the payment of arrears of pensions and state employee wages, which put increasing strain on the budget and on Russia's commitments to the IMF; and by tightening his grip on the media. In February, on the same day that he announced that he would run for re-election, he sacked Oleg Poptsov, the director of the Russian television channel, because of its critical coverage of Chechnya. In March, Malashenko, head of the independent NTV channel, which had frequently been critical of Yeltsin, accepted the position of media adviser in the president's campaign team.

The liberal media was, however, inclined to support Yeltsin despite rather than because of official pressure and interference. They had grave doubts about Yeltsin's claim to be the guarantor of freedom of the press and media, but no doubts at all that Zyuganov would suppress it.

The candidacy of Zyuganov was duly endorsed by a CPRF conference in Moscow on a platform which included stopping the war in Chechnya, restoring state ownership of energy, transport and basic industries and restoring a "voluntary" new union of former Soviet Republics. Zyuganov had the advantage of the support of the only well-organized nation-wide political party and a solid and loyal electorate in the countryside and among the elderly. His problem was to broaden the base of his support. He attempted to solve it by standing officially as the candidate not of the Communist Party but of the "Popular and Patriotic Forces" and mounting a charm offensive at home and abroad (notably at the World Economic Forum at Davos in early February) to convince people that he was at heart a social democrat. Yeltsin by contrast had only a very small loyal political constituency left, but he did have the possibility of drawing on broad anti-Communist support, including from some nationalists and from the democrats who were thoroughly disillusioned but in the end had nowhere else to turn. He also had the advantage of an ex-officio high public profile magnified by the growing support of the media. His energetic campaigning was to allay for the moment concerns about his health.

Doubts were still being aired as to whether the elections would in fact go ahead and, following the Duma resolution on 15 March denouncing the Belovezhskaya Pushcha Agreement of December 1991 (which effectively abolished the USSR), there were persistent reports that draft decrees on a state of emergency had been prepared. The new Duma's provocative resolution was not typical of its generally restrained posture during the first six months of its term. The dominant CPRF fraction, which had secured the post of Speaker (Seleznev) and the chairs of 9 of the 28 Duma committees for Communist deputies, was mainly focused on the presidential elections and not anxious to rock the boat. Fears that the elections might still be aborted were raised again in early May when Korzhakov told journalists that he favoured postponement for the sake of stability. His remarks were disavowed by Yeltsin and Korzhakov was told publicly not to meddle. Suspicions remained that he had been flying a kite. There was also alarmed speculation in some quarters about the implications of Yeltsin's refusal to sign a Duma bill on the transfer of power to a newly-elected president.

Election Campaign

In early May, the CEC officially registered 11 candidates of the 17 who had submitted lists containing the requisite one million signatures in their support. There were five more or less serious contenders: Yeltsin, Zyuganov, Zhirinovsky, Yavlinsky and Lebed. The also-rans included Svyatoslav Fedorov, the businessman/eye surgeon, and Gorbachev. By April–May, opinion polls were showing that Yeltsin had gained ground and was only a few percentage points behind Zyuganov with Yavlinsky well back in third place (although a VTSIOM poll also suggested that only 29 per cent of the electorate trusted Yeltsin against 63 per cent who distrusted him). Yavlinsky, Lebed and Fedorov (who in March had jointly issued a statement condemning the Duma's Belovezhsky resolution) discussed the possibility of combining to form a "third force", but negotiations predictably foundered over the reluctance of any of them to concede primacy to one of the others. Lebed, now freed from the liability of his implausible alliance with Skokov, was coming to be seen as the dark horse of the contest. A deal between Yavlinsky and Yeltsin was also mooted but again predictably came to nothing in face of Yavlinsky's exorbitant demands.

Chechnya

The war in Chechnya continued to be a serious electoral burden for Yeltsin. But, despite continuing heavy Russian losses, some of the heat was taken out of the issue by Yeltsin's plan for a comprehensive peace settlement announced on 31 March, although the cessation of hostilities it called for did not materialize, and by Dudaev's death on 22 or 23 April, apparently as a result of a Russian rocket attack. His successor, Yandarbiev, initially at least, took an even more intransigent line and promised revenge for Dudaev's death. However, in May he came to Moscow for negotiations and on 27 May an agreement providing for a cease-fire as from 1 June was signed by Yandarbiev and Chernomyrdin in the presence of Yeltsin, who on the following day paid a brief visit to Chechnya.

First Round, 16 June 1996

Under the electoral rules, each candidate was allocated a total of 90 minutes on the main television channels beginning on 14 May in an order determined by lot. Zyuganov drew the longest straw and spoke last on 14 June. However, the election broadcasts by the other candidates had relatively little impact in view of the blanket coverage of Yeltsin's official and electoral activities.

In the first round of the elections on 16 June with a turn-out of 69.8 per cent, Yeltsin received 35 per cent, Zyuganov 32 per cent,

Lebed 14.5 per cent, Yavlinsky 7.5 per cent and Zhirinovsky 6 per cent. All other candidates (including Gorbachev) received less than 1 per cent. As predicted, Yeltsin's support was strong in large towns and in the north; Zyuganov did well in the country-side and in the south. Yeltsin's margin of victory was less than had been predicted towards the end of the campaign and he and his team by no means felt assured of victory in the second round, especially in the event of a low turnout.

Turbulent Interval

The interval between the two rounds was a period of political turbulence, rapid manoeuvring and some confusion. Yeltsin moved quickly to do a deal with the third placed candidate, Lebed (a deal had evidently been discussed earlier, if not prearranged). Lebed was appointed National Security Adviser in place of Baturin and Secretary of the Security Council in place of Lobov, whose role as Presidential Plenipotentiary for Chechnya he also inherited. Yeltsin announced that his and Lebed's electoral programmes would be "integrated". Doubtless as a result of the deal, Defence Minister Grachev was dismissed. On 20 June, Yeltsin sacked the Head of the Presidential Security Service Korzhakov, the Head of the Federal Security Service, Barsukov, and the First Deputy Prime Minister Soskovets, in the wake of an extraordinary incident in which two members of the presidential campaign team were arrested by Korzhakov's men for allegedly trying to smuggle hard currency out of the White House. But Yeltsin later hinted that more had been at stake than that incident alone: in his televised announcement of the sackings he said the three had "taken more than they had given" for some time now. (It was alleged by Chubais at a press conference that the arrests were in some way linked to a conspiracy to abort the second round of the elections.) The removal of Korzhakov, and Barsukov in particular, had earlier figured as one of the conditions for a political alliance between Yavlinsky and Yeltsin and it could have been part of the deal when Lebed joined the administration. It is also possible that Korzhakov had merely exceeded his authority once too often and finally exhausted Yeltsin's patience. The removal of these three was welcome to liberal political circles but the manner of their departure aroused concerns once more that the administration was riven by in-fighting and not fully under control. A series of extravagant and naive public statements by Lebed, who declared that he had prevented an army coup and revealed ambitions to become vice-president, aggravated the all-too-familiar atmosphere of confusion and disarray. It was further compounded by Yeltsin's disappearance from public view in the week prior to the second round because of what was officially said to be a cold but was generally assumed to be something worse.

He was well enough, however, to deliver a somewhat stilted final election appeal and to vote on 3 July, but again, as in the December parliamentary elections, he voted at the Barvikha sanatorium instead of central Moscow where journalists were awaiting him.

Second Round, 3 July 1996

The second round had been brought forward to 3 July, a Wednesday, at the instigation of the presidential team to try to maximize the turnout (by the following Sunday many voters might have left for their holidays or been at their dachas). The turnout in the event was down only by 2 per cent compared to the first round and Yeltsin secured a relatively comfortable victory with 53.8 per cent against 40.3 per cent for Zyuganov.

The result did not reflect much positive enthusiasm for Yeltsin or reform policies. A majority of the electorate probably regarded him as the lesser of two evils and many democrats voted for him with a heavy heart. Many uncertainties and anxieties remain. The democratic system rests largely on the fragile shoulders of an ailing President who must deal with a parliament still dominated by the Communists and their hard-line allies. There is no democratic successor to Yeltsin, or strong democratic political party clearly in view. But the fact that elections took place in December 1995 and June/July 1996 was in itself a landmark in Russia's transition to democracy. And the fact that the electorate when faced with a clear choice preferred Yeltsin's problematic democracy to a return to the past may mark a very significant watershed.

Note

1   The requirement for official registration was 200,000 signatures, which proved very easy to obtain commercially if popular support was lacking.

Chronology 1: USSR 1989–1991

1989

25 April	Central Committee Plenum (purge of old guard).
25 May–	**First Congress of USSR People's Deputies.**
9 June	
19 Sept.	Central Committee Plenum on nationalities question.
9 Nov.	Berlin wall opened.
9 Dec.	Central Committee Plenum.
20 Dec.	Lithuanian Communist Party leaves CPSU.
20–25 Dec.	Second Congress of USSR People's Deputies. Death of Sakharov.
25 Dec.	Ceausescu executed.
25–26 Dec.	Central Committee Plenum on Lithuania.
30 Dec.	Havel elected President of Czechoslovakia.

1990

10–14 Jan.	Gorbachev on visit to Lithuania.
15 Jan.	Stasi headquarters in Berlin occupied and ransacked.
20–21 Jan.	All-Union conference of Party reformists establishes Democratic Platform in CPSU.
5–7 Feb.	Central Committee Plenum on Platform for Party Congress and Lithuania. Gorbachev's proposal for USSR Presidency approved.
25 Feb.	Radical demonstration in Moscow of 200,000–300,000 people despite heavy policing.
27 Feb.	USSR Supreme Soviet session debates Presidency.
3 March	*Pravda* publishes text of Democratic Platform for Twenty-eighth Congress.
4 March	Elections in RSFSR, Ukraine and Belorussia.
11 March	Lithuania declares independence.
11–14 &	Central Committee Plenum: approves revision of Article 6.
16 March	of Constitution; nominates Gorbachev for President; decides procedure for electing Congress delegates; approves holding of Russian Party Conference.
12–15 March	**Third Extraordinary Congress of USSR People's Deputies. Gorbachev elected President** by Congress with 59.2 per cent.
18 March	Second round of RSFSR elections.

10 April	Central Committee "Open Letter" attacks Democratic Platform.
21–22 April	Hard-line conservatives set up "Russian CP in CPSU" at meeting in Leningrad.
1 May	Mayday parade. Gorbachev jeered by radicals at end of parade.
16 May– 22 June	**First Congress of People's Deputies of RSFSR.**
29 May	**Yeltsin elected chairman of RSFSR Supreme Soviet.**
May	Yeltsin injured in plane crash in Spain.
12 June	RSFSR Congress adopts **Declaration on State Sovereignty of RSFSR** by 907 votes to 13.
16–17 June	Second all Union conference of Democratic Platform in CPSU.
19 June	Russian Party Conference transforms itself into Congress and elects Polozkov First Secretary.
2–13 July	**Twenty-eighth CPSU Congress.** Gorbachev re-elected General Secretary by Congress. Yeltsin resigns from Party.
16 July	Declaration of sovereignty by Ukraine.
July	Riots in Osh, Kirgizia.
27 July	Belorussia adopts declaration on state sovereignty.
1 Aug.	Law on press enters into force.
2 Aug.	Gorbachev and Yeltsin sign document on joint economic programme.
Aug.	Strikes and protests over tobacco shortage in Russian provinces. Tatar Autonomous Republic declares state sovereignty.
4–6 Sept.	Second part of RCP Founding Congress.
16 Sept.	Demonstration organized by Moscow Soviet demands resignation of Ryzhkov government. Rumours of military movements and plans for coup.
8–9 Oct.	Central Committee Plenum on economy.
9 Oct.	USSR Supreme Soviet adopts law on political organizations.
Oct.	Gorbachev abandons support for 500 Days Programme at USSR Supreme Soviet session.
16 Oct.	Yeltsin responds sharply at Russian Supreme Soviet session to Gorbachev's rejection of 500 Days.
11 Nov.	Meeting between Gorbachev and Yeltsin on Union Treaty, etc.
13 Nov.	Gorbachev addresses military deputies of USSR Supreme Soviet.
14 Nov.	Kravchenko appointed head of Gostelradio.
16 Nov.	Poorly received speech by Gorbachev to USSR Supreme Soviet.
17 Nov.	Second speech by Gorbachev proposes constitutional changes: Cabinet subordinated to President; National Security Council, etc.
27 Nov.	Instruction issued by Minister of Defence Yazov, to military units to use weapons if attacked.

3 Dec.	Bakatin dismissed as Minister for Internal Affairs. Replaced by Pugo with Gromov as First Deputy.
12 Dec.	Kryuchkov, head of KGB, gives hard-line television interview.
17–25 Dec.	**Fourth Congress of People's Deputies.** Shevardnadze resigns as Foreign Minister, warning of impending dictatorship. Yanaev elected Vice-President. PM Ryzhkov suffers heart attack.
22 Dec.	Kryuchkov speech in USSR Supreme Soviet uses cold war language about West and criticizes market economy.
Dec.	RSFSR Supreme Soviet decides to reduce five-fold Russia's contribution to Union budget.

1991

2 Jan.	OMON take-over of Communist Party printing works in Riga.
13 Jan.	**Attack on Vilnius television station.**
14 Jan.	V. Pavlov appointed Prime Minister in place of Ryzhkov.
20 Jan.	Omon attack on Latvian MVD building in Riga.
22 Jan.	Decree on monetary exchange (R50 and R100 notes).
6 Feb.	Hard-line *Pravda* article attacks Democrats.
Feb.	Pavlov alleges Soviet and Western banks plotted to destabilize Soviet economy.
19 Feb.	Yeltsin in television interview calls for Gorbachev's resignation.
21 Feb.	Leading RSFSR Supreme Soviet officials call for Extraordinary Congress to remove Yeltsin.
23 Feb.	Hard-line demonstration in Moscow on Army Day.
26–28 Feb.	Gorbachev during visit to Belorussia attacks Democrats but advocates "centrism".
9 March	Yeltsin calls for strong opposition movement and "declaration of war" on Soviet leadership.
10 March	Huge demonstration in Moscow in support of Yeltsin.
17 March	**All-Union referendum on preservation of the Union.** Additional RSFSR question on Russian presidency.
28 March	Pro-Yeltsin demonstration in Moscow of 150,000 people. 50,000 militia and MVD troops deployed.
29 March–3 April	**Third RSFSR Congress of People's Deputies.** Yeltsin given emergency powers to reform Russian economy by decree. Date for presidential elections fixed for April. Workers strike in Minsk over higher food prices.
9 April	Georgian declaration of independence. Gorbachev presents economic anti-crisis programme to Federation Council.
23 April	Meeting at Novo-Ogarevo of Gorbachev and nine Republic leaders discuss measures to deal with economic and political crisis.
25 April	Central Committee Plenum. Gorbachev threatens to resign in face of right-wing attack which collapses.
24 May	Gorbachev chairs 8-hour meeting of Republic leaders to discuss Union Treaty.

21–25 May	**Fourth RSFSR Congress**. Draft laws on Presidency adopted.
3 June	Further 9 + 1 talks on draft Union Treaty.
11 June	Gorbachev delivers Nobel Prize lecture in Oslo.
12 June	**Yeltsin elected President of RSFSR**. Popov and Sobchak elected Mayors of Moscow and Leningrad.
17 June	Prime Minister Pavlov requests extra powers during USSR Supreme Soviet session. Hard-line speeches by Pugo, Kryuchkov and Yazov at subsequent closed session.
21 June	Tough speech by Gorbachev at Supreme Soviet in response to hard-line criticism.
25 June	Central Committee Plenum adopts Platform for Extraordinary CPSU Congress.
1 July	Movement for Democratic Reform founded by Shevardnadze, Yakovlev, Sobchak, Popov et al.
3 July	9 + 1 meeting at Novo-Ogarevo to discuss Union Treaty.
5 July	Gorbachev meets Chancellor Kohl near Kiev. **Fifth Congress of RSFSR People's Deputies (first part)**. Khasbulatov proposed but not approved as Chairman of Supreme Soviet.
8 July	9 + 1 meeting to agree common policy on London Economic Summit.
17 July	G7 meeting in London.
20 July	Yeltsin decree on removing Party organizations from RSFR structures.
23 July	**Sovetskaya Rossiya** publishes **"A Word To The People"** by 12 prominent right-wing personalities attacking reforms and calling for a new patriotic movement.
25–26 July	Central Committee Plenum approves Gorbachev's draft Party programme for publication.
29 July	Meeting at Novo-Ogarevo between Gorbachev, Yeltsin and Nazarbaev.
30 July	President Bush in Moscow for talks with Gorbachev.
1 Aug.	Chancellor of Exchequer, Lamont, in Moscow for talks with Gorbachev on follow-up to G7.
17 Aug.	Kryuchkov convenes meeting with Yazov, Yanaev, Pavlov joined by Lukyanov to plan coup.
18 Aug.	Delegation of plotters arrives in Foros: Baklanov, Varennikov, Shenin and Boldin. Gorbachev's communications cut off.
19–21 Aug.	Attempted coup.
19 Aug.	Statement issued by State Committee for State of Emergency; Yanaev "Acting President"; armoured troops moved into central Moscow; demonstration at White House; Yeltsin denounces coup and appeals to citizens of Russia; tank unit of Taman division defects to Yeltsin; press conference by 5 members of SCSE.
20 Aug.	Demonstrations in Moscow and Leningrad; growing crowd defends barricades outside White House; three demonstrators killed in late night clash with APCs on Ring Road near White House.

21 Aug.	Emergency session of Russian parliament in White House; Kryuchkov asks Yeltsin to go with him to Foros; Yazov orders troops out of Moscow; Kryuchkov, Yazov, Baklanov, Tizyakov fly to Foros (Lukyanov, Ivashko separately). Russian delegation led by Rutskoi and Silaev brings Gorbachev back from Crimea to Moscow. Kryuchkov and Yazov arrested. Pugo commits suicide.
22 Aug.	Statue of Dzerzhinsky in front of KGB headquarters dismantled; demonstrators attack CPSU Central Committee headquarters.
23 Aug.	Gorbachev addresses RSFSR Supreme Soviet session. Yeltsin decree suspends CPSU in Russia.
24 Aug.	**Gorbachev resigns as Party General Secretary** and calls for dissolution of CPSU Central Committee. Suicide of Akhromeev. Ukraine declares Independence.
25 Aug.	Belorussia declares Independence.
26 Aug.	Gorbachev addresses emergency session of USSR Supreme Soviet; Lukyanov removed as Chairman. Yeltsin press statement raises issue of republic borders.
27 Aug.	Moldova declares Independence.
29 Aug.	USSR Supreme Soviet suspends CPSU; dissolves itself; Russian / Ukrainian agreement on borders signed.
30 Aug.	Azerbaijan declares Independence.
2–5 Sept.	**Extraordinary session of USSR Congress of People's Deputies**: creates Council of State (Gorbachev plus republic leaders); endorses plans for new Union Treaty.
6 Sept.	State Council recognizes independence of Estonia, Latvia and Lithuania. **Coup in Chechnya; Dudaev comes to power**. Leningrad officialy renamed St Petersburg.
9 Sept.	Tajikistan declares Independence.
10 Sept.	Baltic Republics join CSCE.
23 Sept.	Armenia declares Independence.
2 Oct.	RSFSR State Council declares Russia should be legal successor to USSR.
10 Oct.	Yeltsin returns from three-week holiday in Sochi.
11 Oct.	Soviet USSR KGB dismantled.
15 Oct.	Yeltsin speaks of "completing destruction of Centre".
21 Oct.	New USSR Supreme Soviet meets with representatives from only 7 Republics.
27 Oct.	Turkmenistan declares Independence.
28 Oct.–	Second part of **Fifth Russian Congress of People's Deputies**:
5 Nov.	Khasbulatov confirmed as Chairman of Supreme Soviet; Yeltsin speech calls for rapid economic reform; Yeltsin granted additional powers to appoint Ministers and implement economic reform by decree; Congress rejects proposals to end moratorium on sale and purchase of land.
4 Nov.	State Council reduces USSR MFA by one-third; MVD and MOD and single army to remain.
6 Nov.	Yeltsin decree ends activity of CPSU and RCP on Russian

	territory. Yeltsin becomes head of government for duration of reforms.
7 Nov.	Yeltsin decree imposing state of emergency in Chechnya revoked by RSFSR Supreme Soviet.
8 Nov.	Yeltsin appoints Burbulis First Deputy PM and Gaidar and Shokhin Deputy Prime Ministers.
? Nov.	Bakatin appointed head of Inter-republican Security Service; Primakov, Director of Central Intelligence Service.
14 Nov.	State Council Meeting at Novo-Ogarevo; seven republics agree to support new draft Treaty for Union of Sovereign States (SSG).
15 Nov.	**"Government of Reforms" created**; Yeltsin issues decrees accelerating transition to market economy in Russia.
25 Nov.	At State Council Meeting at Novo-Ogarevo republic leaders, instead of initialling draft Union Treaty as expected, remit text to republic supreme soviets.
1 Dec.	**Ukrainian referendum**; 90 per cent vote for Independence. Kravchuk elected President of Ukraine. Nazarbaev elected President of Kazakhstan (98.9 per cent) (98.8 per cent).
3 Dec.	Yeltsin Decree on "Measures to Liberalize Prices".
7–8 Dec.	Leaders of Russia, Ukraine and Belorussia meet at **Belovezhskaya Pushcha** in Belorussia and at Minsk, and sign agreement denouncing Union Treaty of 1922 and creating Commonwealth of Independence States (CIS).
10 Dec.	Parliaments of Ukraine and Belorussia ratify, with amendments, CIS agreement.
12 Dec.	Russian Parliament denounces 1922 Union Treaty and approves CIS agreement. Presidents of Kazakhstan and four Central Asian Republics meet in Alma Ata and agree to join CIS.
19 Dec.	Yeltsin decree merging Ministries of Interior and Security (later annulled by Constitutional Supervision Committee).
21 Dec.	Leaders of all FSU Republics bar Georgia and Baltic States sign **Alma Ata Declaration on founding the CIS**.
25 Dec.	RSFSR renamed Russian Federation. Gorbachev resigns as President of USSR.
29 Dec.	Azerbaijan votes in favour of Independence.
30 Dec.	Meeting of CIS Leaders in Minsk.
31 Dec.	**Official end of USSR.**

Chronology 2: Russia 1992–1996

1992

2 Jan.   **Radical economic reform** begins with liberalization of prices.

10 Jan.   Russian Government bans export of some consumer goods and foodstuffs.

13 Jan.   Khasbulatov calls for replacement of "incompetent" Government.

18 Jan.   Barannikov appointed Head of Security Ministry.

25 Jan.   Yeltsin states Russian nuclear missiles no longer targeted on USA.

30 Jan.   Yeltsin pays short working visit to UK en-route to New York for Security Council Summit.

6 Feb.   Khasbulatov claims hyper-inflation has begun.

9 Feb.   Hard-line demonstration on Manege Square.

23 Feb.   Pro-Communist march and demonstration on Army Day. Clashes with militia.

25 Feb.   Yeltsin decree makes Ministry of Security, Internal Affairs, Foreign Affairs, Defence and Justice responsible to President.

1 March   **Gaidar appointed First Deputy Prime Minister** with responsibility for reform.

13 March   18 of 20 republics initial Federation Treaty in Moscow.

17 March   Hard-line opposition demonstration on anniversary of referendum on Union.

21 March   Vote for sovereignty / independence in Tatarstan (64 per cent).

30 March   Shakhrai resigns as Deputy Prime Minister.

31 March   Federation Treaty adopted by Congress.

5 April   Visit by Vice-President Rutskoi to Transdniestria.

6–21 April   **6th Congress of People's Deputies**.

7 April   Report to Congress by Yeltsin.

9 April   Yeltsin decree on transfer to Russia of Black Sea Fleet.

29 April   IMF votes to admit Russia and 13 other FSU republics.

7 May   Vodka price freed. State alcohol monopoly abolished. Russia applies for full membership of Council of Europe.

15–16 May   CIS summit in Tashkent.

18 May   Energy prices raised five to six-fold.

20 May	Khizha appointed Deputy Prime Minister.
26 May	Democratic groups begin collecting signatures for referendum on land and constitution.
26 May	Shakhrai resigns as State Secretary.
30 May	Chernomyrdin appointed Deputy Prime Minister and Minister for Energy. Lopukhin dismissed as Minister for Energy.
1 June	Matyukhin resigns as Chairman of Central Bank of Russia.
2 June	Press statement by President's Office accuses Gorbachev of attempting to "destabilize political situation".
2 June	V. Shumeiko appointed First Deputy Prime Minister.
4 June	Yeltsin tells "Reform" Coalition Deputies that "the limits of compromise have been exhausted".
5 June	Popov resigns as Mayor of Moscow. Replaced by Luzhkov.
10 June	Yeltsin meets 700 senior military commanders.
11 June	Supreme Soviet approves privatization programme.
15 June	**Yeltsin appoints Gaidar Acting Prime Minister**.
15–16 June	Yeltsin visits USA.
21 June	Inaugural meeting of Civic Alliance.
12–22 June	"Labour Russia" picketing of Ostankino TV ending in clashes with police.
26 June	Constitutional Court statement warns of threat to constitutional order.
26 June	Supreme Soviet votes to lift sanctions on Serbia.
1 July	Kozyrev article in *Izvestiya* warns of threat from "War Party".
4 July	Yeltsin rebukes Kozyrev for "harmful statement.
6 July	CIS summit in Moscow.
7 July	Yeltsin decree on powers of Security Council.
7–8 July	G7 summit in Munich attended by Yeltsin.
8 July	Ministries of Defence and Security reject rumours of impending coup at joint press conference.
16 July	Civic Alliance publishes alternative economic programme.
17 July	Gerashchenko appointed acting Chairman of CBR.
22 July	Russia / Moldova statement on settlement of Transdniestrian conflict.
3 Aug.	Yeltsin / Kravchuk meeting. Agreement on transfer of BSF from CIS command to Joint Russian / Ukranian control for three years.
19 Aug.	Yeltsin's television address on anniversary of coup attempt.
21 Aug.	Yeltsin's press conference on coup anniversary.
2 Sept.	Yeltsin's meeting with Japanese Foreign Minister Watanabe. Yeltsin's visit to Japan postponed.
11 Sept.	Yeltsin addresses regional leaders at meeting in Cheboksary attended by Khasbulatov and Gaidar.
17 Sept.	"Russia Unity" Parliamentary bloc declares right and left opposition uniting to overthrow President and Government.
15 Sept.	Constitutional court hearings on CPSU resume.
22 Sept.	5th Session of RF Supreme Soviet opens. Political Declaration by right and left opposition published in **Sovetskaya**

	Rossiya.
1 Oct.	Voucher privatization begins.
6 Oct.	Yeltsin speech to Supreme Soviet. Reproaches Government for its "too macroeconomic" policy and criticizes several Ministers by name.
9–10 Oct.	CIS summit in Bishkek.
15 Oct.	Council of Heads of Republics established. Gorbachev banned from travel abroad over the refusal to testify to constitutional court.
17 Oct.	Poltoranin, Kozyrev and Burbulis brief foreign journalists on threat of parliamentary coup.
20 Oct.	Supreme Soviet votes to subordinate *Izvestiya* publishing house to control of Parliament.
21 Oct.	Supreme Soviet rejects President's request to postpone Seventh Congress.
24 Oct.	Nationwide demonstrations against Government's economic policy (low turn-out). Inaugural congress of National Salvation Front.
26 Oct.	Statement by Minister of Defence Grachev on loyalty to Yeltsin.
27 Oct.	Yeltsin in speech to MFA collegium describes Supreme Soviet's refusal to postpone congress as "sheer confrontation"; calls for tougher foreign policy.
28 Oct.	Yeltsin decree bans National Salvation Front. Yeltsin decree disbands parliamentary protection service.
4 Nov.	Supreme Soviet confirms Gerashchenko as Chairman of CBR.
5 Nov.	Shakhrai appointed Deputy Prime Minister and Head of Temporary Administration in North Ossetia.
9–10 Nov.	Yeltsin visits UK.
13 Nov.	Right-wing deputy Andronov tells Supreme Soviet that Parliament will be dissolved on 24 / 25 November. Supreme Soviet adopts Law on Government.
14 Nov.	Yeltsin and Gaidar address Civic Alliance Congress.
18 Nov.	Yeltsin visits South Korea.
17 Nov.	Council of Heads of Regions established.
25 Nov.	Poltoranin resigns as Deputy Prime Minister and Minister of Information. Yegor Yakovlev sacked as Head of Ostankino TV.
26 Nov.	Gaidar addresses Supreme Soviet on economic situation.
26 Nov.	Burbulis' post of State Secretary abolished. He is appointed head of President's group of advisers.
30 Nov.	Constitutional Court verdict on CPSU and RCP. Ban on higher party organs upheld; primary organizations declared legal.
1–14 Dec.	**7th Congress of People's Deputies**.
8 Dec.	Yeltsin concession to Congress. Four key Cabinet Ministers to be approved by Supreme Soviet. Yeltsin nominates Gaidar as Prime Minister.
9 Dec.	Congress rejects Gaidar by 486 votes to 467.

10 Dec.	Yeltsin confronts Congress and declares people will choose in Jan. referendum between Congress and President. Yeltsin and supporters walk out but Congress remains quoratea and in session.
12 Dec.	Zorkin brokers compromise agreement "on stabilization of constitutional system".
14 Dec.	Gaidar comes third in preliminary vote on candidates for Prime Minister. **Chernomyrdin appointed PM. Gaidar resigns** from Government.
23 Dec.	New Government announced: B. Fedorov and Yarov appointed Deputy Prime Ministers.
25 Dec.	Yeltsin decree sets up Federal Information Centre under Poltoranin with the rank of First deputy Prime Minister.
31 Dec.	Chernomyrdin decree on price regulation (revoked 18 Jan. 1993).

1993

3 Jan.	Yeltsin and Bush sign Start II treaty in Moscow.
9–10 Jan.	Khasbulatov article in the *Rossiiskaya Gazeta* criticizing proposed referendum.
10 Jan.	Sergei Filatov, First Deputy Chairman of Supreme Soviet, appointed head of presidential administration.
14 Jan.	Supreme Soviet reconvenes and adopts a decree on referendum on 11 April.
22 Jan.	CIS Summit in Minsk. Seven states sign CIS charter (not including Ukraine, Moldova and Turkmenistan).
27–28 Jan.	Yeltsin visits India and signs friendship treaty.
28 Jan.	Chernomyrdin reaffirms government's main economic priorities as control of inflation and maintenance of value of rouble.
30 Jan.	Arrest of army major allegedly preparing attempt on Yeltsin's life.
9 Feb.	Yeltsin meeting with republic leaders who speak against proposed referendum.
10 Feb.	Zorkin expresses opposition to referendum.
11 Feb.	Meeting between Yeltsin, Khasbulatov and Zorkin.
16 Feb.	Yeltsin and Khasbulatov establish working group to consider draft constitution.
18 Feb.	Yeltsin proposes constitutional agreement including early presidential and parliamentary elections.
20–21 Feb.	All-army officers' assembly calls for resignation of Defence Minister Grachev.
25 Feb.	Yeltsin establishes Council of Heads of Administration.
28 Feb.	Yeltsin tells Civic Alliance he can no longer tolerate the parliament's parallel government; calls for Russia to be given "special powers" to guarantee peace and stability in CIS.
1 March	One-day warning strike by coal-miners in the Kuzbass and Vorkuta, seeking back pay.
2 March	Yeltsin addressing leaders of the democratic movement

warns that hard-liners could come to power through the Congress and reverse the reforms.

10–13 March **Eighth Congress of People's Deputies** annuls the Dec. 1992 compromise agreement, cancels the April referendum and implements constitutional amendments reducing presidential powers.

15 March Large scale industrial privatization begins.

20 March Yeltsin addresses nation on television announcing decree on "special regime" until referendum to be held 25 April.

21 March Rutskoi and Khasbulatov denounce Yeltsin's move as "attempted coup".

23 March Constitutional Court rules Yeltsin's statement unconstitutional.

24 March Secretary of Constitutional Court tells session of Supreme Soviet that Yeltsin's statement provides grounds for impeachment.

26–29 March **Ninth Congress of People's Deputies** fails by 72 votes to impeach Yeltsin; approves referendum for 25 April with 4 questions formulated by Congress.

26 March Boris Fedorov (Deputy Prime Minister) appointed Minister of Finance.

4–5 April Yeltsin-Clinton summit in Vancouver. Agrees $1.6 billion US aid package for Russia.

9 April G7 Foreign and Finance Ministers in Tokyo announce $4.3 billion package of financial aid for Russia.

14 April Trial of Aug. 1991 coup plotters opens in Moscow.

15 April Oleg Lobov appointed First Deputy Prime Minister.

16 April CIS summit in Minsk expresses support for Yeltsin.

16 April Rutskoi alleges corruption among senior government officials.

23 April Rutskoi relieved of responsibility for agriculture.

25 April **Referendum**. Yeltsin wins vote of confidence in himself (58.5 per cent) and in his economic and social policy (53 per cent); insufficient majorities in favour of early presidential and parliamentary elections (49 per cent and 67 per cent).

30 April Full text of Yeltsin's draft constitution published in *Izvestiya*.

1 May Hard-liners riot at a May Day demonstration killing militiaman.

6 May Yeltsin television address to nation calls for parliamentary elections by the autumn.

11 May Secretary of Security Council, Skokov and Deputy Prime Minister, Khizha, dismissed.

13 May Rutskoi deprived of last official Vice-Presidential functions.

14 May Yeltsin meeting with Shevardnadze results in decision on cease-fire in Abkhazia from 20 May.

14 May CIS Summit in Moscow calls for greater economic integration within CIS.

21 May Yeltsin decree convening constitutional conference for 5 June.

22 May	Government and Central Bank of Russia sign joint statement on commitment to financial stabilization.
1 June	Rouble falls below 1,000 roubles to the dollar.
4 June	President Dudaev's forces attack opposition headquarters in Chechnya killing 14.
5 June	Constitutional conference opens in Moscow. Heckling by Yeltsin's supporters forces Khasbulatov from the tribune.
17 June	Constitutional conference adopts statement on draft new constitution.
17 June	Yeltsin–Kravchuk summit in Moscow agrees on division of the Black Sea fleet.
24 June	Supreme Soviet calls for dismissal of Shumeiko and Poltoranin for alleged corruption.
26 June	Constitutional conference fails to conclude as originally scheduled.
1 July	Coal prices liberalized.
? July	Sverdlovsk Soviet votes for formation of Urals republic.
7–9 July	G7 summit in Tokyo agrees $3 billion privatization and restructuring programme for Russia.
10 July	Prime Ministers of Russia, Ukraine and Belarus agree to accelerate the integration of their economies.
10–11 July	Yeltsin–Kohl summit at Lake Baikal.
12 July	Constitutional conference concluding its first phase votes by large majority to approve Yeltsin's draft constitution.
16 July	Yeltsin's draft constitution submitted to parliament.
20 July	Parliament suspends Yeltsin's decree of 8 May authorizing speeding up of privatization process.
22 July	Parliament approves budget for 1993 providing for large increase in expenditure and deficit.
23 July	Supreme Soviet votes to authorize Procurator-General to bring criminal charges against Shumeiko.
24 July	Central Bank of Russia announces withdrawal from circulation of pre-1993 bank notes.
24–25 July	Second Congress of National Salvation Front.
25 July	Yeltsin cuts short holiday and returns to Moscow in response to crisis atmosphere.
27 July	Yeltsin dismisses Minister of Security, Barannikov for "violation of ethical norms" and mistakes in leadership of the border troops.
1 Aug.	President's press spokesman denies reports that Yeltsin seriously ill (e.g. in *Pravda* of 31 July).
1 Aug.	Head of Russian provisional administration in North Ossetia and Ingushetia, Polyanichko, assassinated.
6 Aug.	Government approves medium term economic programme with financial stabilization as immediate priority.
10 Aug.	Shaposhnikov resigns as Secretary of Security Council.
12 Aug.	Supreme Soviet votes to introduce changes to law on government increasing powers of parliament.
12 Aug.	Yeltsin tells press conference September will be "super combative month" when his struggle with parliament would be

	resolved.
13–14 Aug.	Yeltsin meets republic and regional leaders in Petrozavodsk and proposes setting up "Federation Council" to comprise two members from each subject of Federation.
18 Aug.	Security Council's anti-crime and corruption commission accuses Rutskoi of holding dollar account in Swiss bank.
19 Aug.	Yeltsin tells press conference on August putsch anniversary that he is determined to hold autumn parliamentary elections.
21 Aug.	Resignation of Minister for Foreign Economic Relations, Glaz'ev (accused in anti-corruption commission report).
24–26 Aug.	Yeltsin visits Poland, Czech Republic and Slovakia.
31 Aug.	Russian troop withdrawal from Lithuania completed.
1 Sept.	Yeltsin suspends Rutskoi and First Deputy Prime Minister Shumeiko pending outcome of investigations into corruption.
1 Sept.	Supreme Soviet rejects 1993 budget.
3 Sept.	Yeltsin–Kravchuk summit at Massandra.
9 Sept.	Yeltsin sets up working group under Ryabov to reconcile rival draft constitutions.
12 Sept.	Yeltsin briefs "power" Ministers on planned dissolution of parliament.
17 Sept.	Rutskoi warns Yeltsin proposing to introduce Presidential Rule.
18 Sept.	Khasbulatov addressing all Russian conference of People's Deputies claims President has been sounding out reactions in West to dissolution of parliament and imposition of state of emergency.
18 Sept.	**Gaidar appointed First Deputy Prime Minister**; Lobov appointed Secretary of Security Council.
20 Sept.	Golushko appointed Acting Minister of Security.
21 Sept.	Yeltsin addresses nation on TV and issues **decree no. 1400** on "staged constitutional reform" dissolving parliament and ordering elections on 11–12 December.
21 Sept.	Rutskoi declares himself Acting President.
22 Sept.	Constitutional Court declares Yeltsin's decree unconstitutional.
23 Sept.	Yeltsin decree on presidential elections on 12 June.
24 Sept.	CIS summit in Moscow. All leaders attend.
24 Sept.	Blockade of White House implemented.
29 Sept.	Ultimatum by Russian and Moscow governments for evacuation of White House by 4 October.
2 Oct.	Violent demonstrations by hard-line supporters of parliament.
3 Oct.	Hard-line White House supporters seize Mairie and attack Ostankino television station.
3 Oct.	**State of emergency imposed** in Moscow (from 16:00 hrs until 10 Oct.).
4 Oct.	Following **shelling of White House**, army units storm parliamentary building and crush resistance. Rutskoi and

	Khasbulatov are among those arrested; 144 dead in fighting on 3–4 October.
4 Oct.	Hard-line opposition groups suspended.
6 Oct.	Yeltsin addresses nation on TV about recent tragic events.
6 Oct.	Press censorship lifted after 48 hours.
7 Oct.	Day of Mourning.
7 Oct.	Constitutional Court suspended until new parliament, the Federal Assembly, meets.
8 Oct.	Minister of Interior, Yerin, made hero of Russian Federation.
9 Oct.	Yeltsin decree on reform / dissolution of regional city and local Soviets.
10 Oct.	State of emergency extended to 18 October.
11–13 Oct.	Yeltsin visits Japan.
15 Oct.	Fifteen hard-line publications banned.
18 Oct.	State of emergency lifted.
19 Oct.	Six parties / movements including National Salvation Front banned from participation in December elections.
22 Oct.	Yeltsin decrees elections to new regional Dumas by March 1994.
27 Oct.	Yeltsin decree on private ownership of land.
7 Nov.	Twenty-one electoral blocs submit list of 100,000 signatures to Central Electoral Commission to qualify for party lists contest. Eight disqualified, 13 to contest elections.
10 Nov.	Draft constitution published in final form for referendum on 12 December.
18 Nov.	Yeltsin decree imposing limits on foreign banking activity in Russia.
21 Nov.	Official three-week election campaign begins.
22 Nov.	Yeltsin-Kohl meeting in Moscow.
26 Nov.	Yeltsin warns politicians against attacking the constitution in their election broadcasts.
3 Dec.	Rally of opponents to the constitution addressed by Zorkin and Rumyantsev.
6–7 Dec.	Yeltsin visits North Caucasus.
8–9 Dec.	Yeltsin visits Belgium and attends EU summit meeting.
12 Dec.	**Referendum approves new constitution** (58 per cent in favour from 55 per cent turnout). **Elections to Duma and Federation Council**. Zhirinovsky's LDP wins most votes in party lists contest (23 per cent to 15 per cent for Russia's Choice).
21 Dec.	Poltoranin resigns as Minister of Information.
22 Dec.	Yeltsin gives press conference on election results. States that President and constitution are bulwark against neo-fascism.
23 Dec.	Yeltsin decree on restructuring of government.
23–24 Dec.	CIS summit in Ashkhabad.

1994

11 Jan.	Opening sessions of Federation Council and Duma. Rybkin elected Chairman of Duma.
12 Jan.	Shumeiko elected Chairman of Federation Council.

16 Jan.	**Gaidar resigns as First Deputy Prime Minister.**
28 Jan.	Boris Fedorov resigns from government.
9 Feb.	Duma votes to set up commission to investigate events of 3–4 Oct. 1993.
10 Feb.	Gaidar launches new party based on Russia's Choice.
14–16 Feb.	Prime Minister Major visits Moscow.
15 Feb.	Agreement between Federal authorities and Tatarstan signed in Moscow.
23 Feb.	**Duma adopts resolution on political amnesty,** memorandum of accord etc.
24 Feb.	Yeltsin delivers State of Nation address to two houses of parliament.
26 Feb.	Leaders of Oct. 1993 insurrection released from Lefortovo.
3 March	*Nezavisimaya Gazeta* list of 100 leading politicians places Yeltsin second to Chernomyrdin.
4 March	Yeltsin proposes Civic Accord Agreement at expanded session of government.
14 March	Yeltsin leaves for holiday following second bout of flu.
17 March	"Accord In Name Of Russia" launched.
20, 27 March	Local elections. Very low turn-out.
23 March	Attempt to table "no confidence" motion in government fails.
6 April	Federation Council rejects Yeltsin's request to dismiss Procurator-General Kazannik.
7 April	Text of Civic Accord Memorandum published.
26 April	Yeltsin in interview published in Nezavisimaya Gazeta says no decision yet on whether he will stand for re-election in 1996.
28 April	**Civic Accord signed at Kremlin ceremony.**
28 April	Yeltsin launches second book of memoirs, "Notes of a President".
27 April	Murder of Duma deputy Aidzerdzis.
17 May	Yeltsin at meeting with Prime Minister Chernomyrdin puts pressure on him to speed up implementation of economic reforms.
May	Yeltsin signs 12 decrees designed to give impetus to economic reform.
28 May	Inaugural meeting of Accord In Name Of Russia (new version of National Salvation Front).
8 June	Duma passes budget at second reading.
12–13 June	Inaugural Congress of Russia's Democratic Choice party. Gaidar elected leader.
12 July	Federation Council approves law on Constitutional Court (first constitutional legislation adopted by new parliament).
15 July	Expanded session of government. Chernomyrdin's half-year report on economy takes predominantly reformist line.
29 July	Russian government statement denouncing Dudaev regime and declaring situation in Chechnya out of control.
3 Aug.	Bilateral agreement on division of powers signed by Yeltsin and President of Bashkortostan.

31 Aug.	Yeltsin's exuberant demeanour at troop withdrawal ceremony in Berlin sharply criticized in Russian press.
21 Sept.	Small hard-line demonstration in Moscow on anniversary of Yeltsin's decree dissolving parliament.
30 Sept.	Yeltsin fails to emerge from aircraft for stop-over meeting at Shannon with Irish Prime Minister.
4 Oct.	Yeltsin at press conference rejects speculation on postponement of Presidential elections; and reaffirms commitment to reform.
5 Oct.	New Duma session opens.
11 Oct.	**"Black Tuesday"**. Rouble value falls 25 per cent against dollar.
16–19 Oct.	HM The Queen's state visit to Russia.
21 Oct.	CIS meeting in Moscow. Russian and Moldovan Prime Ministers sign agreement on withdrawal of 14th Army within three years.
27 Oct.	"No confidence" motion in government fails: 194 in favour, 55 against, 54 abstentions.
28 Oct.	Solzhenitsyn's address to Duma.
30 Oct.	Sergei Mavrodi (head of collapsed MMM Investment Company) elected Duma deputy at by-election.
6 Nov.	Communist Duma deputy dies after street mugging.
11 Nov.	Head of government Administration, Kvasov, sacked.
Nov.	Government reshuffle. Chubais promoted First Deputy Prime Minister.
26 Nov.	Assault by opposition forces on Grozny fails.
2 Dec.	Presidential security forces raid headquarters of MOST financial group in Moscow.
10 Dec.	Yeltsin in hospital for nasal operation.
11 Dec.	**Russian forces enter Chechnya**.
14 Dec.	Vice-President Gore in Moscow for session of Gore-Chernomyrdin Commission.
31 Dec.	Russian ground forces launch assault on Grozny.

1995

19 Jan.	Russian forces capture Presidential palace in Grozny.
24 Jan.	Polevanov dismissed as Chairman of State Property Committee.
7 Feb.	Constitutional Court resumes activity following election of last member.
8 Feb.	Sergei Belyaev appointed Chairman of State Property Committee.
10 Feb.	Yeltsin attends CIS Summit in Almaty.
13 Feb.	Vladimir Tumanov elected Chairman of Constitutional Court.
16 Feb.	Yeltsin delivers State of Nation address to parliament.
24 Feb.	Duma adopts 1995 budget.
1 March	Murder of TV journalist Vladislav List'ev.
2 March	Yeltsin orders dismissal of Moscow procurator and chief of police.

10 March	Duma revokes appointment of Sergei Kovalev as Russia's Human Rights Commissioner.
30 March	Capture by Russian forces of Dudaev stronghold, Gudermes.
25 April	Chernomyrdin announces formation of electoral bloc "Our Home, Russia".
27 April	Yeltsin signs decree on moratorium on combat operations in Chechnya during VE anniversary celebrations.
9 May	VE 50th Anniversary celebrations in Moscow.
10 May	Presidents Yeltsin and Clinton hold summit meeting in Moscow.
26 May	Yeltsin attends CIS Summit in Minsk.
14 June	Chechen gunmen seize hospital in Budennovsk.
21 June	Duma passes vote of no-confidence in the government.
30 June	**Yeltsin dismisses Ministers for Interior, Yerin, and Nationalities, Yegorov, and Head of FSB, Stepashin.**
1 July	Second motion of no-confidence in the government fails.
11 July	**Yeltsin hospitalized with heart problems**.
12 July	Duma vote to set up Commission to impeach the President fails to achieve majority.
19 July	Duma fails to confirm Paramonova as Chair of Central Bank.
24 July	Yeltsin leaves hospital. Barsukov appointed Head of Federal Security Service (FSB).
30 July	Cease-fire agreement signed by Russian and Chechen negotiators.
7 Aug.	Yeltsin returns to work at the Kremlin.
2 Sept.	President Yeltsin and Chancellor Kohl begin two-day meeting in Moscow.
6 Oct.	Commander of Federal forces in Chechnya, General Romanov, seriously wounded.
8 Oct.	Yeltsin dismisses Acting Procurator-General Ilyushenko.
16 Oct.	Yury Kuratov appointed Procurator-General.
24 Oct.	Doku Zavgaev appointed head of government in Chechnya.
26 Oct.	**Yeltsin hospitalized following heart attack**.
22 Nov.	Sergei Dubinin confirmed by Duma as Chairman of Central Bank.
27 Nov.	Yeltsin leaves hospital for convalescence at Barvikha sanatorium.
28 Nov.	Federation Council rejects Duma's law on formation of the Upper House.
6 Dec.	Duma adopts 1996 budget.
14 Dec.	Chechen fighters reoccupy Gudermes (driven out after one week).
17 Dec.	**Duma elections**. Communists win party list contest with 22.3 per cent; LDP 11.18 per cent; NDR 10.13 per cent; Yabloko 6.89 percent.

1996
3 Jan.	General Tikhomirov appointed Commander of Federal

	Forces in Chechnya.
5 Jan.	**Kozyrev resigns as Foreign Minister**.
9 Jan.	Primakov appointed Foreign Minister.
9 Jan.	Chechen gunmen seize hospital in Kislyar, Daghestan, and take hostages.
10 Jan.	Vyacheslav Trubnikov replaces Primakov as Head of Foreign Intelligence Service.
13 Jan.	**Filatov resigns as Head of Presidential Administration**.
15 Jan.	Nikolai Yegorov appointed Head of Presidential Administration.
16 Jan.	First session of new Duma.
	Chubais dismissed as First Deputy Prime Minister.
17 Jan.	Gennady Seleznev elected Chairman of State Duma.
18 Jan.	Bungled assault by Russian forces on Chechen gunmen at Pervomaiskoe leaves many hostages dead.
22 Jan.	Gaidar leaves Presidential Council over Pervomaiskoe operation.
23 Jan.	Sergei Kovalev resigns as Chairman of President's Human Rights Commission.
25 Jan.	Vladimir Kadannikov appointed First Deputy Prime Minister.
15 Feb.	**Yeltsin announces in Yekaterinburg that he will run for re-election as President**.
21 Feb.	Duma ratifies Russia's accession to the Council of Europe.
23 Feb.	Yeltsin delivers State of Nation address to the Federal Assembly.
15 March	Duma denounces Belovezhsky Agreement of December 1991.
31 March	Yeltsin announces plans for peace settlement in Chechnya.
2 April	Presidents Yeltsin and Lukashenka (of Belarus) sign treaty on formation of a Community of Sovereign Republics.
16 April	73 Russian soldiers killed in ambush in Chechnya.
21 April	Presidents Yeltsin and Clinton hold talks in Moscow.
22–23 April	Djohar Dudaev reported killed in rocket attack.
5 May	Korzhakov suggests postponement of Presidential elections.
27 May	Yanderbiev begins talks with Yeltsin in Moscow.
	Agreement announced on cease-fire from 1 June.
28 May	Yeltsin pays visit to Chechnya.
16 June	**First round of Presidential elections**: Yeltsin 35 per cent, Zyuganov 32 per cent, Lebed 14.5 per cent, Yavlinsky 7.5 per cent, Zhirinovsky 6 per cent.
18 June	**Lebed appointed National Security Adviser and Secretary of Security Council.**
	Minister of Defence Grachev dismissed.
20 June	**Head of Presidential Security Service, Korzhakov, Head of FSB, Barsukov and First-Deputy Prime Minister Soskovets dismissed.**
3 July	**Second round of Presidential elections: Yeltsin 53.8 per cent**; Zyuganov 40.3 per cent.
15 July	**Chubais appointed Head of President's Administration.**

Bibliography

In English

A. Aslund, *Gorbachev's Struggle for Economic Reform*. Pinter, 1991.
——, *How Russia Became a Market Economy*. The Brookings Institution, Washington, 1995.
I. Banac (ed.), *Eastern Europe in Revolution*. Cornell University Press, 1991.
H. Carrère d'Encausse, *The End of the Soviet Empire*. Basic Books, 1991.
T. Colton and R. Levgold (eds), *After the Soviet Union*. W. W. Norton & Co., 1992.
M. S. Gorbachev, *The August Coup*. HarperCollins, 1991.
G. Lapidus and V. Zaslavsky (eds), *From Union to Commonwealth*. Cambridge University Press, 1992.
G. Lapidus (ed.), *The New Russia*. Westview Press, 1995.
A. Nove, *An Economic History of the USSR, 1917–1991*. Penguin Books, 1992.
D. Remnick, *Lenin's Tomb*. Viking, 1993.
A. Roxburgh, *The Second Russian Revolution*. BBC Books, 1991.
R. Sackwa, *Russian Politics and Society*. Routledge, 1993.
G. Schöpflin, *Politics in Eastern Europe, 1945–1992*. Blackwell, 1993.
S. Sestanovich, *Rethinking Russia's National Interests*. CSIS Washington, 1994.
J. Steele, *Eternal Russia*. Faber and Faber, 1994.
R. Szporluk (ed.) *National Identity and Ethnicity in Russia and the New States of Eurasia*. M.E. Sharpe, New York, 1994.
S. White, G. Gill and D. Slider (eds), *The Politics of Transition*. Cambridge University Press, 1994.
S. White, *Gorbachev and After*. Cambridge University Press, 1992.
D. Yergin and T. Gustafson, *Russia 2010*. Nicholas Brealey, 1994.

Studies in Public Policy, University of Strathclyde:
No. 186, *Transition to Democracy in Central Europe*.
No. 205, *Russia Between State and Market*.
No. 226, *Distrust as an Obstacle to Civil Society*.
No. 227, *Getting by Without Government*.
No. 228, *New Russia Barometer III*.

262 *Bibliography*

In Russian

V. Bakatin, *Osvobozhdenie ot ilyuzii*. Kemerovo, 1992.
——, *Izbavlenie ot KGB*. Novosti, Moscow, 1992.
E. Chazov, *Zdorov'e i Vlast'*. Novosti, Moscow, 1992.
A. Chernyaev, *Shest' let s Gorbachevym*. Progress, Kultura, Moscow, 1993.
B. Yeltsin, *Ispoved' na zadannuyu temu*. 'Novy Stil'', Moscow, 1990.
B. Yeltsin, *Zapiski Prezidenta*. Moscow, 1994.
Ye. Gaidar, *Postrouit' Rossiyu*. Moscow, 1994.
——, *Gosudarstvo i evolyutsiya*. "Evraziya", Moscow, 1995.
M. Gorbachev, *Dekabr'-91, moya pozitsiya*. Novosti, Moscow, 1992.
A. Grachev, *Kremlevskaya Khronika*. EKSMO, Moscow, 1994.
V. Pavlov, *Avgust iznutri* Delovoi Mir, Moscow, 1993.
V. Pechenev, *Gorbachev: K. Vershinam Vlasti*. Moscow, 1991.
A. N. Yakovlev, *Gor'kaya chasha*. Yaroslavl', 1994.
——, *Muki prochteniya bytiya*. Novosti, Moscow, 1991.
V. Zhirinovsky, *Posledny brosok na yug*. Moscow, 1993.

Gorbachev–Yeltsin: 1500 dnei politicheskogo protivostoyaniya. "Terra", Moscow, 1992.
Revansh. Nedoperevyvorot: Versiya Tsentra "RF-politika". Moscow, 1994.
Putch: Khronika trevozhnykh dnei. Progress, Moscow, 1991.

Index

264 *Index*

Barsukov, Mikhail, Head of Chief
    Security Directorate (1992–5), Head
    of Federal Security Service (FSB)
    (1995–6), 175, 176, 232, 241
Bashkiria, 159
"Basic Guidelines", 54
Baturin, Yury, President's Legal Adviser
    (1993–4), National Security Adviser
    (1994–6), 175, 241
Beer Lovers, 236
Belaya Vezha, 85, 90
Belorussia/Belarus, 15, 60, 65, 66, 80, 90,
    178, 201
Belovezhsky (Minsk) Agreement, 24, 89,
    90, 91, 221, 239, 240
Berlin, 224, 225, 226
Berlin Wall, 15
Bessmertnykh, Alexander, Foreign
    Minister, USSR (1990–91), 60
Black Sea Fleet, 97
"Black Tuesday" (11 October 1994), 227
Boldin, Valery, 77
Boldyrev, Yury, 58
    co-leader of Yabloko, 190
Bolsheviks, 14
Bolshakov, Aleksei, Deputy Prime
    Minister for CIS Affairs (1994–5), 228
Bragin, Vyacheslav, Head of Ostankino
    TV, (1993), 131, 196
Budennovsk, 233, 234
budget, 95, 138, 167, 170, 218, 219, 226,
    227, 233, 238
Building Russia (Ye. Gaidar), 22, 33
Burbulis, Gennady, First Deputy Prime
    Minister, State Secretary, Russia
    (1991–2), 25, 43, 85, 87, 90, 100, 104,
    114, 116, 119, 120, 124, 125, 126,
    151, 188
Bush, President George, 34, 71, 89
by-elections, 58

Cabinet of Ministers (USSR), 57, 79
Cabinet changes/appointments (Russia),
    119, 122, 123, 125, 128, 157, 158, 202,
    203, 206, 207, 226, 228, 237, 238
Cabinet crisis (January 1994), 201–3, 211
Cancer Ward (A. Solzhenitsyn), 14–15
capitalism, 35
Central Asian Republics, 91
Central Bank of Russia (CBR), 107, 122,
    137, 153, 168, 178, 202
    Chairman of, 202, 206, 227, 228, 233
Central Committee (of CPSU), 17, 18, 20,
    21, 45, 47, 49, 50, 77, 79
    Conference (July 1989), 42
    "Open Letter", 48, 50
    Plenums of, 41, 42, 43–4, 46, 61, 63, 67,
        69, 71, 72
    Presidium, 49

Russian Buro, 49
Secretariat, 63, 77
see also Politburo
Central Electoral Commission (CEC), 189,
    190, 191, 194, 239
Centre (USSR), 6, 12, 20, 25, 50, 56, 57, 58,
    63, 64, 67, 68, 70, 76, 79, 80, 84, 87,
    88, 90, 91
"Centrist bloc", 63, 195
Chechnya, 2, 16, 100, 154, 191, 193, 214,
    228–30, 231, *233–4*, 237, 238, 240
Chelnokov, Mikhail, 169
Chernavin, Admiral Vladimir, 62
Chernomyrdin, Viktor
    Deputy Prime Minister Russia (1992),
        106
    Prime Minister (1992–), 125, 126,
        128, 137, 138, 142, 143, 144, 146,
        148, 149, 161, 175, 197, 198, 201,
        202, 205, 207, 208, 216, 217, 218,
        225, 227, 228, 229, 232, 234, 235,
        237, 240
Chernyaev, Anatoly, Gorbachev aide, 45,
    52, 65, 67, 71
Chikin, Valentin, 111
Christian Democrats, 96
China, 17, 27, 28, 121, 128
Chubais, Anatoly, 10, 31, 114, 138, 145,
    151, 158, 188, 222, 241
    Deputy Prime Minister (1992–4), 108,
        202
    First Deputy Prime Minister (1994–6),
        228, 237
    Head of President's Administration
        (1996–), 36
Chubais, Igor, 48
Chuvash Republic, 205
CIS (Commonwealth of Independent
    States), 89, 90, 91, 98, 100, 104, 106,
    110, 114, 141, 142, 152, 176, 178, 203,
    207, 212, 228, 230, 231
Civic Accord, *212–15*, 217, 218, 219, 220
Civic Alliance, 110, 113, 115, 116, 119, 122,
    128, 134, 137, 150, 187, 189, 190, 193,
    197, 221
Civil Code, 219, 220
civil liberties, 32
Clinton, President Bill, 233
CMEA, 140
Cold War, 35, 62
Committee for Defence Conversion, 98
Committee of National Salvation, 59
Communist Party of the Soviet Union
    (CPSU) 3, 5, 7, 8, 10, 21, 44, 50, 54,
    60, *63*, 65, 82, 86, 195, 234
    apparat/apparatus, 22, 28, 41
    and August coup, 77
    ban/suspension (1991), 21, 23, 80, 81
    Constitutional Court hearings, 23